Game Audio Programming

Principles and Practices

Game Audio
Programming
Principles and Practices

Edited by **Guy Somberg**

CRC Press
Taylor & Francis Group
Boca Raton London New York

CRC Press is an imprint of the
Taylor & Francis Group, an **informa** business

CRC Press
Taylor & Francis Group
6000 Broken Sound Parkway NW, Suite 300
Boca Raton, FL 33487-2742

© 2017 by Taylor & Francis Group, LLC
CRC Press is an imprint of Taylor & Francis Group, an Informa business

Printed on acid-free paper
Version Date: 20160701

International Standard Book Number-13: 978-1-4987-4673-1 (Hardback)

Library of Congress Cataloging-in-Publication Data

Names: Somberg, Guy, editor.
Title: Game audio programming : principles and practices / editor: Guy
Somberg.
Description: Boca Raton : Taylor & Francis, CRC Press, 2016. | Includes
bibliographical references and index.
Identifiers: LCCN 2016016015 | ISBN 9781498746731 (alk. paper)
Subjects: LCSH: Computer games--Programming. | Computer sound processing. |
Computer game music. | Sound--Recording and reproducing--Digital
techniques.
Classification: LCC QA76.76.C672 G327 2016 | DDC 794.8/1525--dc23
LC record available at https://lccn.loc.gov/2016016015

Visit the Taylor & Francis Web site at
http://www.taylorandfrancis.com

and the CRC Press Web site at
http://www.crcpress.com

Printed and bound in the United States of America by Publishers Graphics,
LLC on sustainably sourced paper.

To my wonderful wife, Emily.

Thank you for your patience and support as I worked on (and freaked out over) this book.

Contents

Preface

INTRODUCTION

Welcome to *Game Audio Programming: Principles and Practices*! This book is the first of its kind: an entire book dedicated to the art of game audio programming. There have been plenty of books in this style—contributed works, often called "Gems"—for many different videogame-related subjects, from GPU programming to artificial intelligence to general game programming. But game audio programming has, for many years, been something of a black art practiced by isolated monks. Before starting this book, I only knew of one other audio programmer, although I was certain that others must exist. This book, therefore, is an attempt to spread knowledge of game audio programming so that we can further the art.

I have, more than once, heard game audio programmers described as "unicorns"—mythical beasts that everybody wants, but that don't seem to actually exist. This is true for two reasons—first, all of the existing audio programmers already have jobs. Second (and related), there aren't very many new audio programmers. This second point is where this book comes in. If there are no resources for audio programming, how will people learn? Answer: they will figure it out on their own, and go off to practice their dark art in an isolated monastery.

Of course, I am exaggerating for effect, but the truth is that one of the big problems with audio programming is that there are a scant few resources available to learn anything beyond the very basics. This book is the first step in fixing this problem.

THIS BOOK

I searched far and wide throughout the game development world to find top-notch audio programmers to contribute their knowledge to this book. We have chapters in this book on audio programming subjects of every sort: one chapter each for a number of major audio middlewares (CRI ADX2, FMOD Studio, and Audiokinetic Wwise), audio engine design, granular synthesis, music, and even a couple of chapters from sound designers giving their perspective on the subject.

Here are brief summaries of all of the chapters in this book:

- **Principles of Audio** (Chapter 1)—Audio is a complicated beast. There's so much theory and fundamentals that are valuable to understand, from how the ear works to how audio is represented.

- **Sound Engine State Machine** (Chapter 2)—There are many ways to organize an audio engine, but only a few which are truly effective, extendible, and easy to use. This chapter shows one way to put an audio engine together such that it will be a joy to work with, rather than a burden.

- **Streaming Sound** (Chapter 3)—As much as we have gigantic amounts of memory on modern systems, you still can't load everything into RAM. Learn how to work with the filesystem to prioritize your streaming data, and how to prime your streamed audio data.

- **An Introduction to ADX2** (Chapter 4)—CRI ADX2 is the *de facto* standard in Japan, but is virtually unknown to Western audiences. See how to use ADX2, as well as the fundamental principles by which it operates.

- **Wwise and the Audio Programmer** (Chapter 5)—Wwise is another of the most popular audio middleware engines. This chapter shows you how to use Wwise in your game engine, from the very basics of triggering an event through to some more advanced topics.

- **Programming FMOD Studio** (Chapter 6)—FMOD Studio is one of the most popular audio middleware engines. This chapter shows how to use FMOD's low-level API and Studio API, and then touches on a couple of advanced topics on using FMOD.

- **CRYENGINE's Audio Translation Layer** (Chapter 7)—As a game engine vendor, Crytek can't afford to limit which audio middleware their customers choose. See how Crytek built an audio engine that abstracts the middleware so completely that you can swap it out at runtime.

- **A Sound Designer's Perspective on Audio Tools** (Chapter 8)—Sound designers are your customers. They have entire worlds to create, and the only tools that they have to do it with are the ones that you make. Should it surprise you that they are opinionated?

- **Working with Audio Designers** (Chapter 9)—The audio department should really be part of the design process from day one. Here is the perspective from a sound designer on procedures and practices for working together.

- **Open Sound Control** (Chapter 10)—OSC is one of the protocols of choice for the offline audio world, competing with MIDI and a few others. This chapter explains what OSC is, how to use it, and even builds up an implementation in C#.

- **Listeners for Third-Person Cameras** (Chapter 11)—It's not as easy as "put the listener in the camera." Learn why that's true, and how you can easily implement a system that will work in all situations.

- **Interactive Music Systems for Games** (Chapter 12)—An overview of dynamic music systems in games. This chapter is a sampling of the different routes you can take in creating a dynamic musicscape for your games.

- **Granular Vehicle Engines** (Chapter 13)—Learn how to take a single recording of a vehicle sweeping through its RPM range and turn it into a sequence of grains that can be played back to create a realistic-sounding car engine effect.

- **Debugging Features for Middleware-Based Games** (Chapter 14)—As programmers, we spend most of our time debugging. This chapter contains tips and techniques for debugging your audio engine with a focus on Wwise-based tools, but with handy techniques for any audio programmer no matter what back-end you use.

- **Open World Game Optimizations and Limiter Systems** (Chapter 15)—Open-world games pose a particularly challenging problem for game audio—the world is gigantic, so you can't play all of it at once. See how the *Far Cry* franchise solved this tricky problem over the various games.

- **Vector-Based Amplitude Panning** (Chapter 16)—There is some pretty heavy math behind panning a channel around a surround-sound speaker setup. Find out the nitty-gritty details, and see an implementation.

- **Dynamic Game Data** (Chapter 17)—Getting data to and from the audio engine is, ultimately, what drives the audio in your game. See how to build a first-class system to route game data and events into parameters for the middleware.

By its nature, a book like this must leave content out—sometimes painfully so. All the contributors to this book want to do one gigantic brain dump: "*Thwump.* Here is your 20,000-page monster tome containing all the collected knowledge and wisdom of the game audio programmers of the world." Such an epic work, of course, is not realistic. But it is my hope that the volume you hold in your hands now is but the first in a series that will put us on that path.

PARTING THOUGHTS

As you read this book, I hope that you get inspired. Inspired to be an audio programmer; inspired to overhaul your game's audio engine; inspired to speak with your sound designers and work with them more closely; inspired to try some of the techniques that you read in this book… If we have done that, then we have accomplished our task.

Acknowledgments

Thanks to Thomas Buckeyne, who first introduced me to audio programming and helped me to write my first low-level mixer.

Thanks to Tyler Thompson, who took a chance and hired a kid, then told him "spend a quarter of your time on audio, but DON'T TELL US WHAT YOU'RE DOING." I still have that caveman.

Thanks to David Steinwedel, who has traveled with me throughout most of my audio programming journey. David is a contributor to this book as well—thanks for not minding me freaking out over your chapter!

Thanks to Delaney Gillilan, who befriended me early on in my career and whose passion and enthusiasm has led down some paths that would not have opened up otherwise.

Thanks to Rick Adams from CRC Press, without whom this volume would not exist. Thanks also to the rest of the publishing team: Sherry Thomas, Delroy Lowe, and all of the other people who worked hard on this book.

Thanks to my wife Emily, who has supported me wholeheartedly throughout this endeavor.

Editor

Guy Somberg has been programming audio engines for his entire career. From humble beginnings writing a low-level audio mixer for slot machines, he quickly transitioned to writing game audio engines for all manner of games. He has written audio engines that shipped AAA games like *Hellgate: London*, *Bioshock 2*, and *The Sims 4*, as well as smaller titles like *Minion Master*, *Tales from the Borderlands*, and *Game of Thrones*. Guy has also given several talks at the Game Developer Conference.

When he's not programming or writing game audio programming books, he can be found at home reading, playing video games, and playing the flute.

Contributors

Stéphane Beauchemin's education pathway could seem quite chaotic. He made several program changes: from music to science, back to music, to mathematics, to music technology, and finally to computer science. Given that he now works as an audio programmer in the video game industry, suddenly all that makes sense. Stéphane began his career at Audiokinetic as a software developer. During that period, he learned to use Wwise from the inside out. Although working for Audiokinetic was really fulfilling, he could not pass on when he was offered an audio programmer role at WB Games Montreal. He is now the lead audio programmer at the studio, and he is using Wwise to develop AAA games.

Blair Bitonti has worked as an audio programmer in video games for over 15 years. Fortunate enough to be hired into the Tools and Libraries group at Electronic Arts Canada straight out of college, Blair had the opportunity to collaborate with the best in the industry on critically acclaimed titles such as *NHL, NBA Live, FIFA, SSX, Knockout Kings*, and *Medal of Honor*. For the past 10 years, Blair has worked at Activision and Treyarch, helping push sound technology forward on many titles, most notably the *Call of Duty Black Ops* franchise.

Matthieu Dirrenberger has been a sound programmer for 6 years at Ubisoft Montreal. He mainly worked on the *Far Cry* brand with the Dunia engine. After earning his MS in Mathematics and Graphic Computing at the University of Strasbourg (Strasbourg, Alsace, France), he quickly started to work in the video game industry as a sound specialist. As a musician, he has released a few electronic and heavy metal albums (most recently KARNON first EP).

Nicolas Fournel has more than 25 years of experience in the development of audio tools and engines for the music and video game industries, for companies such as Factor 5, Konami, Electronic Arts, and Sony. He holds several patents in the field of digital audio and is a regular speaker at international conferences. He is currently the CEO of Tsugi, a company specializing in audio R&D for the game industry.

Florian Füsslin had a 10-year audio background when he entered the game industry with Crytek in early 2006. Being a dedicated gamer and living the passion for game audio, he is now audio director in the company's Frankfurt HQ, having shipped all major Crytek titles including the *Crysis* franchise, *Ryse: Son of Rome*, and several *Warface* missions; he continues to contribute to and improve the audio pipeline for CRYENGINE.

Jorge Garcia has been working in the audio field for more than a decade under different roles in broadcasting, music, and more recently, games. He has participated in the engineering and programming of game franchises like *FIFA* and *Guitar Hero*.

His interests and skill set span from R&D to digital signal processing, tools, and engine design and development.

Stephen McCaul was born in the backwoods of Arkansas. His childhood interests were music, electronics, and video games. Never one to follow the normal route, Stephen's undergraduate experience was full of detours, eventually ending up with a BS in mathematics from the University of Arkansas. Both before and after earning his degree, he worked as a systems programmer for large-scale mainframe applications including doing Linux driver development on IBM mainframes. In the quest for a sexier job, Stephen became a part of the Guildhall at SMU's third cohort. Two sleepless years later, he accepted a job at Treyarch as an audio programmer for *Spider-Man 3*. For the next 10 years, he worked as a sound engineer on *Spider-Man 3* and four *Call of Duty* titles. He also developed shared sound technology used in all current *Call of Duty* titles.

Aaron McLeran is a game audio veteran with AAA development experience as an interactive music composer, sound designer, and audio programmer for a number of award-winning games. He is currently the senior audio programmer at Epic games working on the audio engine for UE4.

Jon Mitchell has been an audio programmer for 15 years, having gotten his start at Revolution Software. After that, he moved to Codemasters, where he worked on *Colin McRae Rally 2005* and *Redline*, before transitioning to Radical Entertainment (where he worked on *Scarface*), and finally United Front Games.

Tomas Neumann discovered his passion for interactive audio while he was studying computer graphics in Braunschweig, Germany. For more than 5 years, he worked at Crytek, prominently on the *Crysis* series. He started as a junior programmer and when he left as the technical audio lead, he had developed systems and workflows which, until recently, were still in use in CryEngine and its licensed games. In 2010, he joined Blizzard as the first dedicated audio programmer and contributed on *Overwatch* and *World of Warcraft* to eliminate the gap between the game and audio ranging from asset deployment, multiple sound features, a criteria-based voice-system, localization, and more.

David Steinwedel has spent 14 years in game development and audio production. In that time, he has shipped titles of all sizes as a sound designer, audio director, and audio tools engineer. David's work has been awarded by the Motion Picture Sound Editors Guild and has been nominated for multiple Game Audio Network Guild awards.

Dave Stevenson is an audio programmer with a background working in the games industry, mostly focusing on audio systems at companies including Ubisoft Reflections and Codemasters. He started in the games industry after graduating from Strathclyde University with a BSc degree in computer science, working on various games including *Farscape: The Game, Medal of Honor: Rising Sun, Driver San Francisco, Just Dance 3*, and the *Formula One* games. He is now working at Krotos on DSP audio software, using his insight into the games industry to help bring the audio technology over to game engines. Outside of work, Dave is a Cub Scout leader, working up a skillset that will serve him well in the zombie apocalypse.

Thomas Wollenzin is a German national who, for many years, lived in New Mexico, USA, where he worked as an aircraft technician. During that time, he discovered a passion for general programming and so decided to pursue a professional career in the games industry.

During his academic studies as a general game programmer, he discovered a passion for audio in games and audio technology in general and so decided to specialize in that field.

In 2009, after endeavors at other companies he touched down at Crytek as a junior audio engineer, and since then has risen to the position of lead audio software engineer. Thomas is also the engineer behind Crytek's Audio Translation Layer—a technology first for the industry. Currently, he has a small team of three people who are responsible for all areas of audio technology starting with build pipelines, audio tools through enhancing the ATL technology and up to creating full-blown dynamic response systems.

Shipped games within his portfolio include *Crysis 2* and *Crysis 3*, *Ryse: Son of Rome*, as well as many other contributions to Crytek games.

I

Fundamentals

CHAPTER 1

Principles of Audio

Stephen McCaul

CONTENTS

1.1 INTRODUCTION

A very senior engineer I worked with long ago once asked me "What is sound?" A bit stunned, I gave him a brief description of acoustics and how acoustic signals are represented in a computer. Almost every engineer in video games can give a basic explanation of how a TV works with your eyes to convey visual information, but often dedicated audio engineers cannot give an analogous explanation about aural information.

The goal of this chapter is to give anyone with a basic technical background an index to understand audio and its perception with a focus on issues relevant to video games. Acoustics and psychoacoustics are huge topics with large bodies of research, so out of necessity I will only discuss points that I have found useful in my day-to-day work as a game audio engineer. The references are all books I wish had known about when I was just starting to work in game audio.

1.2 WHAT IS SOUND?

The scientific study of sound is called acoustics and is defined by the American National Standards Institute as the "Science of sound, including its production, transmission, and effects including biological and psychological effects."[1] The majority of the human-relevant physical properties of sound can be modeled as waves in an elastic medium using the acoustic wave equation. There are, as always, interesting exceptions such as the trombone and supersonic airplanes, both of which compress air enough to bring out significant nonlinearities.

As with all wave phenomena, sound can interact through diffraction, interference, reflection, and refraction. Given the speed of sound (approximately 340 m/s) and the frequencies that humans can hear (more on this later), everyday objects such as walls, chairs and cups can create all of these interactions. The number and complexity of these interactions makes accurate simulation of the transmission of audio more difficult than the simulation of light across frequencies of interest to human perception.

A comprehensive explanation of physical acoustics is well outside the scope of this chapter, but I will provide a drop of history with references for those interested in learning more.

The earliest written explorations of the physics of sound go back to the Greeks. Both Pythagoras and Aristotle spent significant amounts of time studying and writing about the nature of vibrating strings, both from a physical and musical perspective. The Renaissance brought many advances in our understanding of the physics of sound. Good modern references for physical acoustics are *Fundamentals of Physical Acoustics*[2] and *Theoretical Acoustics*.[3]

The first exhaustive work treating sound as both a physical and psychological phenomenon was not published until the nineteenth century with the work of Helmholtz et al., *On the Sensations of Tone as a Physiological Basis for the Theory of Music*.[4] This book is still very relevant for musical acoustics and gives a good first-order model of the functioning of the ear. The twentieth century brought a tremendous growth of understanding of the functioning of the ear and brain's perception of sound. This field of study is called psychoacoustics, which is directly responsible for wonders of modern technology such as mpeg audio compression and today's amazing hearing aids.

The single most important concept to understand from acoustics is frequency. Frequency is defined as the number of times in a given period a repetitive phenomenon repeats; in audio, the unit of frequency is hertz, which measures repetitions per second. What makes frequency particularly useful is that any bandlimited signal can be decomposed using the Fourier transform into an integral number of pure tones (sinusoids).[5] These pure tones have integral frequency and may vary in amplitude and phase. When analyzing or modifying a signal, it is extremely useful to consider the signal as a finite sum of linearly separable simple parts rather than a complex whole. Your sense of hearing thinks so as well: the single most important behavior of the ear is to separate frequencies.

1.3 HOW DO WE HEAR AUDIO?

Sound surrounds us. Everywhere we go we are enveloped in a field of vibrating air. These waves interact with our heads and pinnae (the part of the ear that sticks out from the head proper) and are funneled into our ear canal. In the ear canal, the waves displace the eardrum, a thin membrane, proportionally to the pressure of the air. This membrane conducts the pressure vibrations to a set of bones that act as levers to transfer and amplify the vibrations to the cochlea.

The cochlea is a complicated organ that acts as an adaptive noise-reducing pressure-to-frequency detector. Its physical form is a rolled up cone with a line of hair cells inside spaced down its length. The dimensions of the cochlea act as a sort of filter giving a differing frequency response at every point along the cone. This frequency response difference causes the vibrations to differ at every point along the length of the cochlea (tonotopic mapping). Thousands of hair cells exist along the length of the cochlea that act as signal detectors by conducting the vibrations into the follicles, which transduce the physical vibration into electrical pulses in the nervous system. These signals undergo processing within the cochlea as well as in the brain itself to form our perception of sound. Figure 1.1[6] shows a diagram of the various parts of the human ear.

A fantastic beginning reference on this topic is *An Introduction to the Psychology of Hearing*,[7] which covers most of the content presented in this section in significantly more depth. I consider it a must-read for anyone working in audio, technical or not. A more in-depth book is the eponymous *Psychoacoustics*.[8]

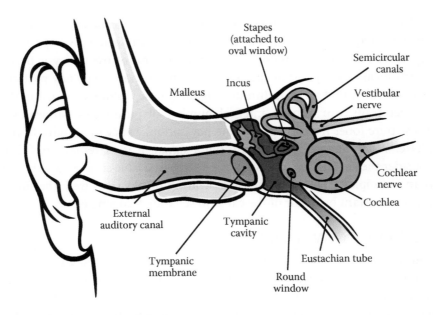

FIGURE 1.1   Anatomy of the human ear.

1.3.1 Dynamic Range

An amazing fact about our hearing is the ear's dynamic range. Human hearing has a range of about 120 decibels (dB). A decibel is a logarithmic unit used to express a ratio of two values. When used to measure sound pressure level, the reference level in the ratio is the quietest sound a human can hear. 120 dB represents a range of 1,000,000 to 1. The primary way the ear achieves this is by the bones that transmit the signal from the eardrum to the cochlea. They have the ability to dynamically reconfigure themselves to adapt their gain in real time according to the incoming signal.

1.3.2 Spatial Hearing

Humans have the ability to tell the direction that a sound is coming from, primarily due to the geometry of the head and ears. Two physical cues that are used by the brain for directionality are the interaural time difference (ITD) and the head-related transfer function (HRTF).

Sound moves slowly enough for your brain to measure the time delay between when a wave hits one ear versus the other. This time difference is called ITD. If a sound is directly in front of a person, the delay will be zero as the wave will hit both ears simultaneously. As the sound moves to one side, this delay changes as the distance from the sound to each ear changes. This is a primary cue to the brain for the angle that a sound is coming from relative to the front of the head.

The structure of the head and the pinnae of the ear act as a filter that varies frequency response by the angle of the signal. For example, if a sound is transmitted through the pinnae, it will lose power at high frequencies. We can model these effects by defining a filter for each ear that has a differing frequency response depending on the incidence angles of the sound with the ear. This angle-based filtration is the HRTF. The brain infers directional information by analyzing the frequency response of a signal. This is a learned behavior as the specific shape of an individual's ear impacts the HRTF, and thus the HRTF can vary significantly between individuals.

The information presented to the brain is not enough for the brain to disambiguate all incoming angles of sounds. The ambiguity forms the shape of a cone and is aptly called "the cone of confusion." The brain uses input from the other senses (e.g., matching a sound source to a visual input) and contextual knowledge (e.g., helicopters are seldom below one's feet) to help narrow down the actual direction of a sound.

An exhaustive review of this is presented in the book *Spatial Hearing*.[9]

1.3.3 Reflections

The environment that surrounds us interacts with our sound environment primarily by reflection. When a sound wave interacts with a surface, the surface reflects it. At higher frequencies with smooth surfaces, this works much like specular reflection. Reflections contain a significant amount of information about the surrounding environment. The structure of the reflections comprises primary cues to the brain about the distance between the listener and the sound. It also allows us to estimate the size of the surrounding environment.

Reflections also interfere with more important signals, and the ear ignores certain reflections because of this. When a sound is immediately followed by another sound, only the first of these is used by the brain to determine the direction of the sound. This is called "the precedence effect."[10]

1.3.4 Time and Sensory Fusion

Human perception of time is nonintuitive. For example, there are documented phenomena where a stimulus changes the perception of a previously received stimulus, thus apparently violating our notion of causality. A lot of interesting and extremely game-relevant research has been done in what is called "sensory fusion." This is the study of how close two stimuli need to be for the brain to think they are part of the same physical cause. For example, how close can two audio pulses occur and the brain still distinguish them as distinct sounds (about 5 ms); and how temporally separated can a voice be from a video of someone talking before the listener no longer perceives the voice and audio as one (lip sync). This particular example shows the sorts of complexity common in psychoacoustics as lip sync timings are not symmetric in time. You will notice the synchronization being off at far shorter intervals if the audio is leading the visual rather than the reverse. The variance infusion sense across the population is large, possibly as large as a factor of five between those with the most accurate and the least accurate. Musicians and others with formal audio training tend to have a much lower threshold than the general population. My oversimplified rule of thumb for lip sync is to keep audio within 50 ms of video. The chapter "Perceivable Auditory Latencies" in *Audio Anecdotes: Tools, Tips, and Techniques for Digital Audio*[11] has an excellent overview of the research relating to sensory fusion that anyone working in interactive audio should be familiar with.

1.3.5 Frequency

A good first approximation of hearing is of a windowed time-to-frequency converter. Windowed means that it looks only at a small amount of time. The ear can precisely detect frequencies from about 20 Hz to at most 20 kHz. The spacing is similar to exponential so the accuracy (in Hz) of the ear decreases as the pitch increases. There are quite a few units that have been developed to more closely approximate the ear's pitch space, e.g., Mel, Bark, and ERB.[8]

1.3.6 Masking

One of the most dramatic abilities of our hearing is the ability to filter out frequency content in a signal based on the time–frequency content of that same signal. The broad gist is that a loud sound can cause a quieter sound to be inaudible. The details are quite complicated and somewhat outside the scope of this document. Models of masking are what lossy audio compression algorithms such as mpeg use to reduce the amount of information in stored audio as any signal the ear would remove need not be kept in the compressed audio.

To give a bit of character to this complexity, I will give two examples of masking behavior. First, a quieter broadband sound can mask a louder pure tone sound (frequency masking). This is common in games as guns and explosions are very common sounds. These sounds are extremely broadband, meaning they have power at nearly all perceptible frequencies. Because of this, they are very effective at masking sounds that are more localized in frequency. In my experience, it is common to have a nearly inaudible broadband sound (typically an explosion) cause a wide variety of other sounds to become inaudible. Merely removing big noisy explosions causes everything else to pop and often makes the entire scene seem louder as the other sounds are no longer being masked.

Another example is a sound that happens after another can cause the sound that occurs first in time to be inaudible (temporal masking). Causality is a fuzzy quantity in perception within 100 ms or so.

1.4 HOW IS AUDIO REPRESENTED, PROCESSED, AND REPRODUCED?

Any one-dimensional physical property can be used to represent air pressure at an instant in time. If that property can change over time, it can represent audio. Common examples are voltage (the most common analog), current (dynamic microphones), optical transmissivity (film), magnetic orientation (magnetic tape), and physical displacement (records). The selected property is varied over time to represent the changing of pressure over time. In storage media, time is usually represented by length (tape, optical, record). In many sound analogs, time is represented by time itself (e.g., voltage via cable).

The majority of source audio comes from recording physical sound using microphones. Microphones translate air pressure into one of these pressure analogs (voltage and current are the two most common). Speakers convert current or voltage (almost always current) into pressure.

The ubiquitous representation for processing sound in games (and in all digital audio processing) is pulse-code modulation, or PCM. This representation consists of a sequence of integers that represent the sound pressure at equally spaced times.[12]

As with all approximations, the digital representation is imperfect. As we are capturing a continuous quantity with a fixed-size integer, there is information loss by quantization. The size in bits of the integer used to represent pressure is called bit depth. The most commonly used bit depth is 16 bit. Sampling at a fixed rate also causes information loss, although the specifics are difficult to quantify.

One of the most powerful tools for understanding how sampling affects the signal is the Nyquist–Shannon sampling theorem. This theory, somewhat oversimplified, states that for a band-limited signal, you need to sample at more than twice the rate of its highest frequency in order to correctly reconstruct the signal. High-frequency components above the Nyquist are reflected onto frequencies within the bandwidth of the sampled signal, a phenomenon known as aliasing. From an audio perspective, aliasing is unnatural sounding and is generally to be avoided. This material is covered in many books. One of my favorites is *Theory and Application of Digital Signal Processing*.[13]

Nearly all audio digital signal processing (DSP) is performed by basic operations (+, −, *) on these sequences of integers. This also is a huge topic that is well-covered. I highly recommend the Julius O. Smith III Audio DSP series, which are available both online and in print.[14–17] They give a comprehensive overview of basic audio DSP.

1.5 CONCLUSION

Hearing is a complicated and sometimes nonintuitive sense. Understanding its peculiarities is necessary to achieve both technical and artistic success in video game audio. A grasp of audio relevant to game programming requires a significant breadth of knowledge across the fields of physics, psychology, and signal processing. This chapter has given a brief overview of topics that I frequently find useful in my role as an audio programmer with the hopes that others will have a better place to start than I did.

NOTES

1. American Standards Association. 1960. *Acoustical terminology SI*, 1–1960. New York: American Standards Association.
2. Blackstock, David T. 2000. *Fundamentals of Physical Acoustics*. New York: John Wiley & Sons.
3. Morse, Philip McCord, and K. Uno Ingard. 1968. *Theoretical Acoustics*. Princeton: Princeton University Press.
4. Helmholtz, Hermann L.F., and Alexander J. Ellis. 2009. *On the Sensations of Tone as a Physiological Basis for the Theory of Music*. Cambridge: Cambridge University Press.
5. Smith, Julius O. 2007. *Mathematics of the Discrete Fourier Transform (DFT): With Audio Applications*. W3K.
6. Brockmann, Chittka L. A diagram of the anatomy of the human ear. https://commons.wikimedia.org/wiki/File:Anatomy_of_the_Human_Ear_en.svg licensed under Creative Commons Attribution 2.5 Generic license.
7. Moore, Brian C.J. 2012. *An Introduction to the Psychology of Hearing*. Leiden, The Netherlands: Brill.

8. Zwicker, Eberhard, and Hugo Fastl. 2013. *Psychoacoustics: Facts and Models*. Vol. 22. Berlin: Springer Science & Business Media.
9. Blauert, J. 1997. *Spatial Hearing*. Cambridge, MA: MIT Press.
10. Toole, Floyd E. 2008. *Sound Reproduction: Loudspeakers and Rooms*. Burlington, MA: Taylor & Francis.
11. van den Doel, Kees, and Dinesh K. Pai. 2004. Modal synthesis for vibrating objects. *Audio Anecdotes: Tools, Tips, and Techniques for Digital Audio*, ed. K. Greenebaum and R. Barzel. Natick, MA: A.K. Peters.
12. Watkinson, John. 2001. *The Art of Digital Audio*. London: Taylor & Francis.
13. Rabiner, Lawrence R., and Bernard Gold. 1975. *Theory and Application of Digital Signal Processing*. Englewood Cliffs, NJ: Prentice-Hall.
14. Smith, Julius O. 2007. *Mathematics of the Discrete Fourier Transform (DFT): With Audio Applications*. W3K.
15. Smith, Julius O. 2007. *Introduction to Digital Filters: With Audio Applications*. W3K.
16. Smith, Julius O. 2010. *Physical Audio Signal Processing*. W3K.
17. Smith, Julius O. 2011. *Spectral Audio Signal Processing*. W3K.

CHAPTER 2

Sound Engine State Machine

Guy Somberg

CONTENTS

2.1 THE NEED FOR A STATE MACHINE

When writing a very basic audio engine, the "jukebox" metaphor is quite apt. You need functions to load, play, pause, and stop sounds—all of the basics. And it turns out that you can actually do quite well and ship award-winning content using just those very basic tools. By abstracting the concept of a "sound" to an "event," modern audio middleware provides even more power to the sound designers without any sort of advanced engineering.

But simply wrapping the middleware with jukebox methods leads to a big mess of code as the audio engine grows to accommodate new features, because those features rarely map to the simple jukebox pattern. This is why a lot of audio engines, even ones that have shipped great games, are (frankly) terrible—if you can ship AAA award-winning Game-of-the-Year content on an audio engine that has no functionality other than playing wav files, why would you bother to update it?

The answer to that question lies in the expressivity of the sound designers. Inevitably, a sound designer will come to you and say "I want to do Thing X." Whatever Thing X is, your audio engine doesn't have that functionality right now, and it's your job to figure out how to bring a new feature into your audio engine. If you're working with an audio engine that is a simple "wrap the middleware" deal, you'll find that your code starts to look like a horrible tangled mess very quickly.

The question, then, is how to implement an audio engine that expresses the fundamentals, but provides easy and clean hooks to add new features. There are, of course, many ways to do it correctly, and in this chapter I'll be presenting a method that I have developed over a number of years, and which has shipped all sorts of games.

2.2 THE STARTING POINT

An audio engine that simply wraps the middleware is likely to have a very simple interface that just plays sounds in the `Play()` call and updates their state in the `Update()` call, thus:

```
void AudioEngine::Update()
{
  vector<ChannelMap::iterator> pStoppedChannels;
  for(auto it = mChannels.begin(),
        itEnd = mChannels.end();
        it != itEnd;
        ++it)
  {
    bool bIsPlaying = false;
    it->second->isPlaying(&bIsPlaying);
    if(!bIsPlaying)
    {
      pStoppedChannels.push_back(it);
    }
  }
}
```

```
  for(auto& it : pStoppedChannels)
  {
    mChannels.erase(it);
  }
  mpSystem->update();
}

int AudioEngine::PlaySound(
  const std::string& strSoundName,
  const Vector3& vPosition,
  float fVolumedB)
{
  int nChannelId = mnNextChannelId++;
  auto tFoundIt = mSounds.find(strSoundName);
  if(tFoundIt == mSounds.end())
  {
    LoadSound(strSoundName);
    tFoundIt = mSounds.find(strSoundName);
    if(tFoundIt == mSounds.end())
    {
      return nChannelId;
    }
  }
  FMOD::Channel* pChannel = nullptr;
  mpSystem->playSound(tFoundIt->second,
                      nullptr, true, &pChannel);
  if(pChannel)
  {
    FMOD_VECTOR position = VectorToFmod(vPosition);
    pChannel->set3DAttributes(&position, nullptr);
    pChannel->setVolume(dBToVolume(fVolumedB));
    pChannel->setPaused(false);
    mChannels[nChannelId] = pChannel;
  }
  return nChannelId;
}
```

Although this is a functional model, it's not very extensible. In fact, if we wanted to express the lifetime of a playing channel under this model as a state machine, it would look like Figure 2.1.

That's not much of a state machine, is it? Just one state: Playing. Nevertheless, we're going to use this state machine as a starting point.

Playing

FIGURE 2.1   A trivial state machine.

We're going to iterate on this state machine by implementing three new features: Fadeouts, Async Loading, and Virtual Channels. Once we've put the state machine together, we'll take a look at what the code might look like.

2.3 FADEOUT

We'll warm up by implementing fadeout. Fadeout is a simple feature and the change to our state machine is relatively minor, but it'll give us a taste of the sorts of changes that we'll be making to the state machine in order to implement other more complex features.

The feature itself is trivial: when a channel is requested to be stopped, it can optionally have a fadeout time requested. The channel fades out to silence over that amount of time, and then its lifetime ends.

To implement this feature, we'll adjust our state machine to look like Figure 2.2.

We start with a Playing sound, just as we had before. Now, when a stop request comes in, we jump to a new Stopping state. The Stopping state handles whatever fadeout logic it needs to. It may adjust the volume of the underlying channel by performing a linear interpolation on the volume down to silence over the requested time; it may implement an ADSR curve; or it may simply wait for the middleware to say "yes, the channel has finished playing."

Regardless of the details of the logic, the end result of the Stopping state is that the channel has finished playing. When the channel is completed,

FIGURE 2.2   State machine implementing fadeout.

our state machine switches to the Stopped state. Once a channel is in the Stopped state, the audio engine cleans it up and releases its resources.

And that's it! We've now implemented fadeout support.

2.4 ASYNC LOADS

Well, that wasn't too hard! We just added a couple of states, and now our feature is implemented! Let's go again, this time with a more complicated feature.

Asynchronous loads are, on the surface, a relatively simple feature. When a sound is requested to be loaded or played, we make sure that we don't block the main thread while the load happens. Instead, we load the sound data asynchronously and then start playing the sound once the load is complete.

But if you think about it, this one feature is completely incompatible with our nice simple idea of the lifetime of our playing channel. Our happy middleware-wrapping world comes falling apart if we try to do this naively. The reason that this happens is that now there is potentially some nonzero length of time between when the game asks for the sound to be played and when the audio engine actually plays the audio. Fortunately, by adjusting our state machine to look like Figure 2.3 to implement the feature, we can implement the feature while keeping a clean interface.

Under this new model, we no longer play a channel immediately upon creating it. Instead, when the channel is created from the ether, we put

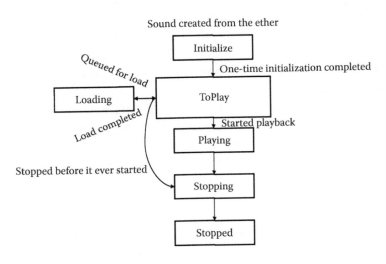

FIGURE 2.3   State machine implementing async loads.

it into a one-time `Initialize` state. Note that this state is not the same as a constructor, which initializes the invariants for the object itself. The `Initialize` state prepares any initialization parameters that should only happen once. Under certain circumstances, this state may be empty, but we'll see an example later on in this chapter of a use case for this state.

Once the one-time initialization is completed, we switch to the `ToPlay` state, so called because it is for sounds that are ready *to play*. You'll note that the box for this state is extra large. We'll come back to why that is in a bit, once we hit the Virtual Channels feature. In the `ToPlay` state, we actually start the playback of channels—we create any runtime context and start to play the sound data. Once the playback is started, we jump to the `Playing` state, and proceed just as we did before.

All of that is only true, though, if our sound data is actually loaded. If it is not loaded, then the `ToPlay` state will start the asynchronous load of the sound data and switch to the `Loading` state. The `Loading` state sits and waits for the sound data to finish loading. Once the async load is complete, it switches back to `ToPlay`, and the state machine continues on as normal.

There is one more arrow that we need in order to make this feature complete. Because of the nonzero length of time from when a sound is triggered to play until the channel is prepared to play in the `ToPlay` state, there is now a window of opportunity for the state of the channel to be modified by the game. It is possible that, during that timeframe, we received a request from the game code to stop the channel. In fact, it's entirely possible that we received this stop request on the same game frame that we got the play request!

To handle this case, we draw our last arrow directly from `ToPlay` into `Stopping`. If a stop request has come in before we actually had a chance to play the sound, then there's no point in playing it just so that we can stop it immediately.

Asynchronous loads have forced us to detach the lifetime of our channels from the "jukebox" functions that we've exposed to the game API. This is a good thing, because that connection was artificial, and detaching the lifetimes allows for far greater expressiveness and functionality when implementing new features.

2.5 VIRTUAL CHANNELS

Our state machine is still fairly linear. If the sound data is fully loaded before we play the sound, then we progress directly through `Initialize`,

ToPlay, Playing, Stopping, and Stopped states. For our next feature, we'll actually get some more complicated structure to our state machine.

Virtual channels are a mechanism in a sound engine to control the entire mix of sounds, while at the same time managing performance in the face of an overwhelming number of play sound calls. A virtual channel is a channel that is not important enough to be heard. There are many reasons why this could be: it is outside of the 3D max distance; it has a maximum number of playbacks; its volume is below a certain threshold; or there are too many similar sounds currently playing.

The possibilities for selecting sounds for virtualization are endless, and will vary from game to game. Some games (such as adventure games) may not need this feature at all. Highly randomized action adventure games will need a healthy dose of virtualization in order to prevent the mix from becoming a muddy mess.

The simplest check for virtualization is to check if a sound is outside of its 3D max distance. It's a trivial check, and a valuable one, but the result is more valuable for performance optimization than for mix control. A more useful check is testing a sound's audibility, which is a sound's combined volume from 3D attenuation, obstruction/occlusion, volume control, and any other pieces that may control its overall volume. If a sound is insufficiently audible, then it may be a good candidate for virtualization.

2.5.1 Max Within Radius

One particularly effective, but advanced, technique for virtualization is called *Max Within Radius*. To understand this feature, we need to go to the film world and reference Walter Murch's *Rule of Two and a Half*.[1] In short, the Rule of Two and a Half states that we humans can only keep track of two things at a time. As soon as we have more than two things, the "two and a half" things to keep track of, then it becomes more about "the sound of many of those things together" than each individual sound.

The canonical example of this rule (and the one where Walter Murch first discovered this principle while mixing *THX1138*) is footsteps. When you have one set of footsteps, it's important that each footstep sound syncs up precisely with each animated step. When you have two sets of footsteps, it's likewise important to sync them up. But once you have three or more sets of footsteps, it's more about the sound of walking feet than about each person's footsteps.

Of course, Walter Murch was working in the world of film, where he had the luxury of precisely tailoring the mix to every moment in time. So, when adapting this technique to game audio engines, we have to generalize it for a game mix where sounds can be triggered willy-nilly, at arbitrary (and sometimes downright inconvenient!) times.

So, to implement the *Max Within Radius* feature, each sound is given a radius around itself and a maximum number of playbacks within that radius, both configurable by the sound designers. As the sound is played on a channel, the audio engine checks within the given radius around itself for duplicate sounds. If the maximum number of sounds is hit, then it virtualizes that channel until the other channels either finish or until they move apart.

You can see an example of this technique in Figure 2.4. The triangle is the listener, and each of the smaller circles represents a sound source. The sounds check within their assigned radius (the larger outer circles), and then virtualize the highlighted sounds where there are more than the maximum (two in this example) within the radius.

2.5.2 Virtual Channels in the State Machine

Ultimately, there will be a single function call ShouldBeVirtual() that your audio engine will contain that performs all of the necessary heuristics to decide whether a particular channel is "important" enough to be heard. Since virtual channels aren't important to the mix, we can simply stop playing them (while still tracking their position and other metadata, of course). This frees up resources that are used to play the sound, improves performance, and cleans up the mix.

In practice, you can follow somewhat different rules for one-shot sounds than looped sounds. Because most one-shot sounds are short, if a one-shot

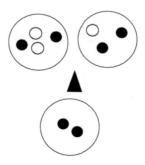

FIGURE 2.4   Max Within Radius.

sound is not important enough to be heard when it first starts playing, you can skip playing the sound entirely. Once it's playing, you don't need to bother checking it for virtualness again. Looped sounds, however, do need to go through the virtual check during their update. When a looped sound is virtualized, it needs to be faded out over a short period—I've found that a quarter-second to a half-second is best, although that time could vary per game. Similarly, when channels are getting devirtualized, they should have a quick fade-in as well.

The question is, then, how do we implement virtual channels into our state machine? As you can see in Figure 2.5, this time we needed to add some more complexity. Although, in truth, it's only two new states, there are now a lot more arrows coordinating them.

Let's start with the Playing state. We need to do a ShouldBeVirtual() check on the channels as they're playing. If the channel should be virtual, then we need to implement a quick fadeout. Similar to the Fadeout state, we add a new Virtualizing state, which implements the fade. Once the fadeout is complete, we stop the channel and release the resources for the sound, and then switch to the Virtual state. However, because the fade takes some time, the environment can change during the fadeout. So, we need to continue to do the ShouldBeVirtual() check while we're fading out. If it ever comes back as not virtual, then we can fade the sound back up to full volume and switch back to the Playing state.

In the Virtual state, we can simply check ShouldBeVirtual() periodically. If we decide that it should continue to be virtual, then there is

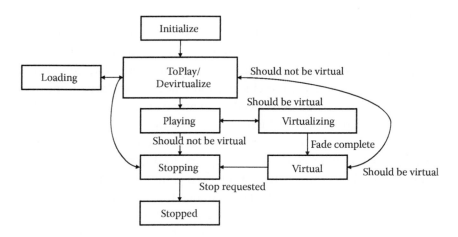

FIGURE 2.5   State machine implementing virtual sounds.

nothing to do. If it shouldn't be virtual any more, then we need to restart the sound. Fortunately, we already have a state for that—ToPlay!

Except that the behavior when devirtualizing a channel is slightly different than when playing a sound from scratch. We need do a quick fade-in, we need to select parameters from the state instead of randomizing them, and perhaps other slight differences. There are a few ways to implement this—we could store a bool or we could set a bit-flag on the channel object. But then, we're lugging around a bunch of data in the channel object for a state that is extremely transient.

Instead, we add a new state—Devirtualize, which is the same as ToPlay, except that it does the extra behaviors for devirtualization. Implementing this as a state is by definition transient, and so it doesn't waste any space in the channel object. Most of the code can be shared, and the extra behaviors are easy and fast to check.

There are just two more state transitions to complete the picture. When we're in either the ToPlay or Devirtualize state, we can perform a pre-emptive ShouldBeVirtual() check. If the check indicates that the channel should be virtual, then we can either jump straight to Virtual state (if it's a looped sound) or jump straight to Stopping (if it's a one-shot sound). Finally, channels in the Virtual state can be stopped by the game code and can simply transition to Stopping.

Whew! That's a lot of transitions for just two new states. But what we have now is a single function call to ask whether a channel should be virtual, and a set of very simple rules to implement the feature.

2.6 THE STATE MACHINE

We've now finished making edits to this state machine for a couple of reasons. First of all, because we've fully implemented everything that we set out to do—by just making state machine changes, we've gotten three features fully implemented, including some fairly complicated ones. The second reason is that we don't need to go any further. This state machine that we've ended up with, which you can see in Figure 2.6, has shipped numerous games. I have used this exact state machine (or, rather, minor variations of it as it developed over the years) to ship first-person shooters, action RPGs, dungeon crawlers, simulation games, and adventure games. That doesn't account for every genre under the sun (brawlers and real-time strategy games are notably missing, off the top of my head), but I feel confident that this state machine would account for any behaviors that you might find in any game genre.

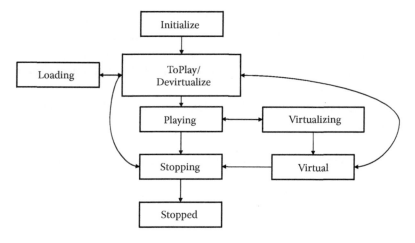

FIGURE 2.6 Final state machine.

2.6.1 The Code

Enough talk—let's see the code! Above, I presented hypothetical Play()
and Update() functions for a simple jukebox-style sound engine. The
beauty of this setup is that the jukebox interface does not need to change.
Play(), Stop(), Pause(), Update(), and all of your other interface functions don't need to change, just their underlying implementations. Let's
start by looking at Play():

```
int AudioEngine::PlaySound(
    int nSoundId,
    const Vector3& vPosition,
    float fVolumedB)
{
  int nChannelId = mnNextChannelId++;
  auto tSoundIt = mSounds.find(nSoundId);
  if(tSoundIt == mSounds.end())
    return nChannelId;
  mChannels[nChannelId] =
    make_unique<Implementation::Channel>(nSoundId,
      tSoundIt->second->mSoundDefinition,
      vPosition,
      fVolumedB);
  return nChannelId;
}
```

All of a sudden our `Play()` call is really trivial. All we need to do is allocate memory for our channel, and we're done! In the example code, I've used C++14's make_unique<> to allocate off of the heap, but there's no reason why you can't keep a cache of unused channel objects and reuse them as an optimization.

As it turns out, the guts of the `Update()` function don't need to change much either:

```
void AudioEngine::Update(float fTimeDeltaSeconds)
{
  vector<ChannelMap::iterator> pStoppedChannels;
  for(auto it = mChannels.begin(),
        itEnd = mChannels.end();
        it != itEnd;
        ++it)
  {
    it->second->Update(fTimeDeltaSeconds);
    if(it->second->meState == Channel::State::STOPPED)
    {
      pStoppedChannels.push_back(it);
    }
  }
  for(auto& it : pStoppedChannels)
  {
    mChannels.erase(it);
  }
  mpSystem->update();
}
```

Really, the only difference is that we're calling `Channel::Update()` to run through our state machine, and then check to see if the state is Stopped instead of whether the underlying channel has stopped.

So, let's take a look at the actual implementation of `Channel::Update()`. This function is long, so we'll break it up into one state at a time.

In this example code, our Initialize state does nothing. However, we'll leave it in there for future extendibility. In the next section, we'll show an example of the sort of logic that would go into the Initialize state.

```
void Channel::Update(float fTimeDeltaSeconds)
{
  switch(meState)
```

```
{
case State::INITIALIZE:
// Intentional Fallthrough
```

The most complicated state of this machine is the `ToPlay` and `Devirtualize` state. The thing to notice is that each conditional check maps to an arrow in our state machine. If a stop is requested, we jump to the `Stopping` state. If it should be virtual, we go to either `Stopping` or `Virtual` depending on whether it's a one-shot sound. If the sound isn't loaded, we load it and go to `Loading`. Finally, we can play it just as we did in the earlier function.

And note also that the code to actually play the sound is virtually identical to the code that we had before—the only thing that's changed is the state machine harness surrounding it.

```
case State::DEVIRTUALIZE:
case State::TOPLAY:
   {
     if(mbStopRequsted) {
       meState = State::STOPPING;
       return;
     }
     if(ShouldBeVirtual(true)) {
       if(IsOneShot()) {
         meState = State::STOPPING;
       else {
         meState = State::VIRTUAL;
       }
       return;
     }
     if(!SoundIsLoaded(mSoundId)) {
       LoadSound(mSoundId);
       meState = State::LOADING;
       return;
     }
     mpChannel = nullptr;
     auto tSoundIt =  mSounds.find(mSoundId);
     if(tSoundIt !=  mSounds.end())
       mpSystem->playSound(
           tSoundIt->second->mpSound,
           nullptr, true, &mpChannel);
     if(mpChannel) {
```

```
      if (meState == State::DEVIRTUALIZE)
        mVirtualizeFader.StartFade(SILENCE_dB, 0.0f,
                                   VIRTUALIZE_FADE_TIME);
      meState = State::PLAYING;
      FMOD_VECTOR position = VectorToFmod(mvPosition);
      mpChannel->set3DAttributes(&position, nullptr);
      mpChannel->setVolume(dBToVolume(GetVolumedB()));
      mpChannel->setPaused(false);
    }
    else
    {
      meState = State::STOPPING;
    }
  }
  break;
```

The next state is the Loading state, which is pretty trivial:

```
case State::LOADING:
  if (SoundIsLoaded(mSoundId))
  {
    meState = State::TOPLAY;
  }
  break;
```

In the Playing state, we are watching for any changes. The mysterious UpdateChannelParameters() call is applying 3D position, volume effects, panning, and any other game state that needs to be accumulated into the underling playing channel. As before, each conditional maps to a line in our state machine. If we've stopped, jump to the Stopping state. If we should be virtual, jump to the Virtualizing state.

```
case State::PLAYING:
  mVirtualizeFader.Update(fTimeDeltaSeconds);
  UpdateChannelParameters();
  if (!IsPlaying() || mbStopRequsted)
  {
    meState = State::STOPPING;
    return;
  }
  if (ShouldBeVirtual(false))
  {
```

```
mVirtualizeFader.StartFade(SILENCE_dB,
                            VIRTUALIZE_FADE_TIME);
    meState = State::VIRTUALIZING;
}
break;
```

Next come the Stopping and Stopped states. Here, there are many fewer conditionals and transitions. The clock is ticking until the channel will be going away entirely. In the Stopping state, our channel is simply whiling away the moments until the sound has finished playing or its fadeout is complete.

```
case State::STOPPING:
  mStopFader.Update(fTimeDeltaSeconds);
  UpdateChannelParameters();
  if(mStopFader.IsFinished())
  {
    mpChannel->stop();
  }
  if(!IsPlaying())
  {
    meState = State::STOPPED;
    return;
  }
  break;
case State::STOPPED: break;
```

Finally, the Virtualizing and Virtual states. Virtualizing is similar to Stopping, except that it has the extra ShouldBeVirtual() check to see if it should switch back to the Playing state. The Virtual state should do very little, but we do need to do another ShouldBeVirtual() check to see if we should restart the sound with Devirtualize.

```
case State::VIRTUALIZING:
  mVirtualizeFader.Update(fTimeDeltaSeconds);
  UpdateChannelParameters();
  if(!ShouldBeVirtual(false))
  {
    mVirtualizeFader.StartFade(0.0f,
                                VIRTUALIZE_FADE_TIME);
    meState = State::PLAYING;
    break;
```

```
    }
    if(mVirtualizeFader.IsFinished())
    {
      mpChannel->stop();
      meState = State::VIRTUAL;
    }
    break;
  case State::VIRTUAL:
    if(mbStopRequsted)
    {
      meState = State::STOPPING;
    }
    else if(!ShouldBeVirtual(false))
    {
      meState = State::DEVIRTUALIZE;
    }
    break;
  }
}
```

It turns out that you can implement an entire audio engine (albeit a simple one), including this state machine and all of the supporting code, in about 600 lines of code and a few hours' worth of work. This is only slightly more than double the lines of code that it takes to do a simple "wrap the middleware" deal (which I was able to do in about 250 lines of code) but it is so much more feature-full, approachable, maintainable, and extendable.

A couple of notes about this code:

- Some of the functionality is simplified for effect. For example, the code uses a "fader" object to implement fades, but you can use the Channel::addFadePoint() API (or other middleware-specific APIs if you're not using FMOD) to automate this.

- Similarly, the implementation of this code is using the FMOD Studio low-level API. The playback code will be different if you use the FMOD Studio API, or another middleware such as Wwise or CRI ADX2.

- Finally, although I have presented this as an Update() call, you can also implement it as an event-driven system.

2.7 WHERE TO GO FROM HERE

This state machine is just to give you a framework to get started and hooks to add features, of course. Let's see some examples of how to leverage this state machine to add yet more features.

2.7.1 Randomizing Sounds

Let's say that we want to add a feature where every time a sound is played, the audio engine randomizes the volume and pitch of the sound, within some parameters based on the sound itself. Easy enough! We'll pick the randomized volume and pitch inside the Initialize state, then apply the values in the UpdateChannelParameters() call. UpdateChannelParameters() is already called at the appropriate times, so we don't need to worry about when and where to apply the parameter changes. So that's it! We're done!

Note that we use the Initialize state to implement this feature, which has heretofore been an unused stub. The reason that we use Initialize instead of ToPlay for this feature is because we want to make sure that, when a channel goes virtual and then gets devirtualized, it ends up playing at the same randomized volume and pitch as it was before it went virtual. Initialize is there exactly for that situation.

2.7.2 Make Virtual Channels Cheaper

Depending on your game, virtual channels can actually be a majority of the sounds in the game at any given time. You may end up having thousands of virtual channels, and only a dozen or so actually playing sounds. As a result, you want to make sure that your virtual channels are as cheap as possible.

There are, of course, many ways to effect this, but the simplest one is simply to update them less often. Pick a number N, and only update sounds in the Virtual state every N frames or seconds. The specific number will vary based on your game—how many virtual channels you have, how expensive it is to check whether a channel should be virtual, and what sounds the best. The one thing to be careful of is that you don't want (for example) every 10th frame to be slow because that's the frame where virtualization checks occur for your several thousand virtual channels. Instead, assign each channel a number as it becomes virtual, and stagger the virtual updates over time, so that any given frame has a roughly equal number of virtual channel checks.

2.7.3 Play Sound Groups Together

The feature description is that we want to play multiple sounds together and treat them as a single unit. This allows you to, for example, split the impact and tail of an explosion into two separate entities. That allows you to give them different virtualization behaviors and randomization parameters, while still triggering them, mixing them, and treating them as a single unit.

To implement this feature, you'll need to store a container inside of your Channel object (if you're using FMOD, that container will be an `FMOD::ChannelGroup*`), along with a vector of subsounds. Update the `Loading` state to load all of the subsounds, and make sure that `ToPlay` plays them all and combines them into the `ChannelGroup`. Finally, you will have to fix up the `UpdateChannelParameters()` call to apply the parameter changes to the appropriate object. (With FMOD Studio, you can store an `FMOD::ChannelControl*` pointer and assign that to either an `FMOD::Channel*` or an `FMOD::ChannelGroup*`, then just make changes to the `ChannelControl` object.)

And that's it! Make those changes, and now the feature is implemented.

2.8 CONCLUSION

It doesn't take a lot of code, time, or energy to create a functional, maintainable audio engine that is a joy to work with. With a small time investment, and using the state machine described in this chapter, you too can create a powerful, extensible audio engine. And when your sound designers come to you asking for features, you'll be able to work with them to figure out what they're actually after, and then have confidence that you can implement the feature quickly and cleanly.

NOTE

1. Walter Murch. 2005. Womb Tone. *The Transom Review* Vol. 5/Issue 1. http://transom.org/wp-content/uploads/2005/04/200504.review.murch_.pdf (accessed July 14, 2015). Although the whole article is interesting, the Rule of Two and a Half starts on page 15.

Streaming Sound

Blair Bitonti

CONTENTS

Stream (from google.com)

strēm

noun

noun: **stream**; plural noun: **streams**

> 1. a small, narrow river.

synonyms:	creek, river, rivulet, rill, runnel, streamlet, freshet tributary; bourn; brook "a mountain stream"

2. a continuous flow of liquid, air, or gas.

"Frank blew out **a stream of** smoke"

synonyms:	jet, flow, rush, gush, surge, torrent, flood, cascade, outpouring, outflow; *technical* efflux "a stream of boiling water"

3.1 INTRODUCTION

According to Google.com, this is the definition of a stream. These days, when you mention a stream, most people probably think of the constant barrage of media they are consuming through their phones, tablets, and laptops. Nearly everyone is familiar with the term "streaming," but I wonder how many people stop to think about what a "stream" actually is. Does the content-hungry, iPhone generation ever give a second thought to the technology behind their on-demand movie and music delivery services? Probably not, but if they were to look into it they would learn that streaming technology became a viable means of content delivery in the early 1990s—around the same time as the dawn of the optical media era as the first PC CD-ROMs were becoming more popular.

With nearly every new PC game shipping on one to several CDs, this led to the best thing to happen to the PC industry—the death of the floppy disk! In addition, CD-ROM technology allowed game developers in the early 1990s to pack in the content like never before. Game programmers in this time had to devise systems capable of reading this high-quality content off the disk and render it back in-game. Before the Internet was mature enough to handle everyone streaming content, the video game industry was hard at work designing and optimizing CD-ROM-based streaming systems to deliver richer content to their growing mass of consumers. This is what I mean when I talk about a stream during the course of a typical work day as an audio programmer at Treyarch and what I am going to be talking about in this chapter.

3.2 KEY LIMITING FACTORS TO STREAMING PERFORMANCE

Once games started streaming in-game content, it ushered in an era of high-quality, large file/memory-sized assets that helped immerse the gamer in the audio universe that the sound team envisioned for their title. Custom MIDI scores became full-blown Hollywood-style orchestral recordings that rivaled big screen and TV productions. Random world emitters went from the odd RAM-based (short) samples to rich, detailed streamed ambiences that could be designed to match the player's surroundings in the game. Low-quality, seldom-used dialog cues gave way to sophisticated play-by-play systems in sports games and long scripted voiceovers from A-list talents, designed to sell the game as a cinematic experience to the player.

Once sound designers had access to streaming systems capable of rendering all of this content, they wanted to use it more and more. As with any highly optimized system, there are certain trade-offs if you want to push the envelope for greater performance.

CPU cost is always a concern. Early low-level console sound hardware had limited to nonexistent support for streaming requiring the programmer to write code to read waveform data from the physical media into main memory and then shuffle it off down to the sound rendering layer, usually by way of direct memory access (DMA) or some other OS-dependent API. All of this data handling comes at a cost and, even if implemented in a highly optimized way, has both CPU and memory costs associated. "Hardware streams," as this first case describes, would usually be reasonable from a CPU perspective, especially if they relied on any hardware resident decoder abilities. For most consoles, this was usually some flavor of adaptive differential pulse-code modulation (ADPCM), which yields ~3.5:1 compression ratios and fairly noticeable audio artifacts. If the designer was truly going for a high-quality experience they would want to make use of a "main CPU"-based stream that would stream the data into main RAM from the disk, then decompress and mix it in with any other main RAM-based audio for transport to the hardware. Depending on the compression scheme chosen, this could use up to 1–2% of the CPU for a single streamed voice. When working under tight performance budgets (10% of the CPU for audio is considered generous on most titles), you can see how the CPU costs can add up rather quickly and limit the amount of voices you could stream.

In any code system in a game engine, you need to be concerned with memory and ensure that you design in a way that keeps memory costs to a minimum. Both the hardware and main CPU streams mentioned previously will incur some type of memory cost, either in main RAM, "sound" (or "special") RAM, or both. I say "special" RAM as some consoles feature dedicated sound RAM, whereas others have an auxiliary reserve that is shared with sound and other systems. The amount of this RAM that is allocated to the sound system, taking into consideration how much is used by other (loaded) sounds assets, may end up being a limiting factor to the number of simultaneous streams the engine can handle.

3.2.1 "Seek"-ing More Streams

Despite the usual memory and CPU limitations, most games have typically been seek-time bound. Seek time refers to the amount of time required for the physical media to move the read head and "seek" to the next file to be processed in the file system. Seek times have stayed about the same as optical drives have matured, despite read speeds getting faster and faster. Even on modern optical drives it is not unreasonable to have to account for a worst case of 250-ms seek time from a standard DVD or CD. Factor in that double- and sometimes even triple-buffering is pretty standard for streaming sound, the memory costs for multiple streams can balloon quickly. If your engine allocates streaming buffers of 256 KB in a double-buffered streamer and you have 10 streaming channels, then you are allocating 5 MB before you even have any sounds loaded into RAM.

3.3 PRIORITY

A well-designed game audio engine requires a good priority system to help determine what sounds are most important to the gamer and to make sure that these sounds always play and are never interrupted in favor of sounds that are not crucial to gameplay or the overall goals of the sound team. In most cases, the audio programmer is going to want to devise a system where streams are handled differently than RAM-based sounds. This is because you are going to want to set a limit to the amount of simultaneous streamed channels that are supported and also because your streamed sounds tend to be the more "important" sounds in the game such as music or dialog. Without a decent priority system that tracks streamed versus RAM-based sounds, you could end up with the unfortunate situation where, for example, the music track disappears during an action sequence in order to start a new sound that could be something way less important, such as a footstep or bullet impact sound. Obviously, this is a situation you would want to avoid at all costs, so make sure that the engine not only tracks which sounds can be interrupted but also pays attention to the type of sound that is trying to play.

3.4 THE FILE SYSTEM IS YOUR FRIEND

Every audio programmer should have a thorough understanding and knowledge of the file I/O layer of whatever target systems they are developing on. In particular, if they are not responsible for any of the low-level file code they will want to consult closely with the person on their team who is. In most cases, the sound engine streamer is going to be pushing the limits of the file system and should have priority over file opens and reads.

As consoles have matured, we have been able to push more and more simultaneous streams. As mentioned earlier in this chapter, this is mainly due to increased memory budgets for systems using the streamer as well as a move to install the game on hard disks rather than streaming the files from optical media at runtime. I mentioned how seek times on optical disks had remained relatively similar to the early devices and had not increased in performance the way read speeds had. The best thing this most recent console generation did was do away with the optical media altogether.

3.4.1 Request Latency—"When Do You *Really* Need Your Data?"

In the heavily optimized console game development world, any system that can be fine-tuned is. That being said, with the PlayStation 4 and Xbox One, we are now provided with an API into the file system that takes into account the time until the rest of your program needs the data. requestLatency is essentially a time (in milliseconds) that the caller requires the data to be returned. As various file I/O operations are queued up by each of the systems in the game, they are expected to provide a reasonable estimate for how long they could go without the read complete callback being fired off to signal the returned data as valid. In a way, this is another type of priority that is used by the file system in the operating system layer to help it determine how to arrange the actual read operations to maximize speed and ultimately streaming bandwidth across the game. For example, during one file system update period, there are four requests made from the texture steaming code, each with a value of 2000 ms for requestLatency, and there is a single request from the sound streamer for a buffer read with a requestLatency of 1000 ms. In this case, the buffer for the sound system will likely be handled and read first by the file system. I say most likely because these numbers are intentionally large to prove a point. Several other factors, such as the size of the reads requested and the location on the disk for the physical files being read, will be taken into account, and it may just be able to handle the requests in the order they were received if all of the values of requestLatency are reasonable and the files system determines it can service them all in that update period.

3.4.2 Sound Is the Most Important

Well, you will never hear that spoken aloud in the hallways of any game studio, but you will in a book about audio programming. In addition to a priority system within the sound engine, the whole engineering team needs to accept the fact that the audio system requires the highest possible priority in the file system layer of the engine. Depending on the different types of game assets that are going to be streamed or read into the game, the sound engine should have the highest priority slot reserved for streaming. The reason for this is simple. If a streamed sound is in the middle of playback and it is preempted in favor of another file read operation, let's say for a texture, the end result can have the potential to be disastrous by leading to audible breakup of the streamed sound. Ask yourself what is worse: having the lead character's voiceover stop in the middle of a line, or having a low-resolution version of a texture pop in a couple of frames later.

3.5 PRELOADING OR PRIMING STREAMS

As consoles have seen dramatic increases in memory capacity and more RAM has been afforded to audio systems, we have had the luxury of using preloading or priming in streaming audio systems. Priming, as I will refer to it, is essentially storing the first portion of a streamed sound in RAM and pointing the sound engine to this data rather than issuing a read request through the file system to the physical media.

So, that explains what priming a stream is if you didn't know, but why would you do this? Why would you spend precious RAM resources that could be better served with maybe higher quality gun or ambient or foley assets? Yes, there has been an increase in RAM in each console generation and we are now fairly spoiled with budgets in the 10s of MBs for sound, but that memory is still at a premium when you have to start accounting for sound coverage on game assets that have increased themselves not only in quality (size) but in variety as well. Every new "thing" in the game also needs a new sound, and all of these new sounds and variety to cover all these new "things" end up consuming RAM. Even if you do have RAM to burn (yeah right), doesn't storing any portion of the sound asset in RAM defeat the purpose of streaming in the first place?

For starters, you don't need or probably even want to prime every single streamed sound in your game. That would be impractical. Rather than make a blanket decision like that, your sound pipeline should be set up to allow any sound to be tagged as primed in your authoring environment and your runtime streamer code, and APIs should all support passing a memory location or copying the primed data and a size.

```
StreamBuffer* StreamBufferReadPrimed(
  StreamBuffer* buffer, int64_t offset,
  const byte* primeData, unsigned int size);
```

Your sound streaming code should call `StreamBufferReadPrimed()` when the streamed sound channel is first triggered to play and it contains a resident primed data chunk.

3.5.1 The StreamBuffer

Most of the functions in the primed streaming example presented here will take a pointer to a `StreamBuffer` variable, which tracks all of the information pertaining to a single buffer of streamed data. When `StreamBufferReadPrimed()` is called on a newly triggered stream for the first time, it essentially just fills out the fields in the `StreamBuffer` structure instance with the information for the primed memory chunk in RAM rather than issuing a read request to the file system. Before we get too far in this example, it helps to take a look at the makeup of the `StreamBuffer` structure that we'll use.

```
struct StreamBuffer
{
  volatile volatile_int32 refCount;
  const char *filename;
  StringHash filenameHash;
  int64_t offset;
  int64_t readSize;
  unsigned int requestLatency;
  unsigned int requestStartTime;
  unsigned int requestEndTime;
  StreamId requestId;
  byte* data;
  bool valid;
  bool error;
  bool invalidateBuffer;
};
```

As found in many threading systems, this streaming example uses reference counting to ensure data validity. `refCount` will be 0 if the `StreamBuffer` is free and there are no pending file I/O operations, and it will be greater than 0 if the buffer is allocated to a stream and has data associated with it and/or any pending file I/O. At various points in the streamer code, we check or assert that this is true to ensure everything runs smoothly. Freeing a `StreamBuffer` with pending asynchronous file I/O operations can result in catastrophic failure depending on the file system and target platform you are working on. We track the `filename` mostly for debugging purposes in this example as the file system used here references the source files by a numerical file ID rather than copying filenames around between buffers and various functions within the system. The `filenameHash` member is part of an optimization of the sound streaming code in this example and is basically a 32-bit cyclic redundancy check (CRC) that is used to track recently used streaming buffers in a cache. The `offset` variable is the byte index into the file that we are streaming from, and the `readSize` is the size of the read issued to the file system. Or, in this case of a primed stream, the size of the primed data that is sitting in resident memory and contains the first `STREAM_BUFFER_SIZE` bytes of the sound file. The `requestId` is a unique identifier assigned by the file system to track asynchronous file requests. The `data` member points to the streamed-in file data from the disk once the request has been completed by the file system or, in this example, it points to the primed data sitting in RAM. The `valid` field is a `bool` that is set to true when the read operation has completed (or `StreamBufferReadPrimed()` has been called), indicating that this buffer is valid and can be used by the sound system. False would indicate that I/O has not been issued or completed yet.

Obviously, `error` is simply a flag to indicate that there is something wrong with this buffer to allow the sound streamer to deal with this situation. The `primed` variable can be confusing for this example as it has nothing to do with primed streams. It is used on all streams, primed or otherwise, to track the status of the buffer and whether it has good data in it. The `invalidateBuffer` bool is there to track whether a buffer has been allocated or freed (valid/true when allocated, invalid/false when it is free and available to be used by the sound streamer).

3.5.2 Primed Streams Functionality and Practical Example

Whether the buffer is read or copied from the primed section in RAM, streamed in via a file read request, or returned from the cache, the data is always contained within an instance of the `StreamBuffer`. The rest of the audio system need not care about where the data comes from. The origin of the data, however, does influence performance and, as stated before, performance needs to be finely tuned to take advantage of every cycle possible.

The primed system yields a significant performance gain when implemented in a game engine. It is not the type of gain that is going to allow you to give back to the rest of the game and render more textures or handle more animations. It's not even the type of optimization that is going to benefit the sound system and allow more simultaneous sound channels or more CPU-hungry DSP effects. The real performance gain afforded by the primed implementation is to eliminate, or delay, the initial seek required to fill the `StreamBuffers` with the first portion of the source audio file. By avoiding this costly seek on the first buffer, we reduce the overall latency that typically plagues the start of a streamed channel and we can ensure better synchronization with the game event that triggered the streamed sound.

As mentioned earlier, it is not necessary to dedicate precious RAM to every stream with an initial primed buffer. For example, if you have a music cue that gets fired off when the player enters an area full of enemy AI in a first-person shooter, it most likely won't matter if the sound starts with the usual latency of a RAM-based sound (different for every game and game engine, but a frame or two latency is usually acceptable and expected). It would be a waste to allocate RAM resources to prime your music cues because even if you get hit with the worst-case file seek penalty (say 250 ms), it likely won't matter as we are just kicking off a piece of music. So long as it starts—that is all we really care about.

What about the situation where we have some really important plot dialog that gets triggered from an in-game cutscene (IGC)? Turns out this is an ideal opportunity to use primed streams. This was exactly the situation we faced on Black Ops II when we had hundreds and hundreds of voiceover lines triggered from cut scenes that were meant to tie together the story as you play through the campaign missions. We were getting dozens of bugs logged that various dialog lines were horribly out of sync with the facial animation of the character speaking the lines. The average human starts to notice sound latency problems when the delta approaches 100 ms. This value is well within the typical seek times that we were experiencing when requesting data from the DVD drive. Overall, 250 ms is the worst case we designed around, but 100 ms seeks were quite common so we had to come up with a solution to this problem. Luckily, we had invested the time to add the primed functionality to the sound streamer so we were able to simply tag each streamed sound that would be used in a lip-synced cut scene. Again, it just makes sense to differentiate primed streams throughout your pipeline in this way to allow the sound designer to mark a sound as primed rather than just prime everything.

3.5.3 Primed Streams Source Code Example

The following is the rest of the primed stream example implementation. Included in the source is the entire stream update function that is called once per frame per stream. It handles all of the high-level logic necessary to service each active stream including interfacing with the decoder and issuing asynchronous read requests to the file system. In the interest of keeping on point, with the exception of the method to handle the primed stream, I have not included the individual functions called within SourceStreamUpdateStep(). I do show all of the high-level code, however, in an attempt to show how the streamer works including the regular read request path.

```
#define STREAM_BUFFER_SIZE (256*1024)
#define STREAM_BASE_LATENCY_MS (1000)

static bool SourceStreamUpdateStep(
  source* source, decoder* decoder)
{
  assert(source->stream);
  stream* stream = source->stream;

  assert(!stream->ioBuffer ||
    stream->ioBuffer->refCount);
  assert(!stream->buffers[0] ||
    stream->buffers[0]->refCount);
  assert(!stream->buffers[1] ||
    stream->buffers[1]->refCount);
  assert(stream->filename);

  bool ioBufferReady = stream->ioBuffer ?
    StreamBufferReady(stream->ioBuffer) : false;

  if(source->error)
  { //error, nothing to do
    assert(source->eos);
    return false;
  }
```

```
else if(decoder->done)
{ //decoder is done, nothing to do
  return false;
}
else if(StreamBufferError(stream->ioBuffer))
{ //check for error in last read
  source->primed = false;
  source->eos = true;
  source->error = true;
  return false;
}
//we have primeData associated with this stream
else if(!source->primed && stream->primeData)
{ // Call StreamBufferReadPrimed() to point the first
  // stream buffer at this memory chunk
  assert(!stream->buffers[0]);
  assert(!stream->buffers[1]);
  assert(stream->primeSize<=STREAM_BUFFER_SIZE);

  StreamBufferReadPrimed(&stream->primeBuffer,
      stream->readOffset, stream->primeData,
      stream->primeSize);
  stream->ioBuffer = &stream->primeBuffer;

  SourcePrime(source);

  stream->readOffset += stream->ioBuffer->readSize;

  if(stream->readOffset == stream->entry->size)
  {
    //single buffer looping files don't issue further IO
    if(source->entry.looping &&
       stream->entry->size > STREAM_BUFFER_SIZE)
    {
      stream->readOffset = 0;
    }
    else
    {
      source->eos = true;
      stream->lastBuffer = stream->ioBuffer;
    }
  }
}
  return true;
```

```
  }
  else if(!source->primed && ioBufferReady)
  { //prime if we have data
    assert(!stream->buffers[0]);
    assert(!stream->buffers[1]);
    SD_SourcePrime(source);
    return true;
  }
  else if(stream->buffersSubmitted[0]
    && DecoderBufferComplete(decoder,
          stream->buffers[0]->data))
  { //see if front buffer is done
    printf(va("decoder %p free buffer %p %d\n",
          decoder, stream->buffers[0]->data,
          stream->buffers[0]->readSize));
    assert(stream->buffers[0]->refCount);
    StreamBufferFree(stream->buffers[0]);
    stream->buffers[0] = 0;
    stream->buffersSubmitted[0] = false;
    return true;
  }
  else if(stream->buffers[1] && !stream->buffers[0])
  { //move back buffer to front
    assert(source->primed);
    stream->buffers[0] = stream->buffers[1];
    stream->buffersSubmitted[0] = stream->
    buffersSubmitted[1];
    stream->buffers[1] = 0;
    stream->buffersSubmitted[1] = false;
    assert(stream->buffers[0]->refCount);
    return true;
  }
  else if(!stream->buffers[1] && ioBufferReady)
  { //grab new back buffer
    assert(source->primed);
    stream->buffers[1] = stream->ioBuffer;
    stream->buffersSubmitted[1] = false;
    stream->ioBuffer = 0;
    assert(stream->buffers[0] != stream->buffers[1]);
    assert(stream->buffers[1]->refCount);
    return true;
  }
```

```
else if(!stream->ioBuffer
  && !source->eos
  && (!stream->buffers[1]
      || stream->buffers[1]->readSize <
          STREAM_BUFFER_SIZE)
      //only triple buffer on loop ends
  )
{ //issue new read request if we need to
  int64_t size =
    stream->entry->size-stream->readOffset;
  assertint(size >= 0,stream->entry->size);

  if(size > STREAM_BUFFER_SIZE)
  {
    size = STREAM_BUFFER_SIZE;
  }
  unsigned latencyMs =
    stream->readOffset != 0 ?
      STREAM_BASE_LATENCY_MS /
        stream->entry->channelCount :
      0;

  stream->ioBuffer = StreamBufferRead(stream->filename,
    latencyMs,
    stream->readOffset + stream->entry->offset,
    size,
    stream->fileHandle
    );

  if(stream->ioBuffer)
  {
    stream->readOffset += size;
    assertint(
      stream->entry->size-stream->readOffset >= 0,
      stream->entry->size);

    if(stream->readOffset == stream->entry->size)
    {
      //single buffer looping files don't issue
      //further IO
      if(source->entry.looping &&
        stream->entry->size !=
          stream->ioBuffer->readSize)
```

```
          {
            stream->readOffset = 0;
          }
          else
          {
            source->eos = true;
            stream->lastBuffer = stream->ioBuffer;
          }
        }

      assert(stream->readOffset <= stream->entry->size);

      return true;
    }
  }

  if(source->primed)
  { //see if decoder can take more data
    for(int i=0; i<SOURCE_BUFFER_COUNT; i++)
    {
      if(!stream->buffersSubmitted[i]
      && stream->buffers[i]
      && DecoderBufferReady(decoder)
        && !decoder->error)
      {
        assert(!decoder->eos);
        assert(stream->buffers[i]->refCount);
        DecoderBufferSubmit(decoder,
          stream->buffers[i]->data,
          stream->buffers[i]->readSize,
          stream->buffers[i] == stream->lastBuffer
          );
        stream->buffersSubmitted[i] = true;

        assert(decoder->eos ==
          (stream->buffers[i] == stream->lastBuffer));
      }
    }
  }

  return false;
}
```

```
stream_buffer* StreamBufferReadPrimed(stream_buffer*
                                      buffer,
                                      int64_t offset,
                                      const byte*
                                      primeData,
                                      unsigned size)
{
  assert(size);
  assert(size <= STREAM_BUFFER_SIZE);
  assert(buffer);
  assert(buffer->refCount == 0);

  buffer->offset = offset;
  buffer->valid = true;
  buffer->error = false;
  buffer->primed = true;
  buffer->filename = 0;
  buffer->filenameHash = 0;
  buffer->data = (byte*)primeData;
  buffer->readSize = size;
  buffer->refCount += 1;

  return buffer;
}
```

The source structure is just a collection of data necessary to describe and handle a single sound source, whether it is a streamed sound or RAM-based. If the source describes a RAM-based sound, then it fills out its loadedData member with the RAM address of the sound. In our case, we care about streams so the stream member points at the stream structure. One other point to note is there is a reference to a bool called primed throughout the code that is also a member of the source structure. This is really just unfortunate naming and really has nothing to do with primed streams. It is simply a flag to keep track of whether the RAM-based sound points to valid memory yet or, in the case of a streamed source, whether the first buffer has been read and is valid.

As you look through the SourceStreamUpdateStep() function, you can see that it is basically set up as a cascading series of if/else clauses that essentially make up a state machine. The current state of the conditionals will determine what needs to happen to the stream on each pass through this function, if anything. As you can see, after taking into account any possible error condition or stream completion, we check if there is primed data and we check the source's primed variable to see if it has had its first buffer serviced yet. The first time this function is called on a stream with primed data, it will enter the if clause and call `StreamBufferReadPrimed()`. This function follows `SourceStreamUpdateStep()` and basically just points the first stream buffer at the passed in `primeData` chunk. It also sets the read size and anything else relevant to the system to make sure the buffer is valid and ready to be passed on to the decoder. In almost all cases, the `readSize` is going to be equal to a single stream buffer size (256 KB in this engine). The reason for this is simple. It wouldn't make any sense to have a partial buffer where some is loaded in RAM and the rest is read off the disk. We really wouldn't see any performance gain, because we'd still have a read request on the first buffer consumed by the system. We also wouldn't want to have a second buffer (or greater than 256 KB of primed data), because it's simply unnecessary. Practice has shown that this single buffer of primed data is more than enough to achieve our expected result of a zero (or as close to zero as possible) latency stream. Using 256 KB buffers and assuming a reasonable compression ratio of ~8:1, a single buffer will hold more than 10 seconds of streamed audio. Since we double buffer, we can issue the actual read request for the second stream buffer just after we handle the primed chunk and will have more than enough time for the request to return with the data.

3.6 DISK LAYOUT CONSIDERATIONS

On previous generations of consoles and PCs, programmers responsible for implementing and maintaining streaming code would issue read requests and then handle the returned data. As has already been mentioned, the seeks caused by resetting the drive head for each read are by far the biggest offender when it comes to coding up an optimized system and getting more simultaneous streams. In the past, there were a couple of optimizations you could make to get a good performance bump out of your system.

Laying out your data in a particular way to minimize the distance that the read head needs to travel is one optimization that many teams have tried to get better performance out of their streamers. Have you ever been playing a game and heard the short bursts of high-speed whining noises? This is the read head on the optical drive seeking around like crazy. If you don't pay any attention at all to how your disk is laid out, then your title's streaming performance is going to suffer because of needless seeking.

For example, if for some reason you have your music files on the disk as single files per track and haven't really paid any attention to where they are located then you could have a situation where you are transitioning from one music track to another so you are reading in the last bit of data from the ending track at the same time as you are reading in the first part of the next track (cross-fading). Since the streamer needs to access two different files, the read head needs to seek from the one file to the other between reads. In a worst case, imagine the first file is located near the outside of the disk whereas the second file is located near the middle. In this case, the seek penalty is going to be significant and will likely cause issues in your system. For this very reason, games have paid careful attention to where files are located on the disk. It only makes sense to have all of your music files in one location on the disk to minimize seeks. Going one step further, it makes sense to have any files you may access on any given level or zone of your game within a similar location on disk.

3.7 CONCLUSION

Hopefully, this chapter has given the reader some insight into the historical uses and limitations of streams and some practical advice on how you can boost the performance of your streaming system. When a new generation of consoles comes out, we all scramble to port our systems over and make them functional and ship our titles. Now is the time to use some of the information and techniques that I have provided you in this chapter to fine-tune your streaming engine and take it to the next level.

II

Middleware

CHAPTER 4

An Introduction to ADX2

Nicolas Fournel

CONTENTS

4.1 INTRODUCTION

ADX2 is a game audio middleware developed by a Japanese company called CRI Middleware. It consists of an authoring tool (AtomCraft) and a runtime library (CRI Atom). Although it is the *de facto* standard in Japan, it may be less known in the West. In this chapter, we will show some of the fundamentals of working with ADX2.

4.2 CREATING THE DATA

Before diving into the programming, let's learn about the data that we will be manipulating. The AtomCraft tool offers a very digital audio workstation (DAW)-like experience to author the sound, while still adding the many features we have come to expect when implementing interactive audio for games. Figure 4.1 shows the main screen, with the project and audio assets trees on the left, the details pane (here showing a timeline) in the middle, and the parameters at the bottom and on the right.

4.2.1 Hierarchy

As can be seen in the tree, an ADX2 project is divided into Work Units. These are nonruntime objects whose sole purpose is to organize the audio in the project by type or function (game location/character/weapons, etc.). This organization makes it easier to distribute the work between several sound designers and use versioning. Work Units can contain one or more CueSheets, each having one or more Cues. Although the terminology is different, you will find many of the same concepts in a Western audio middleware such as FMOD or Wwise. In this case, a CueSheet is basically the equivalent of a sound bank and Cues are the audio events/sounds that you will be triggering from the game.

Therefore, it will come as no surprise that you can have several types of Cues, each exhibiting a different behavior (similar to the blend, random, sequential, etc., containers in Wwise for example). A Cue is composed of several Tracks, each having a timeline on which Waveform Regions (sample data with some extra parameters) can be arranged. The Cue type will determine the way these Tracks are selected and played. All the typical playing behaviors are available—polyphonic, sequential, random, shuffle, etc., as well as some more original ones. For example, a Cue of the combo-sequential type will play the next Track each time it is triggered, but only if it happens within a given time interval, thereby allowing the simulation of combos. If the sound is not triggered in time, it will go back to the first Track.

Each Track (and even each Waveform Region) can have its own parameters (such as a biquad filter). We will talk more about this later, when we see how to update them at runtime. Actions can also be inserted on a Track to provide looping at the Track level (as opposed to the regular sample looping at the Waveform Region level), to set parameters or call other

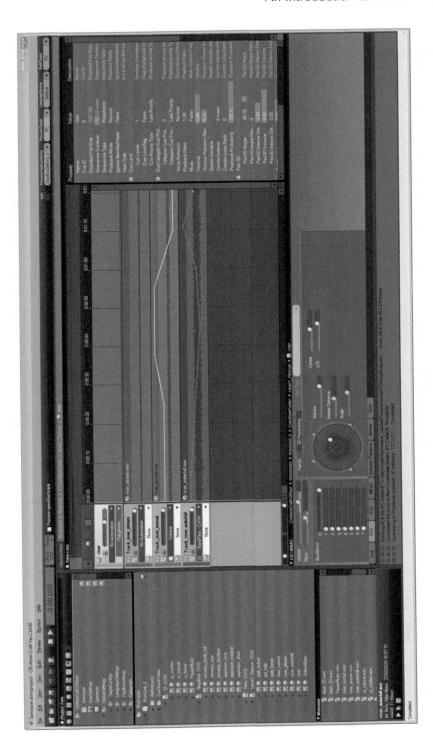

FIGURE 4.1 AtomCraft main window.

Cues. Finally, a Cue can be organized vertically in blocks with transition rules that make it perfect for interactive music.

The bottom tree on the left of the screen is called the Materials tree. This is where you will drag and drop audio files (in WAV or AIFF format) to import them into your project. Once an audio file is registered as a Material, it is possible to specify its looping and encoding parameters, and, of course, to use it as a Waveform Region on a Track.

At the global level, Categories, Voice Limit Groups, REACT (automatic ducking), AISAC (real-time control parameters), DSP buses and more can be defined to control and manage groups of Cues at runtime. We will give a look at some of them a bit later.

The data hierarchy can be seen in Figure 4.2. Fortunately, you don't need to worry about all that to create your first project and start programming. Indeed, generating test data can be done as easily as opening a new project and dragging a couple of wave files onto the default CueSheet that was created for you. They will automatically be registered as Materials, Cues will be created, Tracks and Waveforms Regions added, and we are ready to go!

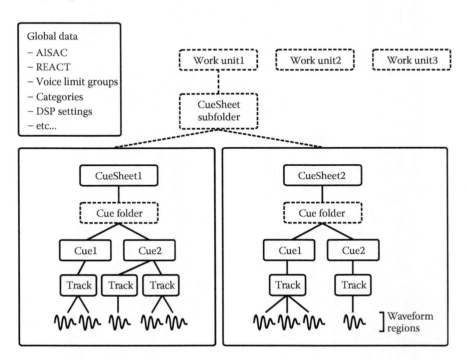

FIGURE 4.2 ADX2 data hierarchy.

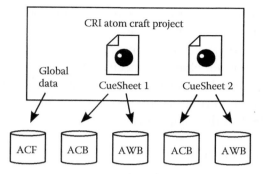

FIGURE 4.3   Data exported to the runtime.

4.2.2 Export

Now that we have examined the different objects that are authored in AtomCraft, let's take a look at Figure 4.3, which details what becomes of that data when it is exported to the game. Three types of files are created:

- The Atom Configuration File (ACF) contains all the global information about a project as well as the list of CueSheets it includes. This is the typical "project file," and it is usually unique for a game.

- The Atom CueSheet Binary (ACB) files contain all the parameters of a specific CueSheet as well as any sample data destined to be played from memory by the Cues in that CueSheet. If the audio is expected to be streamed, it is stored in the third type of file.

- The Atom Wave Bank (AWB) file contains the encoded data for the streams referenced by the CueSheet of the same name (the parameters for the streams themselves are still stored in the ACB file).

In addition to these files, C++ headers with the right definitions will be written. It is also possible to generate specific files required for integration with Unity, Unreal, or CryEngine, should you need them.

4.3 PROGRAM FLOW

After this quick overview of the data, we can start the actual programming. Thankfully, the application program interface (API) is very consistent, making things very easy for the programmer, starting with the names of the functions that all follow this convention: cri + (Atom or AtomEx) + module name + "_" + name of the function. The name of the function itself is of the form verb + object. Most objects can be specified both by name and by ID. For example, a typical function name is `criAtomExPlayer_SetCueId`. Unsurprisingly, you would call this to assign a Cue to a player object by specifying its ID.

Similarly, the initialization and configuration of the different modules or the update of the various parameters are all consistent across the API. Actually, let's look at this right now!

4.3.1 Initialization and Termination

In reality, the Atom library is composed of a series of modules responsible for very specific tasks, such as loading ACB files, managing voices, or playing sounds. All the functions whose purpose is to initialize modules or to create objects will require memory as well as some configuration parameters. To that effect, they all have arguments to pass the address of a work buffer and its size. All modules or objects also provide a function to calculate the size of the work buffer required. This size is often based on the values of the parameters of the configuration structure. Moreover, each configuration structure has a matching macro to automatically set the default values. When you pass NULL for the structure, these same default parameters will be used. For example, let's give a look to the initialization of the main library:

```
CriAtomExConfig config;  // Configuration structure
                         // used to initialize the
                         // library
void *work;              // Address of the work buffer
CriSint32 work_size;     // Size of the work buffer

// Macro that sets the default values to the configuration
// structure
criAtomEx_SetDefaultConfig(&config);

// Calculate the size of the work buffer required
work_size = criAtomEx_CalculateWorkSize(&config);

// Allocate the memory for the work buffer
work = malloc((size_t)work_size);

// Initialize the library
criAtomEx_Initialize(&config, work, work_size);
```

Like any good middleware, you can also register a user-allocator that will be called whenever memory needs to be allocated or released, in which case the two last arguments of `criAtomEx_Initialize()` can be NULL and 0.

Therefore, if you registered the user-allocator and wanted to use the default configuration parameters, you could simply call:

```
criAtomEx_Initialize(NULL, NULL, 0);
```

The exact same principles would apply to the initialization of the streaming system, the creation of a voice pool, etc. Actually, each target platform has a convenience function that will internally call all these other initialization functions with their default parameters for this specific platform (e.g., on PC: `criAtomEx_Initialize_PC()`) so that you don't have to deal with all the details.

The termination is simply done by calling the corresponding `Finalize()` function, for example, `criAtomEx_Finalize_PC()`.

4.3.2 Loading and Unloading the Data

Once the library has initialized, we need to load the project file, which is done by calling:

```
criAtomEx_RegisterAcfFile(NULL,
"C:\\BestGameEver\\PC\\BestGameEver.acf", NULL, 0);
```

As mentioned earlier, the ACF file contains all the global information about the project. Then, we are ready to load one or more sound banks, or, in ADX2 terminology, binary CueSheets. Remember them? It's the ACB files. To do that, we simply use the

```
CriAtomExAcbHn acbHn = criAtomExAcb_LoadAcbFile(NULL,
"C:\\BestGameEver\\PC\\CommonSFX.acb", NULL, NULL,
NULL, 0);
```

The handle returned by this function will be used when unloading the sound bank later with `criAtomExAcb_Release(acbHn)`. At the end of the game, we will of course need to unload the project file as well, which is done by calling `criAtomEx_UnregisterAcf()`.

4.3.3 Server Process

As with any middleware running concurrently with the game, you must make sure that the CRI Atom library's core function (here called the "server process") is executed at regular intervals. This is the function that is responsible for decoding the audio data, actually starting the voices, updating all the internal parameters, etc.

When initializing the library, several threading models are available, from single-threaded to multithreaded, with automatic or manual creation and management of the threads, etc. In most cases, you will need to call the criAtomEx_ExecuteMain() function from your game loop, which will then run the server process (and work with the different threads as needed).

4.3.4 Putting Everything Together

Let's now review what we have learned so far and examine the basic flow of an audio engine using ADX2.

```
CriAtomExAcbHn acbHn;

// Registration of an error callback
criErr_SetCallback(bestgameever_error_callback);

// Registration of a user allocator
criAtomEx_SetUserAllocator(bestgameever_alloc,
bestgameever_free, NULL);

// Library initialization
criAtomEx_Initialize_PC(NULL, NULL, 0);

// Load and register an ACF file
criAtomEx_RegisterAcfFile(NULL,
"C:\\BestGameEver\\PC\\BestGameEver.acf",NULL,0);

// Load a binary CueSheet (ACB file)
acbHn = criAtomExAcb_LoadAcbFile(NULL,
"C:\\BestGameEver\\PC\\CommonSFX.acb",NULL,NULL,NULL,0);

//
// Do something absolutely fantastic here...
//

// Unload a binary CueSheet
criAtomExAcb_Release(acbHn);
```

```
// Unregister the ACF
criAtomEx_UnregisterAcf();

// Finalize the library
criAtomEx_Finalize_PC();
```

Only one thing remains to be done—you know, actually play sounds.

4.4 PLAYING AND STOPPING SOUNDS

ADX2 has a dual approach, which empowers both the programmer and the sound designer. Although it is possible to create complex behaviors entirely on the tool side (e.g., automatic ducking based on sound categories, combosequential Cues), you can also build objects from scratch and manipulate many audio parameters at runtime, even going as far as creating the ACF data itself! You can, of course, use a combination of these two approaches. In that case, sometimes parameters may be set both on the data side (assigned in the authoring tool by the sound designer) and in code (set at runtime by the programmer). However, they will always be intuitively combined. For example, volumes will be multiplied, pitches will be added, whereas other parameters may be overwritten if it makes more sense. Because ADX2 offers full control over the audio to both the designer and the programmer, it requires a good communication between them beforehand!

4.4.1 Players, Voices, and VoicePools

As illustrated by Figure 4.4, at runtime, a basic sound—or Voice in the ADX2 vernacular—is played by an AtomEx Player object (this applies to both in-memory and streaming sounds). Many of these players can be created, each of them being able to play several sounds simultaneously. They can be used to play the Cues authored in the tool, but also audio files or audio data stored in an AWB file directly. As usual, creating a Player with the default parameters and the user-allocator is straightforward:

```
CriAtomExPlayerHn playerHn;
playerHn = criAtomExPlayer_Create(NULL, NULL, 0);
```

The handle returned by this function will let us update the parameters of the Player and, of course, play Cues (more on that in a moment). It will also be used later to release the Player by calling: `criAtomExPlayer_Destroy(playerHn)`.

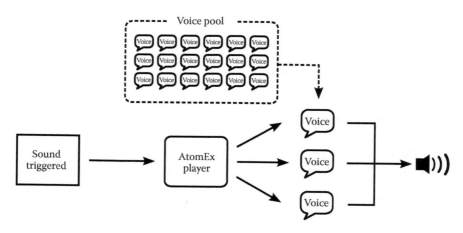

FIGURE 4.4   ADX2 runtime objects.

Whether a specific sound (Voice) can be started actually depends on a number of factors, from instance limiting at the Category or Cue levels to the priority of a Waveform Region (to name a couple of examples). However, at the end it will always come back to the actual number of Voices available in a VoicePool. A VoicePool object manages a set of voices based on priorities (allocation and deallocation) and is also responsible for the decoding of the audio data itself.

Before going any further, now is probably a good time to have a word about the various codecs supported by ADX2. Indeed, in addition to supporting the platform-specific ones, ADX2 comes with a number of very interesting proprietary codecs. ADX is a high-fidelity, high-compression (up to 1/16), and low CPU-load codec. It is available on all game platforms supported by ADX2, from consoles to mobile and embedded systems. The HCA (High Compression Audio) codec offers a compression ratio from 1/6 to 1/12. The CPU load is lower than that of MP3 and AAC and, more importantly, constant during decoding (no hit at the beginning, for example). It also supports seeking. Finally, the HCA-MX codec is a special version of the HCA, which reduces the CPU load even more when playing a large number of sounds simultaneously (several hundred on console). This comes at a price, of course, in that case shared sample rate, pitch, and effects.

Let's go back to the creation of our VoicePool. You will have to choose its type and specify its parameters. A "standard" VoicePool will allow you to play ADX and HCA encoded data. You could also create VoicePools just for ADX or HCA, or for HCA-MX, WAVE, AIFF, or even raw PCM. VoicePool parameters include, for example, the maximum sampling rate and number of channels allowed, the type of audio renderer used to generate the sounds (is it all generated in software or are we leveraging hardware voices), and a flag to determine whether the voices can be streamed. For example, the following code creates a standard VoicePool (i.e., able to play ADX and HCA encoded data) using the default configuration parameters and makes sure it supports streaming.

```
CriAtomExStandardVoicePoolConfig voice_pool_config;
CriAtomExVoicePoolHn voice_pool;

criAtomExVoicePool_SetDefaultConfigForStandardVoicePool(
   &voice_pool_config);
voice_pool_config.player_config.streaming_flag = CRI_TRUE;
voice_pool =
 criAtomExVoicePool_AllocateStandardVoice Pool(
   &voice_pool_config, NULL, 0);
```

When you don't need it anymore, the VoicePool can be released by calling:

```
criAtomExVoicePool_Free(voice_pool).
```

4.4.2 Playback IDs and Status

Once a Player object has been created, it is possible to use it to play a Cue authored in the AtomCraft tool. First, we must specify the Cue's ID (remember that function from Section 4.3?) or its name or its index with one of these functions:

```
void CRIAPI criAtomExPlayer_SetCueId(CriAtomExPlayerHn
   player, CriAtomExAcbHn acb_hn, CriAtomExCueId id);
void CRIAPI criAtomExPlayer_SetCueName(CriAtomExPlayerHn
   player, CriAtomExAcbHn acb_hn, const CriChar8 *cue_
   name);
void CRIAPI criAtomExPlayer_SetCueIndex(CriAtomExPlayerHn
   player, CriAtomExAcbHn acb_hn, CriAtomExCueIndex
   index);
```

The AtomEx player can also play an audio file (such as a.hca) directly with the function criAtomExPlayer_SetFile or a waveform contained in an AWB file with criAtomExPlayer_SetWaveId. In both cases, the format, number of channels, and sample rate can be specified using the following functions:

```
void criAtomExPlayer_SetFormat(CriAtomExPlayerHn player,
  CriAtomExFormat format);
void criAtomExPlayer_SetNumChannels(CriAtomExPlayerHn
  player, CriSint32 numChannels);
void criAtomExPlayer_SetSamplingRate(CriAtomExPlayerHn
  player, CriSint32 srate);
```

Would you believe it? It is finally time to actually trigger the playback! We do it by calling:

```
criAtomExPlayer_Start(CriAtomExPlayerHn player)
```

There are a couple of things are worth noting here.

First, once the data has been assigned to the player, you don't have to set it again if you want to keep playing the same sound/Cue again and again.

Second, it is possible to synchronize precisely the start of several sounds on different players by momentarily disabling the server process using the locking mechanism, like this:

```
// Prevent server process interrupts
criAtomEx_Lock();

// Start playing back multiple voices
criAtomExPlayer_Start(player1);
criAtomExPlayer_Start(player2);
criAtomExPlayer_Start(player3);
criAtomExPlayer_Start(player4);

// Back to normal...
criAtomEx_Unlock();
```

Finally, the criAtomExPlayer_Start function returns a playback ID (CriAtomExPlaybackId). Since a player can play multiple sounds simultaneously, the playback ID is used to reference a single sound. For example, stopping the full player is done by calling criAtomExPlayer_Stop

(CriAtomExPlayerHn player), whereas stopping a single sound will require a call to criAtomExPlayback_Stop(CriAtomExPlaybackId id). Similarly, there will be different functions to call if you want to update the parameters of all the sounds started by a player or just a single one. Note that if an error occurs and an invalid playback ID is returned, it can still be passed to the all the other functions without risk. It will just be ignored and nothing will happen, but this saves you from having to write tests for the return value each time.

In some cases, you may want to know the progress of the playback. The criAtomExPlayer_GetStatus function can be used to get the status of a player. The playback status of an AtomEx Player (or of a single sound, for that matter) can take five values, usually following this order:

```
CRIATOMEXPLAYER_STATUS_STOP
CRIATOMEXPLAYER_STATUS_PREP
CRIATOMEXPLAYER_STATUS_PLAYING
CRIATOMEXPLAYER_STATUS_PLAYEND
(CRIATOMEXPLAYER_STATUS_ERROR)
```

When an AtomEx Player is created, it is in stopped mode (it has the CRIATOMEXPLAYER_STATUS_STOP status). Once the data to be played has been assigned (e.g., using criAtomExPlayer_SetData) and the criAtomExPlayer_Start function has been called, the player status changes to CRIATOMEXPLAYER_STATUS_PREP and the player starts preparing for the playback. When a sufficient amount of data has been provided and the playback is ready, the player status changes to CRIATOMEXPLAYER_STATUS_PLAYING and the audio playback starts. Finally, when all the audio data has been played, the player status changes to CRIATOMEXPLAYER_STATUS_PLAYEND. If an error occurs during playback (e.g., invalid audio data being read), the status is changed to CRIATOMEXPLAYER_STATUS_ERROR.

As we have seen above, a single AtomEx Player can actually play back multiple sounds simultaneously. This has an impact on the status returned by criAtomExPlayer_GetStatus. In particular, if you execute the criAtomExPlayer_Stop function, all sounds currently being played back on the AtomEx Player will be stopped, and its status will return to CRIATOMEXPLAYER_STATUS_STOP. Also, when the criAtomExPlayer_Start function is executed multiple times on a single AtomEx Player, if any sound is in preparation for the playback, the status becomes CRIATOMEXPLAYER_STATUS_PREP. Only after all sounds have started to play does the status change to CRIATOMEXPLAYER_STATUS_PLAYING. Moreover, if the status of the player is CRIATOMEXPLAYER_STATUS_PLAYING and the criAtomExPlayer_Start function is executed again, the status will temporarily return to CRIATOMEXPLAYER_STATUS_PREP.

Finally, while multiple sounds are being played back, if an error occurs for one of them, the status of the player is changed to CRIATOMEXPLAYER_ STATUS_ERROR, regardless of the status of the other sounds.

If you need to track the status of a single sound started by the player, you will have to call the criAtomExPlayback_GetStatus(CriAtom ExPlaybackId id) function that will let you pass a playback ID as an argument.

This distinction between player object and playback ID is very convenient and allows us to do many interesting things programmatically. However, keep track of which one you are manipulating or you may end up with hard-to-find bugs, especially since the functions will have very similar names.

To review some of the points we have discussed in this section, here is a simple program that starts a sound and waits for it to finish playing.

```
CriAtomExPlayerHn player;
CriAtomExVoicePoolHn voicePool;


// Create a voice pool
voicePool = criAtomExVoicePool_AllocateStandardVoicePool(
    NULL, NULL, 0);
// Create a player (will automatically use that
// VoicePool)
player = criAtomExPlayer_Create(NULL, NULL, 0);
// Specify a Cue ID (acbHn is the ACB file handle)
criAtomExPlayer_SetCueId(player, acbHn, CRI_SFX_BOOM);
// Start playback
criAtomExPlayer_Start(player);
for(;;)
{
  CriAtomExPlayerStatus explayer_status;
  sleep(10);
```

```
    // Execute the server processs
    criAtomEx_ExecuteMain();
    // Get AtomEx player status
    explayer_status = criAtomExPlayer_GetStatus(player);
    // Exit the playback loop if the status is PLAYEND
    if (explayer_status == CRIATOMEXPLAYER_STATUS_PLAYEND)
      break;
}
// Destroy the player
criAtomExPlayer_Destroy(player);
// Destroy the voice pool
criAtomExVoicePool_Free(voicePool);
```

4.4.3 Streaming

All of the player starting/updating functions are the same regardless of the type of playback (in-memory or streaming), which is very convenient. However, there are a few things to keep in mind when streaming. In ADX2, the D-BAS module is responsible for managing the streaming buffers for the player objects. It must be initialized early (before the ACF and ACB files are loaded). For example, if you want to use the default parameters, this will suffice:

```
CriAtomDbasId dbas_id =
  criAtomDbas_Create(NULL, NULL, 0);
```

The streaming buffers will be divided into blocks, which D-BAS will assign as needed to the various players.

Also, during the export from the authoring tool, the audio data to be streamed will be stored in an AWB file, not in the ACB file itself. Therefore, this AWB file must be loaded. This is done very easily, by passing the path to the AWB file as an argument when we load the corresponding ACB. For example, loading the ACB file from Section 4.3.2 now becomes:

```
CriAtomExAcbHn acbHn = criAtomExAcb_LoadAcbFile(NULL,
  "C:\\BestGameEver\\PC\\CommonSFX.acb", NULL,
  "C:\\BestGameEver\\PC\\CommonSFX.awb", NULL, 0);
```

Remember also to check that the VoicePool you will use allows streaming (refer to the example in Section 4.4.1 to see how to ensure that it is indeed the case).

When streaming sounds, you can also take advantage of the preparing function:

```
criAtomExPlayer_Prepare(CriAtomExPlayerHn player);
```

It will make it possible to start a stream at the right time without any latency. This function returns a playback ID and is used instead of the `criAtom ExPlayer_Start` function. When it is called, the resources required for the sound playback are allocated and the buffering starts, but when everything is ready, the sound is put in paused mode. The `criAtomExPlayback_Pause` function must then be called to actually start the playback. In-memory sounds can also make good use of `criAtomExPlayer_Prepare` to start many sounds simultaneously (a good alternative to the code in Section 4.4.2).

Finally, you can also provide the blocks of data to stream yourself by registering this callback:

```
void CRIAPI criAtomExPlayer_SetDataRequestCallback(
    CriAtomExPlayerHn player,
    CriAtomExPlayerDataRequestCbFunc func,
    void *obj);
```

If the data is not ready yet, simply call the `criAtomPlayer_Defer Callback` function within the callback to retry during the next server interrupt or pass the last buffer again by calling the `criAtomPlayer_ SetPreviousDataAgain` function.

Thanks in part to proprietary codecs, such as HCA and HCA-MX, and the use of CRI's own file system API underneath ADX2, streaming is usually quite performant.

4.5 UPDATING SOUNDS

4.5.1 Updating Sound Parameters

Most of the time, the sounds you will be playing with ADX2 will be Cues authored in the AtomCraft tool. Their volume, pitch, send levels, or 3D positioning parameters (such as attenuation distance or cone angle) can all be set in the tool but also adjusted at runtime. Moreover, a Cue can consist of multiple Tracks, potentially containing several Waveform Regions each. Each Waveform Region has an amplitude envelope, as well as two filters: a bandpass filter (whose parameters can be inherited from the parent Track) and a biquad filter with the usual cutoff and resonance settings. This envelope and these filters can also be updated at runtime.

With ADX2, changing a parameter and applying that change are two separate actions. This allows us, for example, to prepare for changing the parameters of a player without modifying the sounds currently being played, or to adjust many parameters by calculating their internal values only once during the server process.

The following code first sets the volume of a player to 0.5f by calling the `criAtomExPlayer_SetVolume` function and then starts a sound. Its volume is indeed 0.5f. Then, we set the volume to another value (0.3f). The volume is not immediately changed. It will only be changed when we call the `criAtomExPlayer_Update` function. This function takes a playback ID as an argument, but you can also call `criAtomExPlayer_UpdateAll`, which will change the parameters of all the sounds being played by that particular player object.

```
// Set the Volume
criAtomExPlayer_SetVolume(player, 0.5f);

// Start the playback with the value set to the player
// (0.5f).
id = criAtomExPlayer_Start(player);

// Change the volume
// The volume of the sounds currently playing is not
// affected at this point
criAtomExPlayer_SetVolume(player, 0.3f);

// Apply the new volume to the sounds currently playing
criAtomExPlayer_Update(player, id);
```

Functions similar to `criAtomExPlayer_SetVolume` exist for the pitch, the filter parameters, etc. If needed, the original values of the parameters can be recalled by using `criAtomExPlayer_ResetParameters(CriAtomExPlayerHn player)`.

4.5.2 Playing 3D Sounds

3D audio positioning is activated for a player object by setting the correct pan type:

```
criAtomExPlayer_SetPanType(player,
  CRIATOMEX_PAN_TYPE_3D_POS);
```

ADX2 relies on sound source and listener objects to simulate the 3D positioning. They are created independently from the player and have their own update functions. Therefore, the same sound source can be associated with several players. The following code shows in detail how to make a sound source rotate around a listener.

```
void PlayCueWith3DPositioning(CriAtomExPlayerHn player,
  CriAtomExAcbHn abHn,CriAtomExCueId id)
{
  // Set 3d positoning pan type
  criAtomExPlayer_SetPanType(player,
    CRIATOMEX_PAN_TYPE_3D_POS);

  // Create the listener and source objects
  CriAtomEx3dListenerHn listener =
    criAtomEx3dListener_Create(NULL, NULL, 0);
  CriAtomEx3dSourceHn source =
    criAtomEx3dSource_Create(NULL, NULL, 0);

  // Assign them to the AtomEx player
  criAtomExPlayer_Set3dListenerHn(player, listener);
  criAtomExPlayer_Set3dSourceHn(player, source);

  // Set listener initial position
  CriAtomExVector pos;
  pos.x = 0.0f;
  pos.y = 0.0f;
  pos.z = 0.0f;
  criAtomEx3dListener_SetPosition(listener, &pos);
  criAtomEx3dListener_Update(listener);

  // Set source initial position and distance range
  CriFloat32 distance = 10.0f;
  pos.x = distance;
  pos.z = 0.0f;
  criAtomEx3dSource_SetPosition(source, &pos);
  criAtomEx3dSource_SetMinMaxDistance(source,0,100);
  criAtomEx3dSource_Update(source);

  // Start playback
  criAtomExPlayer_SetCueId(player, acbHn, id);
  id = criAtomExPlayer_Start(player);
```

```
// Make the source rotate around the listener for 10
// seconds
for (CriUint16 i = 0; i < 1000; ++i)
{
  // Wait 10 ms
  Sleep(10);

  // Execute the server process
  criAtomEx_ExecuteMain();

  // Update the position of the source
  pos.x = distance *
       cos(6.28f * (CriFloat32)i / 1000.0f);
  pos.z = distance *
       sin(6.28f * (CriFloat32)i / 1000.0f);
  criAtomEx3dSource_SetPosition(source, &pos);
  criAtomEx3dSource_Update(source);
}
criAtomExPlayer_Stop(player);

// Free sound source and listener objects
criAtomEx3dListener_Destroy(listener);
criAtomEx3dSource_Destroy(source);
}
```

4.5.3 Controlling the Sound from the Game

In addition to simply updating a parameter, there are many ways to control sounds based on the game context with ADX2.

First, an advanced interactive sound and active controller (AISAC) is the equivalent of a real-time parameter control. One or more player parameters can be controlled by an AISAC, which can be either local to a player or global. An AISAC can also control another AISAC, and it can be used as a randomizer or as an LFO (auto modulation). AISACs can control almost any parameter of a Cue. Figure 4.5 shows a simple example where an AISAC controls the volume of the different tracks of a Cue. Here, each Track corresponds to a different layer of a river sound. The AISAC makes it possible to change the sound of the river's flow simply by passing a value between 0.0f and 1.0f from the game to the player object, like this:

```
criAtomExPlayer_SetAisacById(player, AISAC_ID, value);
```

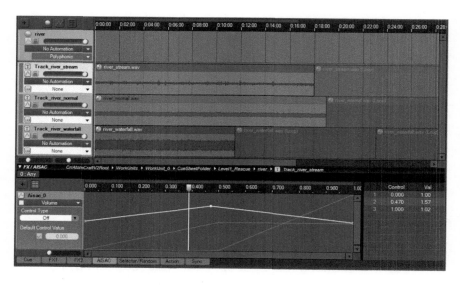

FIGURE 4.5   Using AISAC to control the sounds from the game.

It could not be simpler!

Categories can also be used to update the parameters of whole groups of sounds at the same time. They make it possible to mute a specific type of sounds, to fade them in or out, to apply an AISAC on them, etc.

ADX2 also provides the programmer with easy ways to select the sounds to be played based on what is happening in the game using selectors and blocks.

Think about the selectors as variables that can take several predefined values (here, the selector labels). At runtime, Cues of type Switch will check the value of the selector and play only the Track that is associated with that value. The following function is used to set the value of a selector at runtime:

```
void CRIAPI criAtomExPlayer_SetSelectorLabel(
    CriAtomExPlayerHn player, const CriChar8 *selector,
    const CriChar8 *label);
```

As for blocks, they are well-suited for interactive music (as shown in Figure 4.6) but can also be used advantageously for sound effects. Indeed, they make it possible to jump between different sections of a Cue's timeline and allow the design of complex sonic behaviors. The timing at which the block transitions can occur—as well as the rules to which they obey—can

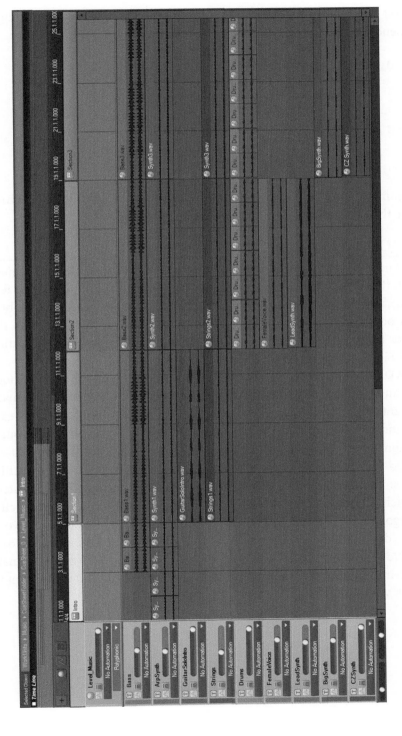

FIGURE 4.6 Using blocks for interactive music.

be set in the authoring tool. This can be overridden at runtime though, depending on the game context, with functions that force transitions:

```
void CRIAPI criAtomExPlayer_SetFirstBlockIndex(
     CriAtomExPlayerHn player,
     CriAtomExBlockIndex index);

void CRIAPI criAtomExPlayback_SetNextBlockIndex(
     CriAtomExPlaybackId id,
     CriAtomExBlockIndex index);
```

Communicating in the other direction, a callback is available to synchronize the game with the block transitions if needed.

4.6 CONCLUSION

This introduction barely scratched the surface of what is possible to achieve with the ADX2 runtime. We could also have talked about the mixing features, the DSP settings for the effects, the ability to provide your own buffers on the run for procedural audio, the seamless integration with the other technologies of CRI Middleware (Softdec2 for the video encoding and FileMajik Pro for the file system), and so on.

ADX2 offers all the typical features you would expect to find in a modern audio middleware and then some. But, as we have seen, one of its main advantages is that it is an extremely coherent system that can be very easily and quickly integrated into a game project. It empowers both sound designers and programmers by providing many ways to implement an audio feature. For example, a ducking system can be entirely created by the sound designer in the authoring tool thanks to the REACT system (which will duck a category of sounds when a sound from another specific category is played, with many options). But you could also program your own ducking system from scratch using calls to criAtomExPlayer_ SetVolume or even attach a Fader object to a player that would automate fade-ins and fadeouts. This makes ADX2 very versatile and convenient to work with.

CHAPTER 5

Wwise and the Audio Programmer

Stéphane Beauchemin

CONTENTS

5.1 INTRODUCTION

Whether you are a complete Wwise neophyte wanting to dive into Wwise, a long-term Wwise user looking for a refresher and tricks, or just an audio programmer looking for great ideas to enrich your in-house engine, this chapter is for you. The intent is not to cover each subject in detail (for that, Audiokinetic has provided thorough documentation), but rather to give you an overview of how you can leverage the full power from an Audiokinetic's audio solution. When audio programmers think about Wwise, they think about the sound engine and the software development fit (SDK), but Wwise has a lot more tools to offer than just that. In this chapter, I will try to present code examples with their authoring tool counterpart. Hopefully, you will see that the Wwise authoring tool is not meant only for sound designers but for the audio programmers, too!

We will begin with the basics: creating an application that plays one sound with Wwise. Since debugging is a crucial part of any video game development, I will introduce you to different tools that Wwise has to help you debug the audio in your game. Finally, I will expose different concepts in Wwise that will allow you to understand the SDK to be able to do the best possible integration in your game engine.

5.2 FIRST STEPS IN Wwise

5.2.1 Hello Wwise

Integrating Wwise into a game can be a daunting task. Wwise has a lot of different modules: Memory Manager, Sound Engine, Music Engine, Communication, and all the plugins (built-in and third party). Each of the different modules needs to be initialized separately. That is why you are required to write a significant amount of code in order to be able to play a sound in your game. Here, I will show you how to play a sound in Wwise using the minimal setup. (Disclaimer: there is no error checking done in this code for the sake of readability.) The music engine and the communication module are optional; therefore, I will ignore those modules for now and come back to them later in the chapter.

```
#include <iostream>
#include <thread>

// Wwise include
#include <AK/SoundEngine/Common/AkMemoryMgr.h>
#include <AK/SoundEngine/Common/AkSoundEngine.h>
```

```cpp
#include <AK/SoundEngine/Common/AkModule.h>
#include <AK/SoundEngine/Common/IAkStreamMgr.h>
//*********************************************************
// Sample low-level I/O implementation !!!
#include <AkFilePackageLowLevelIOBlocking.h>
// To use it you need to compile
// AkDefaultIOHookBlocking.cpp
CAkDefaultIOHookBlocking g_blockingDevice;
//*********************************************************

// Minimal integration of Wwise
// Please link with the follwing Wwise libs:
// AkMemoryMgr AkSoundEngine AkStreamMgr
// CommunicationCentral

namespace AK
{
  void* AllocHook(size_t s)    { return malloc(s); }
  void FreeHook(void * p)       { free(p); }
}

bool InitWwise()
{
  AkMemSettings memSettings;
  memSettings.uMaxNumPools = 20;
  AK::MemoryMgr::Init(&memSettings);

  AkStreamMgrSettings stmSettings;
  AK::StreamMgr::GetDefaultSettings(stmSettings);
  AK::StreamMgr::Create(stmSettings);

  AkDeviceSettings deviceSettings;
  AK::StreamMgr::GetDefaultDeviceSettings
    (deviceSettings);
  g_blockingDevice.Init(deviceSettings);

  // Setting the base path for your banks
  g_blockingDevice.SetBasePath(""); // Set your own!

  AkInitSettings initSettings;
  AkPlatformInitSettings pfInitSettings;
  AK::SoundEngine::GetDefaultInitSettings
    (initSettings);
  AK::SoundEngine::GetDefaultPlatformInitSettings
```

```
    (pfInitSettings);
  AK::SoundEngine::Init(&initSettings, &pfInitSettings);

  // Loading banks from your project
  AkBankID bankID;
  AK::SoundEngine::LoadBank(AKTEXT("Init.bnk"),
    AK_DEFAULT_POOL_ID, bankID);
  AK::SoundEngine::LoadBank(AKTEXT("SFX.bnk"),
    AK_DEFAULT_POOL_ID, bankID);


  return true;
}


void TermWwise()
{
  // Unloading the banks
  AK::SoundEngine::UnloadBank(AKTEXT("SFX.bnk"),
    nullptr);
  AK::SoundEngine::UnloadBank(AKTEXT("Init.bnk"),
    nullptr);


  AK::SoundEngine::Term();
  g_blockingDevice.Term();


  if(AK::IAkStreamMgr::Get())
    AK::IAkStreamMgr::Get()->Destroy();


  AK::MemoryMgr::Term();
}


void PlaySound()
{
  AkGameObjectID myGameObj = 1;
  AK::SoundEngine::RegisterGameObj(myGameObj,
    "GameObj1");
  AK::SoundEngine::PostEvent(AKTEXT("Play_SFX_1"),
    myGameObj);
  AK::SoundEngine::UnregisterGameObj(myGameObj);
}
```

```
void GameMainLoop()
{
  int frameCount = 0;
  while (frameCount++ < 300) // Run 300 frames and exit
  {
    auto time = std::chrono::milliseconds(30);
    std::this_thread::sleep_for(time);
    AK::SoundEngine::RenderAudio();
  }
}

int main(int argc, const char * argv[])
{
  if(InitWwise())
  {
    PlaySound();
    GameMainLoop();
  }

  TermWwise();

  return 0;
}
```

The small program is broken into four different functions: initialization, sound trigger, game loop, and termination. Let's go over them in detail.

The InitWwise() function is where we initialize the different modules. Each module has initialization settings that can be customized depending on your needs. It is important that the modules are initialized in the right order because of dependencies between the modules: memory manager, streaming manager, steaming device creation, and finally the sound engine. When all that is done, we load the banks: Init.bnk and the SFX.bnk bank using AK::SoundEngine::LoadBank(). The Init.bnk file is the bank associated with your Wwise project and must be the first bank to be loaded. In the next section, you will learn how to create the Init.bnk and the SFX.bnk files using the Wwise authoring tool.

In the PlaySound() function, we are simply registering a game object and posting the *Play_SFX_1* event on it. Since the event is a 2D event and we don't need to worry about 3D position, we can unregister the game object right away. However, keep in mind that in a real-life scenario, we would generally keep the game object registered until the sound finishes playing and only then unregister it.

In the function GameMainLoop(), we basically fake a game loop; the game loop is generally where you tick each of your game actors, which makes it the most logical place to call AK::SoundEngine::RenderAudio(). This function sends a signal to the audio thread, telling it to process another audio frame. Before processing the audio samples for the current frame, the audio thread process all the messages sent since the last update: play events, game object positions, as well as other types of messages we will see later.

Finally, in the function TermWwise(), we unload the banks and we unregister the different modules in the opposite order in which they were initialized.

In order to build this example, you will need to compile CAkDefaultIOHookBlocking.cpp, which is part of the Wwise sample code. (We will come back to the IO Hook in Section 5.8.) Also, you will need to link with the following Wwise static libraries: AkMemoryMgr, AkSoundEngine, AkStreamMgr, and CommunicationCentral if you are using debug or profile configuration.

5.2.2 Hello Wwise Authoring Tool

There is still one more thing we need to do in order to be able to hear sounds from our computer speaker: we need to generate the Init.bnk and the SFX.bnk. In order to do that, we need to create a Wwise project with the authoring tool. Open the Wwise executable and create a new project. In your new project, open the "Audio File Importer" (Figure 5.1) by clicking on Project menu and then *Import Audio File...* option. Import a wav file

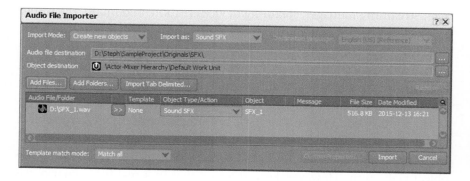

FIGURE 5.1   Audio File Importer.

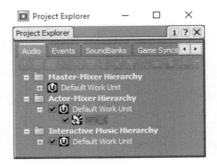

FIGURE 5.2   Actor-Mixer Hierarchy.

into your project (any wav file on your computer will do). This will create a *Sound SFX* object in your *Actor-Mixer hierarchy* (Figure 5.2). In order to be able to play this event in from the sample code, we need to create an event.

On your newly created *Sound SFX*, open the contextual menu by right clicking on the object and select *New Event* and then *Play*. You just created a new event referencing your *Sound SFX* object. This event should be named *Play_SFX_1*.

Next, we need to create the soundbank. In the *Soundbank* tab of your Wwise *Project Explorer* view (Figure 5.3), right-click on the Default Work Unit and create a new soundbank named *SFX*. From there, double click on your newly created SFX soundbank to open the SoundBank editor (Figure 5.4) and drag the Play_SFX_1 event into your bank.

Now that all the data is ready, we can generate the banks. In order to do that, press F7 or open the *Layout* menu and select *SoundBank*. In the *SoundBank Manager* view, select all soundbanks, all platforms, and click on the *Generate* button. This should have created the SFX bank

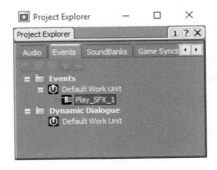

FIGURE 5.3   Project Explorer.

FIGURE 5.4   SoundBank editor.

and the Init bank inside a folder named *GeneratedFolder/[YourPlatform]*, where your Wwise project is located. Please note that you might need set g_blockingDevice.SetBasePath() to point to the location where you generated the soundbanks.

From this point, you should be able to build and run the sample code. However, as you might have experienced as a programmer, things rarely work the first time. As an exercise, I invite you to add error checking when Wwise is initialized and terminated so you can debug more easily.

5.3 DEBUGGING IN Wwise

5.3.1 Wwise Profiler Introduction

So now that we can play a sound using Wwise, we can introduce one of the most powerful and underestimated tool in Wwise: the profiler. Hold on, have you been able to play any sound successfully using the provided sample code? If not, continue reading—it might be helpful to you!

As an audio programmer, you know that debugging audio is not easy. Putting breakpoints in the code will work, but when a breakpoint is hit, the audio is not playing anymore. You need other ways to let you observe the audio activity in your game without disrupting the normal flow. For that, there is the Wwise profiler. Let's build on the sample code we have shown in the previous section and add the code necessary to be able to profile our sample application with Wwise.

```
#include <AK/Comm/AkCommunication.h>

int main(int argc, const char * argv[])
{
```

```
if(InitWwise())
{
  AkCommSettings commSettings;
  AK::Comm::GetDefaultInitSettings(commSettings);
  AK::Comm::Init(commSettings);

  // Gives you 5 seconds to connect
  // before the sounds start
  auto time = std::chrono::seconds(5);
  std::this_thread::sleep_for(time);

  PlaySound();
  GameMainLoop();

  AK::Comm::Term();
}

TermWwise();

  return 0;
}
```

To build the executable properly, you will need to link with CommunicationCentral library. Noticeably, initializing and terminating the communication with Wwise is quite trivial. On the other hand, trying to Connect to Game before the solitary sample event is triggered might be a really challenging task. For this reason, I have added a sleep statement to leave some time to connect before the sound is started. You do need make sure you strip the communication module from your shipping build and, again, this code does no error checking for sake of readability.

Once the application is running and communication has been initialized, the application can be profiled with Wwise. On the Wwise toolbar, click on the *Remote* button; this will show you all the applications running Wwise on your subnet. In the *Remote Connection* view, you should be able to find your application (if it is running).

Once you are connected, you can switch to the *Profiler* layout by pressing F6, or click on the *Layouts* menu and select *Profiler* (Figure 5.5).

The profiler layout is the audio programmer's best friend in Wwise. The *Capture Log* will show various information from the sound engine. There will be a lot of information in the window while you are in the process of debugging your game, but you can always filter out the information you

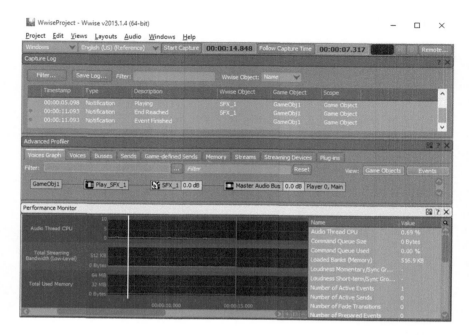

FIGURE 5.5   Wwise Profiler.

don't need using the filter pane. One really useful feature is that you can post your own message from the game code to the Capture Log by using the function AK::Monitor::PostString().

The *Performance Monitor* allows you see the performance on the sound engine graphically in real time when connected to the game. This view will become really useful when it will be time to optimize your game. In this window, you can see the number of active streams, audio thread CPU usage, memory used by the audio media, etc. In fact, you can customize what is shown in the *Performance Monitor* by clicking on the square icon on the top of the window.

The last view in the *Profiler Layout* is the *Advance Profiler*. Each tab basically represents a snapshot of audio activity from a different perspective at a particular time. For example, the *Voice Graph* tab will show all of the mixing graph at time *x*, whereas the *Memory* tab will show a breakdown of the memory usage at time *x*. In order to see a different snapshot for time *x* or time *x'*, you simply need to move the time cursor in the *Performance Monitor*, or activate the *Follow Capture* option to see the information in real time. Like the *Performance Monitor*, you can customize the tabs you are seeing in the Advance Profiler by clicking on the square icon on the top of the window.

5.3.2 Using the Wwise Profiler

As an audio programmer, one of the sentences you hear the most often is probably: "I have integrated sound XYZ and it doesn't play in the game. Can you please debug it?" You can guess that with the Wwise profiler layout, you are well equipped to accomplish this task. Let's see how this would be done in practice. Before starting to debug, we must grab some information from the game. With the Wwise profiler connected to the game, we need to reproduce the scenario where the sound is missing. When this is done, you can disconnect Wwise from the game.

Now that our *Capture Log* is full of information to analyze, the first step would be to find the event in the *Capture Log*. In order to do that, you can type the name of your sound event in the filter and try to find it in the *Capture Log*. If you don't find the event in the *Capture Log*, then the sound engine never received the event so the problem is probably in the game code. If you do find the event, then we need to investigate further to know what is happening.

To begin, shift-click on the event you are trying to debug in the *Capture Log*; this will move the time cursor of the *Performance Monitor* but also update the *Advance Profiler* with the right time. Once this is done, you need to identify the source of the problem. The first thing to look at is errors in the *Capture Logs*—maybe a bank failed to load, or we are running out of memory. If there are no apparent errors, then we need to continue with the *Voice-Graph*—maybe the sound is playing but its volume is really low. At this point, the source of the problem could fork into hundreds of other possibilities. The idea here was to show that the *Wwise Profiler* is a powerful debugging tool to use in conjunction with other tools such as a debugger and performance profiler.

On top of that, I would like to point out that the *Wwise Profiler* is also accessible to the sound designers. This means they can try to debug the issue first themselves. If they are not able to solve the issue or understand the problem, then they can request help from an audio programmer. Since the profiler sessions are stored on disk at root of the Wwise project folder, they can bring their profiling session to someone else for help. The profiling session can be reloaded later from the *remote* button in Wwise; instead of *connecting to IP*, you have to select *connect to file*. This can be particularly useful when you want to debug things remotely or debug issues that are difficult to reproduce. Hopefully, now you understand why I claim that the Wwise Profiler is one of the most powerful and underestimated features of Wwise.

5.4 TRIGGERING AUDIO IN YOUR GAME

5.4.1 Events

Wwise events are what allow your game to interface with the sound engine. An event is a set of actions. There are many actions available, including play, post event, stop, pause, mute, set bus volume, set voice volume, set voice pitch, set switch, bypass effect, seek trigger, and set game parameter. The actions can be of global scope or game object scope. For example, you can request a stop action for a sound sfx object. If the scope is global, all the instances of the sound will be stopped. If the scope is game object, only the game object will be stopped. Calling events from code is rather simple—just call AK::SoundEngine::PostEvent() with the right event and game object. The function returns a playing ID and can be used to target a particular playing event. It could become really useful if one particular game object plays multiple instances of the same sound. This way, you can target a stop action to one particular playing instance rather than the game object.

5.4.2 Soundbanks, Memory, and Streams

As you might recall in the sample code from the first section of this chapter, we have created a soundbank called SFX.bnk. Is this example, we have chosen to include the events, structures, and media inside the same bank (Figure 5.4); but it doesn't have to be this way.

First, let's explain what is serialized into a soundbank. Events consist of the event names contained in your bank. The structures are the objects and buses defined in the actor-mixer hierarchy and the master-mixer hierarchy. Finally, the media is the compressed audio data that will actually be played. The biggest chunk of data is obviously the media!

You can choose to always include events, structure, and media in your banks. This is the simplest strategy. However, there are other strategies available to you. We could have chosen not to include the media in our SFX bank. In that case, the media file would have been copied to the generated soundbank folder by the CopyStreamedFiles.exe of the postgeneration step (accessible in the project settings of Wwise). In this case, you have to call AK::SoundEngine::PrepareEvent() to load and unload the media associated with the event. With this strategy, you can keep the events and structure in memory and load and unload the media on-demand, which will be optimal on the memory but will result in more file access.

Additionally, you can use AK::SoundEngine::PrepareBank() to benefit from this mechanism without having to tell your sound designer to create the banks a certain way. Furthermore, you can push this dynamic loading concept to be used with the media associated with the game syncs with AK::SoundEngine::PrepareGameSyncs().

You can also stream the file from your hard drive or optical media. For that, the sound designer has set the file as a stream in the *sound property* editor of Wwise. They can also activate the zero latency for putting the beginning of the file in memory or make the stream noncacheable. Note that in order to use the cache option, you need to activate bUseStreamCache on AkDeviceSettings when initializing the streaming device.

When generating the banks in Wwise, the media files will also be copied in the generated folder as loose files for access by the streaming device; this is done by the CopyStreamedFiles.exe of the postgeneration step (exactly like for the prepare event case).

5.5 GAME SYNCS (STATES, SWITCHES, AND GAME PARAMETERS)

There are four types of game syncs in Wwise: States, Switches, Game Parameter, and Triggers. As we have seen in the previous section, these can be set using event actions. However, it might become cumbersome to use only event actions, especially for the case of game parameters. Figure 5.6 shows the Project Explorer with a number of game syncs.

5.5.1 States and Switches

States and *switches* are quite similar to C++ enumerations: they represent a list of named values. AK::SoundEngine::SetState() and AK::SoundEngine::SetSwitch() can be used to set values directly in code rather than using Wwise events. You might wonder what the difference is between a *state* and a *switch*. If you look closely at the function signature to set them, you will realize that AK::SoundEngine::SetSwitch() takes a game object ID for one of its parameters. This means that the *switch* scope is the game object, whereas the *state* has a global scope.

In the authoring tool, the *switch* is used with the *switch container*. A typical usage of the *switch container* would be for impact sounds with different materials. For example, you could have a footstep impact sound on the floor. The switch container will be used to create different variations depending on the surface your character is walking on. Although you can use a state with the switch container, this will not work with the footstep

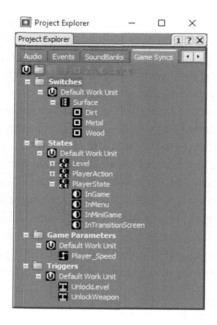

FIGURE 5.6 Game syncs.

example, unless you only have one character in your game. It is important that you and your sound designers understand when it is appropriate to use a switch or a state.

5.5.2 Game Parameters

Game parameters are meant to be used with Real-Time Parameter Controls (RTPCs). In Wwise, any RTPC can be assigned to a game sync parameter. For example, in Figure 5.7, the *voice pitch* RTPC of *SFX_1* is assigned to the game sync parameter *Player_Speed*. In the code, we can set the game parameter at global scope, game object scope, or playing ID scope.

```
// Setting game parameter for all object in game
AK::SoundEngine::SetRTPCValue(
    AKTEXT("Player_Speed"), 50);

// Setting game parameter for one game object
AkGameObjectID myGO = 2;
AK::SoundEngine::SetRTPCValue(
    AKTEXT("Player_Speed"), 50, myGO);
```

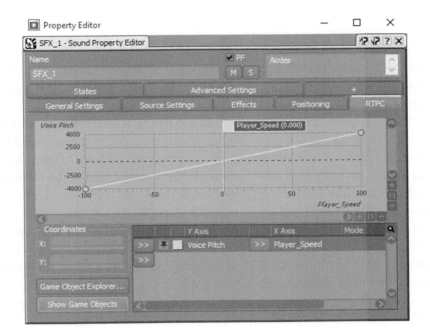

FIGURE 5.7   RTPC.

```
// Setting game parameter for the playing id
AkPlayingID pid = AK_INVALID_PLAYING_ID;
pid = AK::SoundEngine::PostEvent(
    AKTEXT("Play_SFX_1"), myGO)
AK::SoundEngine::SetRTPCValueByPlayingID(
    AKTEXT("Player_Speed"), 50, pid);
```

Another interesting neat trick to know is that you can tell the function AK::SoundEngine::SetRTPCValue() to interpolate to a value over a period of time. The fourth parameter of the function represents the time in milliseconds to ramp to the new value. Instead of doing the interpolation yourself in the game code, you can let Wwise do it for you. Here is an example of how you could do it in the code:

```
// Set the value to 0 and then interpolate to 50 over
// a period of 1000 ms
AkGameObjectID myGO = 2;
AK::SoundEngine::SetRTPCValue(
    AKTEXT("Player_Speed"), 0, myGO);
```

```
AK::SoundEngine::SetRTPCValue(
    AKTEXT("Player_Speed"), 50, myGO, 1000);
```

On the top of that, Audiokinetic has exposed a bunch of different interpolation curves as the fifth parameter of the function. The default is linear interpolation, but you also have access to other curves.

In the *game parameter property editor* of the authoring tool, sound designers also have access to interpolation settings. It is important to understand that it is another layer of interpolation; you have to agree with the sound designer for where you want the interpolation to be applied: using code or the Wwise authoring tool. For complex scenarios, doing the interpolation in code will tend to be more flexible. As a programmer, you can always decide to bypass the interpolation set by the sound designer. `AK::SoundEngine::SetRTPCValue()` allows you to do that. This might be useful especially at initializing time: generally, you want the game parameter to be set to the value right away without any interpolation.

Game parameters can be debugged in-game using the *game sync monitor*. This view can be found in the *Game Object Profiler* of Wwise.

5.6 3D AUDIO

5.6.1 Listeners and Game Objects

If a tree falls in a forest and no one is around to hear it, does it make a sound? We are not here to talk about the perception of the reality, but to model 3D audio we need to have a listener and an emitter for a sound to exist! In Wwise, there can be up to eight active listeners. Why so many? Having different listeners might be useful in the context of split-screen video game, or the feature can also be used for platforms that have controllers with embedded speakers. There are other reasons to use more than one listener in your game. For example, in a third-person game you might want to have some sounds playing out from the main character's perspective whereas other sounds would play out of the camera's perspective.

As an audio programmer, you are responsible for updating the position of the listener with the function `AK::SoundEngine::SetListenerPosition()` and also for game objects with the function `AK::SoundEngine::SetPosition()`. For certain special cases, you could choose not to activate spatialization on a listener. When you do that, all the attenuation curves are ignored. For a implementation details, you can refer to a document of the function `AK::SoundEngine::SetListenerSpatialization()`. For a game object, if you only need to play 2D sounds, you don't need to update its position.

Once you have integrated 3D sound in your game, you can verify your implementation by using the *Game Object profiler*. In order to do that, simply connect to your game (like in the previous section) then switch to the *Game Object Profiler* by pressing F12 or using the *Layout* menu. This profiler renders your game objects and listeners in a 3D world.

For the authoring tool counterpart, the *Attenuation Editor* (Figure 5.8) is where the sound designer will set the attenuation curves based on the distance. There are a lot of curves accessible to the sound designers: bus volume, auxiliary send volume (user defined and game defined), low-pass, high-pass, spread, and focus. There is also the cone attenuation with which you can affect the sound for when the listener is the region behind the emitter. For that to work properly, make sure you normalize the orientation vector when setting the game object and listener position.

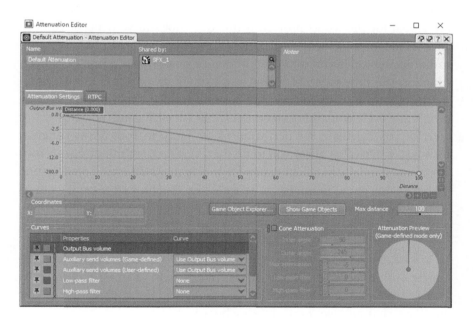

FIGURE 5.8   Attenuation Editor.

5.6.2 Obstruction and Occlusion

Obstruction and occlusion are definitely features that can improve player immersion. When there are obstacles between the emitter and the listener, the sound will be affected: as a result, the sound will probably be quieter and have less low-frequency content. On the other hand, if the sound emitter is placed in a different room from the listener without any direct path, the sound will be occluded. In this scenario, the sound will lose some of its high-frequency content and will be attenuated.

In other words, this means that we can model this phenomenon using a low-pass filter, a high-pass filter, and volume attenuation, which is exactly how Audiokinetic models occlusion and obstruction. As a programmer, you need to call `AK::SoundEngine::SetObjectObstructionAndOcclusion()` per game object and listener pair. However, you are not setting the value of the filters or volume yourself. Rather, you set an occlusion and obstruction factor in the range of 0 to 100.

In the project settings of Wwise, you can access the occlusion and obstruction curves (Figure 5.9). To access it, open the project settings from the project menu or simply type Shift + K, then navigate to the Obstruction/Occlusion tab. As you can see in Figure 5.9, the occlusion factor will be mapped to the curves drawn in this window. The settings are global for the whole project; if this does not suit your need, you can also decide to implement obstruction and occlusion by binding the built-in parameter occlusion and obstruction to one of your game parameter (done in the property window of the game parameter). It is also note-worthy that the advanced profiler has a tab called Obs/Ocl that lets you profile the occlusion and obstruction factor for each game object.

How you calculate the occlusion factor is up to you. Many different techniques exist that allow you to do that, and each technique has its own advantages and drawbacks. Some people pregenerate a sound propagation map by using game geometry, others use line checks, and there are others who use a combination of both.

5.6.3 Dynamic Game Reverb

In Wwise, the game reverbs are implemented using an auxiliary bus. The concept of an auxiliary bus or, if you like, a send channel, is known by every audio mixing engineer. Let's go through a brief explanation of how auxiliary channels work on a mixing board.

There are generally one or more auxiliary channels on a mixing board. The channel has an FX loop that lets the signal out to an external reverb

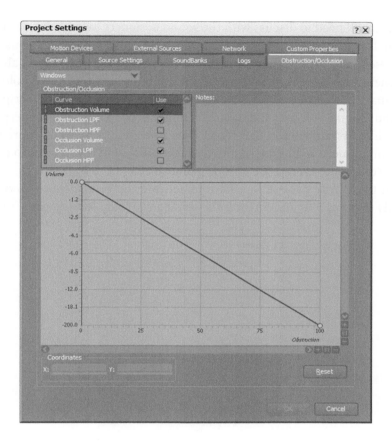

FIGURE 5.9 Obstruction and occlusion settings.

module and loop back into the mixing board from the output of the effect module. Each instrument channel on the mixing board has a send knob in order to send the dry signal of the instrument channel to the auxiliary channel. The auxiliary channel will mix all the signals from the instrument channels and send that to the reverb effect on the FX loop. This is exactly how you can conceptualize the auxiliary bus in Wwise.

As a programmer, your responsibility is to assign each game object to one or multiple auxiliary buses. You are also responsible for the amount of signal you send to the different auxiliary bus channels. This is done with the function `AK::SoundEngine::SetGameObjectAuxSendValues()`. Each game object can send up to four different auxiliary buses, but there is no limit on the total number of auxiliary buses. For example, one game object can send its signal to four auxiliary buses whereas another game object can send its signal to four different auxiliary buses.

You will need to discuss with the sound designers to know how to integrate this feature into your game. Most of the time, an auxiliary bus will represent a room in the game, so your sound designers need to be able to define reverb zones in the game editor. These reverb zones will hold the auxiliary bus name and possibly other settings. Although this description sounds simple, it is only the start. You might need to implement interpolation if your game object can travel from one zone to another. Moreover, you might need to build a sound propagation system if you want to cover more than one reverb zone for one game object.

In the Wwise project, you have to activate the *game-defined auxiliary sends* (Figures 5.10 and 5.11) on the sounds you want to have game reverb

FIGURE 5.10   Aux bus.

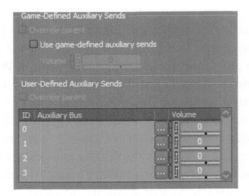

FIGURE 5.11   Game-defined and user-defined auxiliary sends.

on. It is interesting to know that we can also have four *user-defined auxiliary sends*. They work exactly like the *game-defined auxiliary sends* in terms of signal routing, but the user-defined sends are not dynamic. Finally, the amount of signal you route to the auxiliary bus (game defined or user defined) can be affected by the attenuation curve (Figure 5.8). This might sound like a small detail although it might influence the way you set the values when you call `AK::SoundEngine::SetGameObjectAuxSendValues()`. In other words, with the attenuation curve, the sound designer has control over how much dry signal gets into the auxiliary bus based on distance.

5.7 INTERACTIVE MUSIC

5.7.1 Working with the Interactive Music System

The Wwise interactive music system is a powerful but really complex beast, although much of the complexity lies in the Wwise authoring tool. On the programming side, interactive music is done using events, switches, states, game parameters, and triggers. Most of what you need to know as an audio programmer to be able to support interactive music has already been covered in the previous sections of this chapter. The only remaining part is the initialization and termination of the music engine. As you will see in the following snippet, it is quite straightforward.

```
// Initialize the music engine
AkMusicSettings musicInit;
AK::MusicEngine::GetDefaultInitSettings(musicInit);
AK::MusicEngine::Init(&musicInit);

// Terminate the music engine
AK::MusicEngine::Term();
```

Wwise also provides a callback system to receive beats and bar notifications as well as other music-related notifications. These callbacks can be useful if you are doing a music game or you simply want some aspect of your game to be synchronized to the music.

5.7.2 Debugging the Interactive Music

One day, once the music is integrated in your game, the music composer or sound designer responsible for integrating the music will come to you and say that the wrong music is playing whenever the main character "Bobo" is in combat with the boss of level 4: "Big Bad Monsta." Believe me, that day will come! You will start verifying that all the switches are set correctly and the right event is being played, but you won't be able to find any error—everything is set properly. Music can be really complex; you can define crazy rules for transitions in between your music segments, and there is a good chance that the sound designer got confused between "Big Bad Monsta" and "Really Big Bad Final Boss." So how do you solve the issue? This is the time to test in Wwise, not in the game. There are two ways for you to do this: using the *Transport* or using the *Soundcaster*. While you can do a lot of things with *Transport*, it has a huge limitation: it can only play one event.

The *Soundcaster* is basically the Wwise *Transport* on steroids (Figure 5.12). With the Soundcaster, you can play multiple sounds simultaneously, but you also have easy access to all your game syncs. Whether you choose the transport or the *Soundcaster*, the idea is to determine if the bug is caused by a bug in game code or in the transition logic of the interactive music in the project.

Another neat trick to know is that you can profile the internal sound engine of the Wwise authoring tool. To do that, click on the start capture button without being connected. The interactive music system posts a huge amount of information to the *Capture Log* about music transitions, so this can be useful to know. Once you show that to your sound designers, there is a good chance that you won't hear about music transition bugs ever—or at least, you will be hearing about them less frequently.

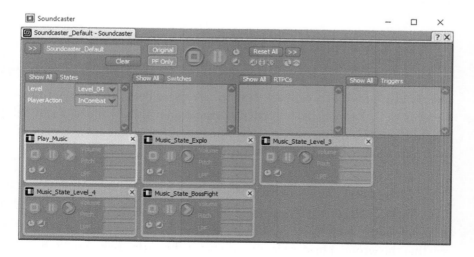

FIGURE 5.12   Soundcaster.

5.8 IMPLEMENTING FILE I/O

If you recall the sample code at the beginning of the chapter, we had to include a file, AkFilePackageLowLevelIOBlocking.h, and compile AkDefaultIOHookBlocking.cpp. The files are provided as sample code from Audiokinetic for how you load soundbanks and stream audio files. The class CAkDefaultIOHookBlocking only implements blocking I/O. There is another sample provided in the Wwise SDK that shows how to do asynchronous file I/O: AkDefaultIOHookDeferred.h and AkDefaultIOHookDeferred.cpp.

In order to be a good citizen, Wwise audio engine I/O requests need to be routed through your game's I/O manager. This way, audio file I/O requests will be processed with all the other media requests of your game like any other data. We won't go into the details of implementing file I/O, because one chapter could have been written solely on this subject. Keep in mind that this subject is complex and that you will need to tackle it. Wwise has plenty of documentation and a good support team if you need help. If there are system or engine programmers on your team, it is definitely the kind of task you want to discuss with them.

5.9 CONCLUSION

There are many other features I would have liked to cover: writing plug-ins, virtual voices, HDR, compression settings, dynamic mixing, localization, dynamic dialog events, soundframe, motion. The list could probably go on. Hopefully, this chapter will encourage you to dig further into Wwise, because a whole book could be written on this very subject. If there is only one thing you need to remember from this chapter, it is the following: knowing the Wwise SDK is important for an audio programmer, but it is even more important to know Wwise as a whole: Authoring tool + SDK. You don't want to work on a sound feature request for a week and then realize that it could have been done in a day using Wwise's built-in features. Now, it is your turn to play with Wwise: learn, experiment, and have fun!

CHAPTER 6

Programming FMOD Studio

Guy Somberg

CONTENTS

6.1 INTRODUCTION

I have been using FMOD for a very long time. Two major rewrites have been released since I first tried it out in 2001, along with countless minor revisions. The thing that struck me about FMOD when I first started using it was how easy it all was: initialize the API, load a file in just about any format under the sun, and play it. Even back then, this ease of use struck me as profound. FMOD has always had an elegant and easy-to-use API that offers a huge degree of control and flexibility to both sound designers and to audio programmers.

In this chapter, we'll be going over FMOD's history and inner workings, then we'll talk about how to use its API to accomplish many of the fundamental tasks that you'll be doing from day to day. Finally, we'll delve into one or two advanced topics. We won't be going into any details on using the FMOD Studio tool—FMOD has a wealth of documentation available for that.

6.2 A BRIEF HISTORY OF FMOD

FMOD is one of the oldest commercial audio engines on the market. Its first public release was March 6, 1995, as the Firelight MOD player. At the time, it was just a program designed to play MOD files and their relatives (XMs, S3Ms, ITs, etc.)—it didn't even have a library! In March 1999, FMOD version 2.13b included a programmers API for the first time, and FMOD version 3.0 was released in December of that same year.

Up through version 3.75, FMOD was provided as just a library for playing sounds. However, with the advent of FMOD 4.0 (also called FMOD Ex), it came with an editor tool, which you can see in Figure 6.1. Finally, in February 2013, FMOD underwent a full rewrite (and reversioning) to

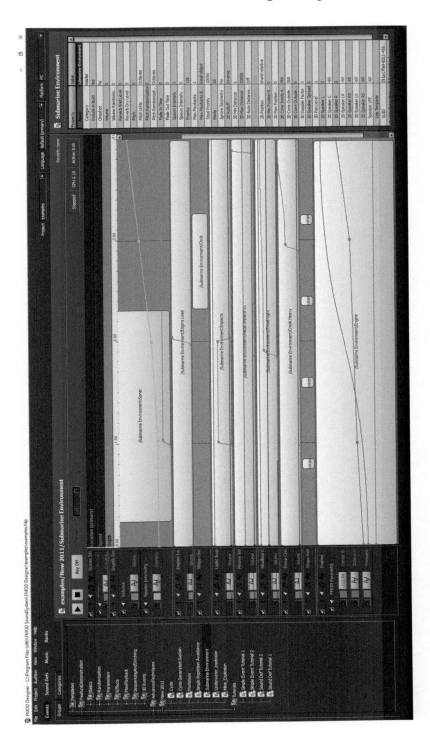

FIGURE 6.1 FMOD Ex Designer tool.

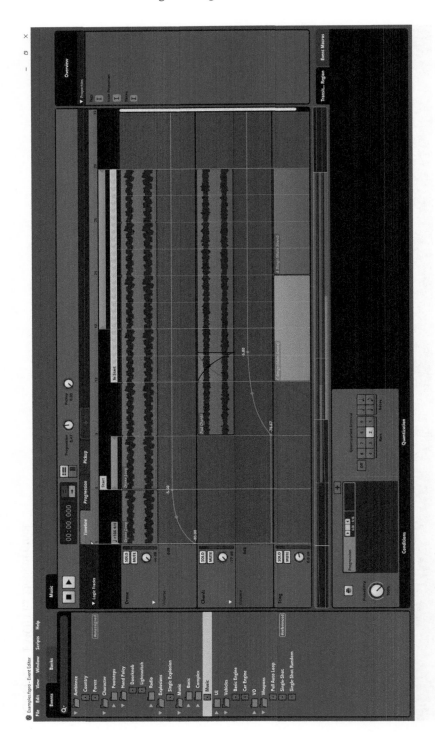

FIGURE 6.2 FMOD Studio tool.

become FMOD Studio version 1.0. The FMOD Studio tool is shown in Figure 6.2. This chapter covers the FMOD Studio API.

6.3 HOW FMOD WORKS

FMOD contains two libraries: a low-level API and a tool API (known as the Studio API). This separation is important, because the Studio API is actually built on top of the low-level API; this means there is nothing that the Studio API can do that you cannot do yourself using the low-level API. Importantly, the Studio API provides hooks into its own low-level implementation. Once you have these hooks, you can start to manipulate or query the internals of the working system in ways that the designers never imagined.

6.3.1 Low-Level API

FMOD's low-level API is responsible for all of the fine details of playing back sound. With a relatively simple set of interfaces, you can load sounds (either individual files or packages called FMOD sound banks [FSBs]), play them, and manipulate them. The low-level engine supports 3D panning, DSP effects using a powerful DSP graph engine (which we'll talk more about later), submixing, reverb, geometry calculations, and a wealth of other features.

6.3.2 Studio API

Whereas the low-level API can operate on individual files in just about any compression format, the Studio API is solely concerned with operating on the output of the FMOD Studio tool—Bank files. Banks contain all of the metadata describing Events along with all of the actual audio data.

The Studio API is quite simple to use, and on the surface, more limited in what you can do than the low-level API. On the one hand, the FMOD Studio tool itself allows the sound designers to be very expressive, so the number of operations that you as the audio programmer will need to do are relatively limited. However, the real power of Studio API is that, if you need to, you can always drop down into the low-level API and manipulate the internals.

6.3.3 FMOD Studio Internals

At its core, FMOD is a graph-based DSP engine. At the very end of the graph is a DSP that outputs to the sound card. Connected to that are one or more DSPs that generate sound (possibly by reading a file), mix sounds

FIGURE 6.3   A simple DSP graph.

together, or manipulate incoming sound data. All of the inputs to each DSP are mixed together before being processed by the DSP. For more advanced use cases, there are alternate inputs (side chain, Send/Return, and Send/Return side chain) that are not audible, but which are available as inputs to the DSP.

You can visualize this DSP graph using the FMOD Profiler tool, which is distributed with the Programmer's API. Figure 6.3 demonstrates a simple audio flow. The audio data flows right to left, and each block is a DSP unit in a DSP chain. The dotted line indicates a logical unit—in Figure 6.3, the right-hand group of two is a Channel and the left-hand group of one is a ChannelGroup. We'll come back to these constructs later in the chapter. A far more complex diagram is shown in Figure 6.4, where we see multiple Channels and ChannelGroups all playing and mixing together in more complicated ways. With practice, these graphs become easy to read.

6.4 API PREAMBLE

FMOD takes great care to separate out the low-level and Studio APIs from each other—when you install the API, they are placed into different folders. As you may expect, the Studio API depends on the low-level API. We'll cover each API separately.

Despite their separation, there are a couple of common aspects to both APIs:

- All of FMOD operates on C++ objects (there is a C API and a C# API, but they end up being wrappers around the C++ API). You get these objects by passing to an FMOD function a pointer to a pointer to an FMOD Object; FMOD then allocates the object and fills the pointer with a handle to that object. It is important to note that this handle is *not* a real pointer. Rather, it is a handle value that FMOD's internals know how to convert into a real object.

- All FMOD functions return an FMOD_RESULT enum. In many cases, it is important to check the return code against FMOD_OK, because the particular code will tell you what happened. When trying to deal

FIGURE 6.4 A mildly complex DSP graph.

with the common "this sound isn't playing" problem, one of the first things to look for is errors being returned from important functions. In this chapter, we won't be doing any error checking for brevity's sake, but that will not absolve you, the reader, from doing so in your own code.

6.5 USING THE LOW-LEVEL API

In this section, we'll go through the basic terminology and objects, then we'll write a program that plays a sound, creates a submix, applies a DSP effect (including reverb), and moves the sound in 3D. Let's get started!

6.5.1 Terminology

There are five fundamental objects in the low-level API:

- **System**—The base object that owns everything. It is responsible for creating the threads, controlling the sound card, and creating all of the other objects on this list.

- **Sound**—Wave data. Usually, it's loaded from a file on disk, but it can be streamed from the Internet, read from memory, or read from within a larger package file. For streamed sounds, the Sound object also holds the file read pointer. We'll discuss samples and streams in a moment.

- **Channel**—A playing Sound. You create a bank of Channels up front when you initialize the System object, and then the System doles them out as Sounds are played in your game.

- **ChannelGroup**—A submix point. ChannelGroups can be used to implement Buses, but they're also used by the Studio API as control points for Events and tracks within Events.

- **DSP**—The fundamental unit of the internal mixer. Underneath the hood, everything is implemented as a DSP. However, DSPs also surface as a way to either generate audio (such as a tone generator) or as a way to manipulate audio (such as a low-pass filter).

6.5.1.1 Sample/Stream Terminology and Consequences

There are three ways to load a sound in FMOD: as a Sample, as a Compressed Sample, or as a Stream. The only thing that you have to do in order to

select a mode is to pass a different flag into System::createSound().
However, there are a number of important differences between the modes
to bear in mind:

- **Sample**—FMOD will decompress the contents of the file into memory and store the data as raw PCM. This has the advantage of being lower CPU at runtime, but has the added memory cost of the decompressed file, which can be 6–10× the size of the file on disk, as well as an added performance cost at load time, because it has to decompress the file.

- **Compressed Sample**—FMOD will load the file into memory in its compressed state, and then decompress it on the fly in the mixer thread. This has the advantage that the memory usage is almost exactly the size as it is on disk, but is more expensive to decompress at runtime. Also, only a subset of the supported formats will work as compressed samples. Specifically, as of this writing: MP2, MP3, IMAADPCM, FSB-encoded Vorbis (without the Ogg wrapper), AT9 (a PlayStation-exclusive format), or XMA (an Xbox-exclusive format).

- **Stream**—FMOD will read chunks of the file at a time off of the disk, keeping only a relatively small buffer for audio data. This is advantageous for larger files, but it is a waste for smaller files. The one thing to be aware of with streams is that the Sound object actually stores the file read pointer. This means that you can only play a streamed sound once per Sound object (although you can have multiple Sound streams pointing to the same file). If you try to play it again while it is already playing, then the new Channel will start from the beginning of the file and the old Channel will be stopped. If you want to play a Stream on top of itself, you must open another Sound for the same file using System::createSound(), and then play that. Samples and Compressed Samples do not have this restriction.

6.5.2 Playing a Sound

At last, we have discussed the fundamentals, and now it's time to play a sound! The root object in the FMOD world is the System object. It is the object that controls and owns everything. The first thing you will need to do in any FMOD implementation is to create one and initialize it:

```
#include "fmod.hpp"

FMOD::System* pSystem = nullptr;
FMOD::System_Create(&pSystem);
pSystem->init(128, FMOD_INIT_NORMAL, nullptr);

// ...
// When you're ready to shut down...
pSystem->release();
```

The first parameter to `System::init()` is the maximum number of `Channels` to create. This value will be your engine's maximum polyphony; the only cost to making it big is memory, so if you can spare the memory, it's worthwhile to make the value much bigger than you would ordinarily expect your maximum polyphony to be. This will allow for brief spikes in the number of playing channels. After that come flags, which are documented in FMOD's help (and are outside the scope of this chapter), followed by platform-specific structures that may need to be passed in that control driver-specific behavior. In this example, we're just passing in `nullptr`.

Now that we have a `System` object, we can use it to load an audio file from disk. The list of file formats that FMOD supports is gigantic, so just about any audio file that you can think of will likely work.

```
FMOD::Sound* pSound = nullptr;
pSystem->createSound(
  R"(c:\path\to\sound.ogg)", FMOD_DEFAULT,
  nullptr, &pSound)

// ...
// When you're finished with the sound...
pSound->release(); // frees up the memory
```

This code will create a `Sound` object, load `sound.ogg` from the disk, and decompress it into memory. The first parameter is the path to the file (note that we're using C++11 raw string literals to avoid having to escape the backslashes). After that comes a set of flags, then a pointer to a `FMOD_CREATESOUNDEXINFO` structure, which is used to control advanced settings. Finally, we pass in the address of our `Sound` variable, which gets filled in.

We are now ready to play the sound! Let's see what that looks like:

```
FMOD::Channel* pChannel = nullptr;
pSystem->playSound(pSound, nullptr, false, &pChannel);
```

That's downright trivial! The first and last parameters are the `Sound` to play, and the `Channel` pointer to fill. The second parameter is a default `ChannelGroup` to assign to (which defaults to the Master `ChannelGroup`). We'll discuss `ChannelGroups` more in the next section. The third parameter is whether to start the Channel in a paused state. This is particularly useful so that you can set properties of the `Channel`, such as its volume, 3D position, pan, pitch, cone settings, and seek point, before it is actually played. A very common pattern is to pass true for this flag in the `System::playSound()` call, set a bunch of parameters, and then call `pChannel->setPaused(false)`.

You do not need to release a `Channel` object. It lives in the pool that the `System` object created. If you run out of `Channels`, then the system will steal a low-priority `Channel`, and you will get a callback indicating that this has happened. You can, of course, control this behavior in very fine detail if you wish.

The last piece of the puzzle is to wait until the sound is finished playing before shutting everything down:

```
bool bIsPlaying = true;
while(bIsPlaying) {
  pChannel->isPlaying(&bIsPlaying);
  pSystem->update();
  Sleep(10);
}
// release() the Sound and System objects here, as
// shown above
```

6.5.2.1 Updating the System

What's with the `pSystem->update()` call in that loop? Won't FMOD play audio without needing to update it every frame? Yes, it does; the mixer runs on an independent thread. The `System::update()` call serves a number of purposes, but the important ones are as follows:

- Updates virtual voices and 3D positioning of sounds. These features will appear to succeed but will not have any effect if you don't call `System::update()`.

- Nonblocking loads will never appear to finish loading if you don't call `System::update()`.

- Callbacks are triggered from the `System::update()` call.

6.5.3 Creating Submixes with ChannelGroups

A `ChannelGroup` is simply a point on the DSP graph where zero or more `Channels` and other `ChannelGroups` mix their audio data together. The `ChannelGroup` can adjust the volume, panning, 3D position, and other properties, and can also act as a point to attach DSP effects. We'll see how to attach DSPs in the next section. For now, let's see how to create a simple bus hierarchy using `ChannelGroups`.

We'll create a Music bus and an Sfx bus, and then a Footsteps bus as a child of the Sfx bus. There is also a Master `ChannelGroup` in the System object that can be queried using `System::getMasterChannelGroup()`.

```
// Declare the ChannelGroup objects
FMOD::ChannelGroup* pSfxChannelGroup = nullptr;
FMOD::ChannelGroup* pFootChannelGroup = nullptr;
FMOD::ChannelGroup* pMusicChannelGroup = nullptr;

// Create the ChannelGroups
pSystem->createChannelGroup("Sfx", &pSfxChannelGroup);
pSystem->createChannelGroup("Footsteps",
  &pFootChannelGroup);
pSystem->createChannelGroup("Music",
  &pMusicChannelGroup);

// Assign the Footseps bus to be a child of the Sfx bus
pSfxChannelGroup->addGroup(pFootChannelGroup);
```

Now, we can assign our `Channel` to a `ChannelGroup` in one of two ways: either when it's played, or by assigning it at runtime.

```
// To assign the ChannelGroup when the Sound is
// initially played
pSystem->playSound(pSound, pFootChannelGroup, false,
  &pChannel);
```

```
// To assign the ChannelGroup at runtime
pChannel->setChannelGroup(pMusicChannelGroup);
```

Now, we have a lot of control. In our example, we can set the volume of the Sfx bus, and it will adjust the volume of every `Channel` being played under the Sfx bus and all of its child buses. It will also combine the parameters recursively. So if the volume of the Sfx `ChannelGroup` is 0.5 (−6 dB) and the volume of the Footsteps `ChannelGroup` is 0.75 (−3 dB), the total volume of any `Channel` being played through the Footsteps `ChannelGroup` is 0.375 (−9 dB).

6.5.4 Applying DSP Effects

Now that we've played our sound and created our submix, it's time to manipulate the audio using DSP effects. DSP effects are filters that modify the audio signal based on a set of input parameters (which can themselves be audio signals!). They can be applied both to `Channels` and to `ChannelGroups`. Let's start by creating a low-pass filter DSP.

```
FMOD::DSP* pLowPass = nullptr;
pSystem->createDSPByType(FMOD_DSP_TYPE_LOWPASS,
  &pLowPass);
```

This DSP object is completely detached from the internal DSP graph. It consumes memory (but not CPU), and has no audible effect until we attach it to either a `Channel` or a `ChannelGroup`.

```
pChannel->addDSP(0, pLowPass);
// Or
pChannelGroup->addDSP(0, pLowPass);
```

If you attach the DSP to a `ChannelGroup`, then the inputs will all be mixed together, and the low-pass filter will be applied to the mixed output.

Great, so we've applied this low-pass filter, but now we need to set its cutoff frequency (and any other parameters, such as its resonance). Each built-in effect has an enumeration for setting the various parameters that control its behavior. We'll show here how to adjust the cutoff frequency.

```
pLowPass->setParameterFloat(
  FMOD_DSP_LOWPASS_CUTOFF, 1200.0f);
```

By creating DSPs and applying them to Channels and ChannelGroups, you can create tools that allow your sound designers to create truly awesome audioscapes.

It's also possible to create your own DSPs to do custom processing if the built-in effects are not sufficient for your purposes. DSPs can also be implemented to generate waveform data, so that you can perform waveform, FM, or granular synthesis.

6.5.5 3D Sound

While there will always be some subset of sounds that will be stereo (such as music and UI sounds), or will be custom-panned, a large majority of sounds will be 3D. In FMOD, manipulating 3D sounds is easy. Let's see how it works.

First, we'll need to set a flag when we create the Sound object.

```
pSystem->createSound(
  R"(c:\path\to\sound.ogg)", FMOD_3D, nullptr, &pSound);
```

The only difference between this createSound() call and the previous one is that we have passed FMOD_3D in the flags section. This tells FMOD that Channels created with this Sound are to be panned in 3D. You can change the mode on a Channel by passing the appropriate flag to Channel::setMode(), which will allow you to override the default from the Sound. To control the 3D min and max distance of the Channel, you can call Channel::set3DMinMaxDistance().

Next, we need to set the 3D position of the Channel.

```
FMOD_VECTOR position = {0.0f, 10.0f, 0.0f};
pChannel->set3DAttributes(&position, nullptr);
```

The second parameter to Channel::set3DAttributes() is a velocity vector. This will adjust the Doppler pitch shift of the sound according to the system settings. Many games just ignore this value by setting it to nullptr, as we have done in this example.

We will also need to manipulate the position of the listener. This is slightly more complicated, because the listener needs not only a position (and an optional velocity), but it also needs an orientation. FMOD does this by requiring you to provide forward and up vectors, which it uses to calculate the reference frame. Typically, you will set the listener position to be in the 3D camera. I have fabricated some accessor functions here, but your game engine may provide you with a quaternion, which will require you to do some math to get these vectors.

```
FMOD_VECTOR pos = GetCameraPosition();
FMOD_VECTOR fwd = GetCameraForward();
FMOD_VECTOR up  = GetCameraUp();
pSystem->set3DListenerAttributes(0,
    &pos, nullptr, &fwd, &up);
```

The first parameter is the listener number; you can configure FMOD to have multiple listeners for split-screen or other custom game reasons. By default, you get one listener at index zero. The `nullptr` in the third parameter is the velocity of the listener, which, like `Channel::set3DAttributes()`, is used for Doppler calculations.

6.5.6 Reverb

FMOD implements reverb by creating a Reverb `DSP` attached to the Master `ChannelGroup`, then adding a second connection path from each playing sound into the Reverb `DSP`'s input. This is demonstrated in Figure 6.5. The `Channel`'s output is routed both to its `ChannelGroup` and to the FMOD Reverb `DSP`. Let's see how to set this up.

```
FMOD_REVERB_PROPERTIES reverb = FMOD_PRESET_CAVE;
pSystem->setReverbProperties(0, &reverb);
```

FMOD comes with a number of reverb presets, but the FMOD_REVERB_PROPERTIES structure contains a dozen different parameters

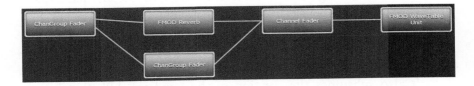

FIGURE 6.5   DSP graph with reverb.

that your sound designers can tweak to their hearts' content. The first parameter to the System::setReverbProperties() function is the reverb instance number. You can have up to four reverbs, and send different amounts of each Channel to each Reverb DSP using Channel::setReverbProperties(). By manipulating the wet level to each reverb, you can control in very fine detail the environment that is perceived for each Channel.

6.5.7 Just the Surface

Unfortunately, in a chapter like this we can only skim the surface of what the low-level API can do. We haven't even talked about 3D cone settings, custom rolloff curves, generic programming with ChannelControls, DSPConnections, Geometry, or any other number of features that are each worth their own section.

The most telling thing about the power of FMOD's low-level API is that the high-level Studio API and tool are actually built on top of it. Let's take a look at the Studio API now.

6.6 USING THE STUDIO API

Now that we have a handle on the low-level API, we can start going into detail on the Studio API. One of the things that you'll notice is that the programming patterns are all the same: we initialize the system, load the audio data, and then play the content that we're interested in. Because the patterns are now familiar, we'll introduce code in bigger chunks in this section. First, as with the low-level API, we'll go through the basic terminology and objects. Next, we'll write a program that plays an Event and moves it in 3D space; finally, we'll talk about mixing with Buses and Reverb.

6.6.1 Terminology

There are five fundamental objects in the Studio API. One important thing to note is that, although the low-level API is all in the FMOD:: namespace, all of the Studio API objects live in the FMOD::Studio:: namespace.

- **System**—Just like the low-level API, the System object is responsible for mixing, playback, and creating all of the other objects. It also subsumes the creation of the low-level API; that is, you only need to create an FMOD::Studio::System object. You don't need to also create an FMOD::System object as well—you can access the underlying low-level System object by using FMOD::Studio::System::getLowLevelSystem().

- **EventDescription**—Metadata about an Event. You can use the EventDescription to play an EventInstance, manage audio wave data, or to query properties of the Event.

- **EventInstance**—Represents a playing Event (or an Event which can be played). You can use the EventInstance to start or stop an Event, or to manipulate Event parameters and properties.

- **Bus**—A handle to an audio Bus, which can be used to manipulate its volume, or to get access to the underlying ChannelGroup.

- **Bank**—A handle to a loaded bank file, which can be used to load and unload audio data, or to query properties and contents of the bank file.

6.6.2 Playing an Event

Just like with the low-level API, now that we've covered the basics, we can now start playing Events. Let's take a look at the code for initializing the System, loading a Bank, and playing an EventInstance from an EventDescription.

```
// Create and initialize the System object
FMOD::Studio::System* pSystem = nullptr;
FMOD::Studio::System::create(&pSystem);
pSystem->initialize(128, FMOD_STUDIO_INIT_NORMAL,
                    FMOD_INIT_NORMAL, nullptr);


// Load the Master Bank and the Master Strings Bank
// Loading the Master Strings bank is optional.
FMOD::Studio::Bank* pMasterBank = nullptr;
FMOD::Studio::Bank* pMasterStringsBank = nullptr;
pSystem->loadBankFile(R"(C:\path\to\Master Bank.bank)",
                    FMOD_STUDIO_LOAD_BANK_NORMAL,
                    &pMasterBank);
pSystem->loadBankFile(
            R"(C:\path\to\Master Bank.strings.bank)",
                    FMOD_STUDIO_LOAD_BANK_NORMAL,
                    &pMasterStringsBank);
```

```cpp
// Load the Bank containing our Event
FMOD::Studio::Bank* pBank = nullptr;
pSystem->loadBankFile(R"(C:\path\to\UI_Menu.bank)",
                      FMOD_STUDIO_LOAD_BANK_NORMAL,
                      &pBank);


// Get the EventDescription for our Event
FMOD::Studio::EventDescription* pEventDescription =
  nullptr;
pSystem->getEvent("event:/Explosions/Single Explosion",
                  &pEventDescription);


// Create an EventInstance from the EventDescription to
// play this Event
FMOD::Studio::EventInstance* pEventInstance = nullptr;
pEventDescription->createInstance(&pEventInstance);


// Start playing the EventInstance
pEventInstance->start();


// Schedule the EventInstance to be destroyed when it
// stops. This is fine for one-shots, but you will
// need to stop looping Events manually with
// EventInstance::stop().
pEventInstance->release();


// Wait for the EventInstance to finish
FMOD_STUDIO_PLAYBACK_STATE eState;
do {
  pEventInstance->getPlaybackState(&eState);
  pSystem->update();
  Sleep(10);
} while(eState != FMOD_STUDIO_PLAYBACK_STOPPED);


// Unload all loaded Banks and free the System object.
// You can also choose to unload individual Banks by
// using Bank::unload().
pSystem->unloadAll();
pSystem->release();
```

As noted above, the general pattern here is the same: initialize the System object, load the data, play the EventInstance, wait for completion, then shut down. Let's go over a few details from the preceding code.

6.6.2.1 Master Bank and Master Strings Bank

When you build a project from the FMOD Studio tool, there is by default one Bank that is automatically created (and which you cannot delete) called "Master Bank." This Bank contains all of the global metadata about your entire project, particularly your mixer hierarchy (Buses, Sends, Snapshots, and VCAs). Technically, loading the Master Bank is optional—each Bank is self-contained and will contain the entire subset of content that it uses, including any Buses. However, there are some components that are only available by loading the Master Bank. For example, if you want to trigger a Snapshot in code that is not referenced by an Event in your project, then you'll need to load the Master Bank.

The Master Strings Bank is always optional. It contains mapping between every content-addressable ID in your project and its human-readable name. If you don't load this Bank file, then you will need to load every item in your project by its ID rather than by name. For many games, this is okay and you can skip the Master Strings Bank. If you want to create your own mapping, FMOD has an option to output an easily machine-parseable and human-readable text file (File->Export GUIDs).

6.6.2.2 FMOD Globally Unique Identifiers

FMOD generates a 128-bit GUID for every single object in your project. You can use these GUIDs with the FMOD_GUID structure, and with functions that look like System::getXXXById(). You can store the FMOD_GUID structure directly in your own data files, or you can keep it as a canonical GUID string ("{xxxxxxxx-xxxx-xxxx-xxxx-xxxxxxxxxxxx}") and use the FMOD::Studio::ParseID() function to convert it into an FMOD_GUID. Ultimately, it does not matter much whether you use names or GUIDs, other than that loading the names costs some amount of memory, and names will have to get converted to GUIDs internally by FMOD in order to look up the matching content.

That said, one advantage to using GUIDs instead of names is that the GUIDs are immutable, whereas the names can change. If a sound designer moves an Event from one folder to another, its name will change, but its GUID will not. If your Event is hooked up by name, then it will be broken after the move. If it's hooked up by GUID, then it will continue to function correctly, and then your tool can look up the name of the Event for display purposes.

6.6.3 Setting Event Parameters

Now that we have our Event set up and played, we want to configure it. The Event we have selected is an Explosion and has a single parameter called "Size," which controls a number of properties, from which sound is played, to the reverb send and the 3D Panner sound size. Let's set this parameter now:

```
// Get the parameter by its name.  There is also
// EventInstance::getParameterByIndex() and
// EventInstance::getParameterCount() if you want to
// use those functions instead.
FMOD::Studio::ParameterInstance* pParameterInstance =
  nullptr;
pEventInstance->getParameter(
  "Size", &pParameterInstance);

// Set to a value.  The range is determined in the tool.
// In this particular example, the range is 0..3.
pParameterInstance->setValue(1.5f);
```

FMOD also has a number of built-in parameters that it fills in automatically for you, such as 3D Distance, Cone Angle, Elevation, and a couple of others. You do not need to do anything to set the values for these parameters, but you can query them using EventInstance::getParameter(). Using ParameterInstance::getDescription(), you can get a data structure that will tell you whether a parameter is built-in or game-controlled.

6.6.4 3D Sound

Setting the 3D position of an EventInstance and the listener 3D position and orientation is very similar to setting it for a Channel and the low-level System object, except that instead of passing each value by itself to the function, we fill in an FMOD_3D_ATTRIBUTES structure. Let's fill in the EventInstance first.

```
FMOD_3D_ATTRIBUTES eventAttributes;
eventAttributes.position = {0.0f, 5.0f, 5.0f};
eventAttributes.velocity = {0.0f, 1.0f, 1.0f};
eventAttributes.forward = {0.0f, 1.0f, 0.0f};
eventAttributes.up = {0.0f, 0.0f, 1.0f};
pEventInstance->set3DAttributes(&eventAttributes);
```

As with the low-level system, the position is used for panning and attenuation and the velocity is used for Doppler shift. The forward and up vectors are passed into the EventInstance and are used to calculate the values for some of the built-in parameters.

Let's fill in the listener's 3D parameters. Once again, I've fabricated a function that will fill in the appropriate values from the game's camera.

```
FMOD_3D_ATTRIBUTES listenerAttributes;
FillListenerAttributesFromCamera(listenerAttributes);
pSystem->setListenerAttributes(0, &listenerAttributes);
```

6.6.5 Buses and Reverb

6.6.5.1 Buses

Buses in the Studio API are the moral equivalent of ChannelGroups in the low-level API, and are in fact implemented using ChannelGroups. The sound designers set up a mixer hierarchy using the FMOD Studio tool, which is made available to the programmer as Bus objects. On the surface, there is very little that you can do with a Bus object—just set its volume, mark it paused, or mark it muted. However, you can get at the underlying ChannelGroup for a Bus in order to perform more advanced manipulations. Let's take a look at how this works.

```
FMOD::Studio::Bus* pBus = nullptr;
pSystem->getBus("bus:/SFX/Explosions", &pBus);

// Here we set the Bus's volume to -6dB.
pBus->setFaderLevel(0.5f);

// If we want to mess about with the internals
FMOD::ChannelGroup* pBusGroup = nullptr;
pBus->getChannelGroup(&pBusGroup);
```

```
// This is a normal ChannelGroup.  We can do anything
// with it!
pBusGroup->setCallback(myCallback);
```

We'll see more about manipulating the internals of the system later in the chapter.

6.6.5.2 Reverb

Although reverb is actually implemented as a feature in the low-level engine, the Studio API and tool do not actually have the idea of reverb built-in. Rather, the sound designers implement reverb in the FMOD Studio tool. They do so by placing a Return somewhere in the mixer hierarchy and adding a Reverb DSP to it. Then they need to hook it up by adding a Send DSP to either a spot on the mixer, or in one or more Events. Figure 6.6 shows the Reverb Return setup, and Figure 6.7 shows the Send setup in the FMOD Studio tool.

FIGURE 6.6   Mixer view with Reverb Return.

FIGURE 6.7   Mixer view with Reverb Send.

There is no limit to the number of Sends, Returns, or DSPs that can be created, so your sound designers have ultimate freedom. Of course, you may run into performance issues if your sound designers go too crazy, so work with them to come up with the proper mix. Once the sound designers have set up their Reverb, you can access it as a Bus object just like any other Bus.

6.6.6 Working with Snapshots

Snapshots describe what a subset of the mixer should look like when the snapshot is active. They are sometimes also called Mix States or Sound

Moods. The Intensity of a Snapshot is the amount that the Snapshot is contributing to the mix. Underneath the hood, Snapshots are implemented as Events that have special tracks that modify the mixer's settings. In fact, if you switch to the Tracks view with a Snapshot selected, you can see the how they are implemented as Events. This is shown in Figure 6.8.

Your sound designers can actually trigger Snapshots directly from inside Events in the Studio tool. However, in order to work with Snapshots in code, they will need to be set up properly. On the surface, you can trigger a Snapshot in code simply by starting it as an Event, but you will not have the ability to adjust its Intensity at runtime. In order to expose Intensity to the programmer's API, the sound designers will need to expose the Intensity as a parameter. Although they can do this by hand, there is a shortcut to automate the process. Figures 6.9 and 6.10 show how to perform this setup. There is, in fact, nothing magical going on here—an Event Parameter is added called "Intensity," and it is hooked up to a curve in the Master track that controls the Snapshot's Intensity linearly from 0% at a value of 0 to 100% at a value of 100.

Let's see how to trigger a Snapshot as an Event.

```
// Snapshots are presented to the API as Events
FMOD::Studio::EventDescription* pSnapshotEvent =
  nullptr;
pSystem->getEvent(
  "snapshot:/InGamePause, &pSnapshotEvent);

// We can trigger this Snapshot by starting the Event
FMOD::Studio::EventInstance* pEventInstance = nullptr;
pSnapshotEvent->createInstance(&pEventInstance);

pEventInstance->start();

// In order to adjust the Intensity, we retrieve it as a
// Parameter
FMOD::Studio::ParameterInstance* pIntensity = nullptr;
pEventInstance->getParameter("Intensity", &pIntensity);

pIntensity->setValue(50);
```

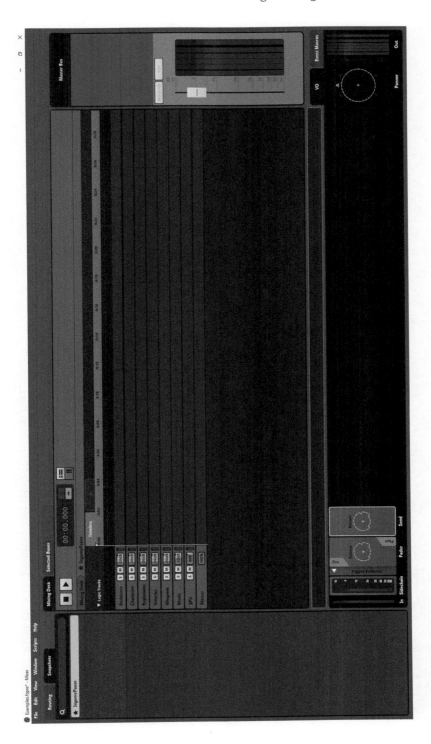

FIGURE 6.8 Snapshot view.

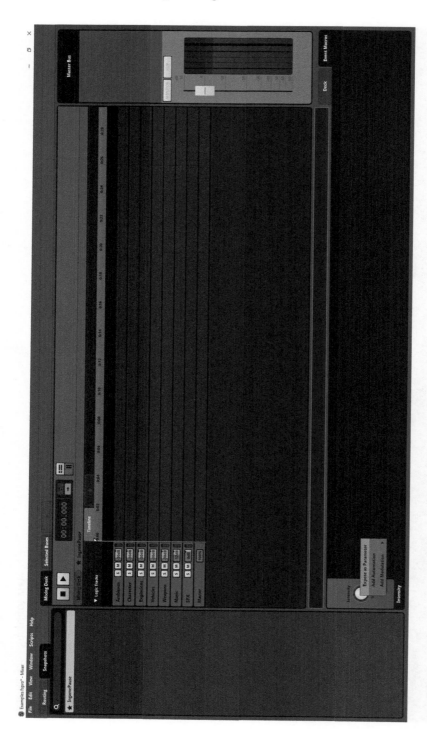

FIGURE 6.9 Right-click on Intensity and select "Expose as Parameter."

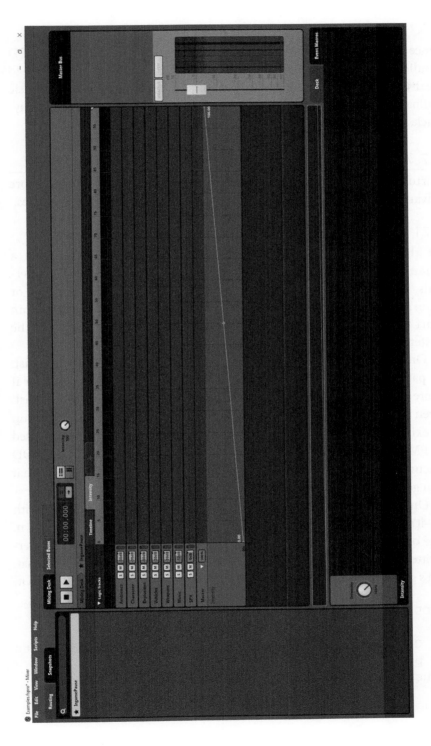

FIGURE 6.10 After "Expose as Parameter."

6.6.7 Just the Surface (Again)

Once again, we have only been able to scratch the surface of the FMOD Studio API in this chapter. Now that you have the basics, you can start to deal with VCAs, CueInstances, various Bank loading strategies, music callbacks for synchronizing with the game, command capture and playback, timeline synchronization, audio tables, and more.

6.7 ADVANCED TOPICS

Fortunately, we do have just a little bit of space to touch on some more advanced features. Let's get a glimpse at just how far the rabbit hole goes.

6.7.1 Messing with Event System Internals

At the head of every EventInstance and Bus object, there is a ChannelGroup that can serve as the entry point to manipulating its internals. You access it by calling EventInstance::getChannelGroup() or Bus::getChannelGroup(). Once you have this ChannelGroup, you can start to manipulate, query, or otherwise muck with the internals of the system.

One thing to be careful of is that the ChannelGroup may not exist. In particular, if your EventInstance hasn't actually been created, or if there are no Events playing on a Bus, then the ChannelGroup won't exist. Even if you call Bus::lockChannelGroup() to force the ChannelGroup to exist, there will still be a length of time while the request is transmitted to FMOD's processing thread, and the response comes back. The FMOD documentation describes a few different options for how to ensure that you get a valid ChannelGroup.

Once you have a ChannelGroup, you can do whatever you want with it—it's just like any ChannelGroup that you may have created on your own. The only catch is that any changes that you make may end up being overwritten by the internals of the Studio API, so you have to be aware of that. Let's grab the ChannelGroup for a Bus and attach a Compressor DSP to it.

```
FMOD::Studio::Bus* pBus = ...;

// Create the ChannelGroup even if there are no Events
// playing on it
pBus->lockChannelGroup();
```

```
// Ensure that the ChannelGroup will exist when we
// query it.
pSystem->flushCommands();

// Get the ChannelGroup for the Bus
FMOD::ChannelGroup* pChannelGroup = nullptr;
pBus->getChannelGroup(&pChannelGroup);

// We need the low-level System object in order to
// create our DSP
FMOD::System* pLowLevelSystem = nullptr;
pSystem->getLowLevelSystem(&pLowLevelSystem);

// Create the DSP
FMOD::DSP* pCompressor = nullptr;
pLowLevelSystem->createDSPByType(
   FMOD_DSP_TYPE_COMPRESSOR, &pCompressor);

// Attach the DSP to the ChannelGroup
pChannelGroup->addDSP(pCompressor);
```

This is, of course, just one example of what you can do—once you have the low-level API at your disposal, you can make magic.

6.7.2 Iterating over Channels and ChannelGroups

One common procedure that you may need to solve is applying a particular operation to all playing Channels or ChannelGroups. To do this, you will need to traverse the DSP graph. There are two ways to do this—at a low level by following through DSP connections, or at a high level by traversing through connections between ChannelGroups and Channels. In this section, we'll be covering the high-level method.

In this example, we want to find a Channel that has an underlying Sound object with a particular piece of user data attached.

```
FMOD::Channel* FindChannel(
   FMOD::ChannelGroup* pChannelGroup
   void* pExpectedUserData) {
   // First iterate over every Channel in this
   // ChannelGroup
   int nNumChannels = 0;
```

```
pChannelGroup->getNumChannels(&nNumChannels);
for(int i=0; i<nNumChannels; i++) {
  // Get the Channel
  FMOD::Channel* pChannel = nullptr;
  pChannelGroup->getChannel(i, &pChannel);

  // Get the Channel's Sound object
  FMOD::Sound* pSound = nullptr;
  pChannel->getCurrentSound(&pSound);

  // Get the Sound's UserData
  void* pUserData = nullptr;
  pSound->getUserData(&pUserData);

  // If it matches, then we've found our return value!
  if(pUserData == pExpectedUserData) return pChannel;
}

// This ChannelGroup doesn't have a matching
// Channel, so we need to recurse for each child
// ChannelGroup
int nNumGroups = 0;
pChannelGroup->getNumGroups(&nNumGroups);
for(int i=0; i<nNumGroups; i++) {
  // Get the SubGroup...
  FMOD::ChannelGroup* pSubGroup = nullptr;
  pChannelGroup->getGroup(i, &pSubGroup);

  // ...and recurse into this same function
  FMOD::Channel* pFoundChannel =
    FindChannel(pSubGroup, pExpectedUserData);
  if(pFoundChannel) return pFoundChannel;
}
  return nullptr;
}
```

6.7.3 DSP Clocks for Synchronization and Fades

The last of the advanced topics we'll be covering is the concept of the DSP Clock. FMOD contains, internally, a 64-bit counter that increments once for each sample that it mixes. (It does so optimally, of course, by incrementing it once for each buffer that it mixes.) This counter is important, because you can use it to synchronize playback of Channels or EventInstances in a precisely sample-accurate manner. FMOD also exposes APIs for performing sample-accurate fades.

Let's see how to fade the volume of a ChannelGroup over 2 seconds.

```
// First, we need to get the system mixer's sample rate
// so that we can calculate how many DSPClocks in 2
// seconds
int nSampleRate = 48000; // reasonable default
pLowLevelSystem->getSoftwareFormat(&nSampleRate,
  nullptr, nullptr);

// Get the ChannelGroup's current DSP Clock
unsigned long long nCurrentClock = 0;
pChannelGroup->getDSPClock(&nCurrentClock, nullptr);

// To set up a fade, we need to add two fade points:
// one at the current time with the current volume,
// and a second one at the desired time with the
// desired volume.  We'll use 1.0 and 0.5.
pChannelGroup->addFadePoint(nCurrentClock, 1.0f);
pChannelGroup->addFadePoint(
  nCurrentClock + 2 * nSampleRate, 0.5f);
```

6.8 CONCLUSION—JUST THE SURFACE (YET AGAIN)

For the last time in this chapter, I'm going to have to say that, once again, we have only managed to scratch the surface of what is possible. We haven't even talked about how to manipulate the DSP graph at a low level, the Geometry API, performing offline processing, built-in debugging tools, generating custom panning matrices, the FSBank API, writing custom DSPs, how FMOD is able to loop MP3s seamlessly, how to implement Programmer Sounds, using memory and file system overrides, scripting the FMOD Studio tool, and more.

In this chapter, we went through the basics of the FMOD API from the low-level to the high-level, and even touched on some advanced features. Hopefully, this has inspired you to learn more and to use FMOD in your products!

CHAPTER 7

CRYENGINE's Audio Translation Layer

Thomas Wollenzin

CONTENTS

7.1 ABOUT Crytek

Crytek is an independent videogame developer, publisher, and technology provider that's dedicated to pushing the boundaries of gaming with their cutting-edge CRYENGINE software. Founded in 1999 by brothers Avni, Cevat, and Faruk Yerli, Crytek has its headquarters in Frankfurt am Main (Germany) along with seven additional studios in Kiev (Ukraine), Budapest (Hungary), Sofia (Bulgaria), Seoul (South Korea), Shanghai (China), Istanbul (Turkey), and Austin (USA).

7.2 ABOUT CRYENGINE

CRYENGINE is a game engine with truly scalable computation, multiaward-winning graphics, state-of-the-art lighting, realistic physics, intuitive visual scripting, high-fidelity audio, designer-friendly AI, and much more—and all straight out of the box.

7.3 HISTORY OF CRYENGINE AUDIO TECHNOLOGY

CRYENGINE's sound solution started out—like most of the other game engines—in the early 2000s as a rather code-driven approach using Microsoft's DirectSound API on PC. *Far Cry* was the first AAA title shipped by Crytek that used this approach, which by today's standards can be considered outdated technology. Shortly after this release, it was decided to implement a dedicated audio middleware—FMOD Ex. This allowed for a more data-driven approach to sound design and coding and additionally allowed for convenient support of other platforms including consoles. Over the following years, this solution was used for all of the games that were shipped by Crytek. During this period, the entire development of CRYENGINE was of a rather game-centric approach that resulted in its technology being tightly coupled to internal game development. However, with the release of the *Crysis* games and the resulting attention that CRYENGINE was receiving, a decision was taken to license the engine to other game developers. Now, the engineers had to deal with the licensee's unique requirements, which forced them to rethink some of their approaches. For audio, this meant adopting a more generic, homogeneous, and user-friendly approach to audio design including coding. At around that time, the idea of an abstracting layer between the engine and an audio middleware was spawned. A proof of concept was introduced in 2013, and work on the actual implementation that led to today's ATL followed shortly thereafter.

7.4 WHAT IS CRYENGINE'S ATL?

The ATL is an abstracting interface between CRYENGINE and an audio middleware such as Wwise, FMOD, SDL_mixer, Miles Sound System, or CRI ADX2. In this way, CRYENGINE can assure an audio middleware-agnostic approach to sound implementation into game assets. Audio designers make use of Audio Controls, which are basically an abstraction of game-specific events and values that need to be communicated down to the audio middleware. That data is then used to generate and manipulate audio. CRYENGINE currently provides five control types: Triggers, Real-Time Parameter Controls (RTPCs), Switches and States, Environments, and Preloads. One big advantage of such an abstract approach is that audio middleware can be swapped out even at runtime.

7.5 WHAT WAS THE MOTIVATION FOR INTRODUCING ATL?

Before the introduction of the ATL, CRYENGINE was basically "married" to a single audio middleware. This was a limiting factor for Crytek not just internally, but also externally as licensees could not use the audio middleware of their choice. Additionally, it was not possible to provide a homogeneous solution toward implementing audio in all regards. Also, the increasing complexity of the engine required more and more maintenance. So, to solve this situation, CRYENGINE's audio technology team came up with the idea of an abstract layer named the ATL. How the ATL fits into CRYENGINE's architecture is illustrated in Figure 7.1.

7.6 ATL ADVANTAGES

The abstractness of the system is certainly an advantage, because no matter what audio middleware your programmers or management choose to implement, it will always feel the same because you are already used to working with CRYENGINE's audio controls that stay the same. Working with audio controls allows for assigning different data to a single control. For example, a single ATL-Trigger could execute any number of different events. This is useful if the audio middleware does not support event chaining, or for example when setting an ATL-Switch-State where designers can choose to set a Wwise switch, state, and RTPC. The freedom is almost endless and lies entirely in the middleware implementation that is written by an audio programmer.

Also, do not underestimate the potential of swapping out the middleware during production or when a game is generally ported. The advantage here

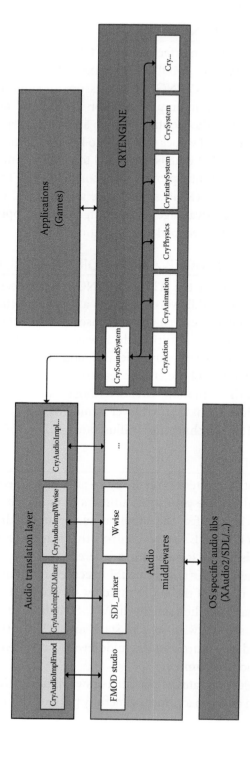

FIGURE 7.1 CRYENGINE ATL component diagram (created using www.gliffy.com).

is that this will not require any game code changes or redesign of audio setups in your game's levels. Game programmers also see the advantages as well as they no longer need to worry about audio behavior. Questions such as "Is the sound still playing?," "Do I need to start or stop this loop now?," "When do I need to pause, resume, or mute?"—these are all things of the past, as all the game programmers now need to do is just inform the audio designers of game events using audio controls, and to update corresponding parameters accordingly. This is sometimes awkward for them as they are more used to hearing results immediately—but this might no longer be the case.

7.7 ATL DISADVANTAGES

The abstractness of the system is a disadvantage, as an approach like this naturally introduces an additional layer of indirection, which has an impact on performance. Fortunately in the case of CRYENGINE, the ATL system is highly optimized and any additional overhead is negligible. For audio designers, this layer can be mostly hidden (if not eliminated), and it can even be argued that this is a must in regard to convenience and workflow. However, in the case of programmers, they will always end up needing to do work in this layer.

7.8 AUDIO CONTROLS EDITOR

The ACE is the single point of access for audio designers in CRYENGINE. It was developed around a single word—convenience. The main goal was to never break the audio designer's workflow. This, in particular, means that there is never a need to restart any of the tools or to enter data manually in any form. The ACE features include hot reloading, drag and drop functionality, error reporting, searching, filtering, and listing. Figure 7.2 illustrates the ACE in conjunction with Wwise. The left pane lists all of the available ATL controls, the middle pane houses the inspector panel with a list of connected middleware-specific controls per selected ATL control, and the right pane is entirely reserved for displaying and handling data provided by the loaded audio middleware.

Audio designers use the ACE to connect ATL controls to the audio middleware controls. For example, any number of FMOD or Wwise events can be connected to a single ATL trigger. All those events would then be executed simultaneously upon trigger execution. Another used case is to connect again any number of audio middleware-specific parameters to a

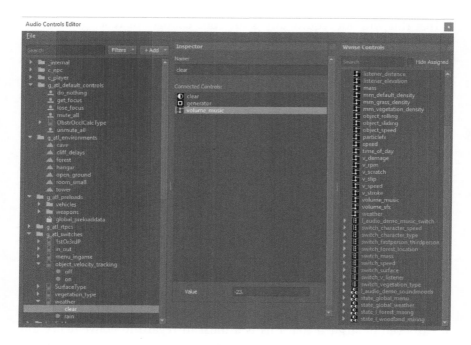

FIGURE 7.2 The Audio Controls Editor.

single ATL RTPC and drive it using a custom offset and multiplication for each parameter if so desired.

In order to have access to the middleware data, the ACE needs to load and parse audio middleware-specific project setups. This is possible because of the ACE operating on the exact same idea as the ATL. This means that the ACE has its own implementations as well, which adjust at runtime whenever the middleware is swapped out. That said, the ACE is not a classical sound design tool, but rather an audio data connector and handler that is used to connect work done in sound design tools such as Wwise or FMOD to ATL-specific controls. Currently the ACE stores all data in an XML format; however, there is a plan to change this to the JSON format sometime in the future.

7.9 IMPACT ON DESIGNERS

This radical new approach to general audio design requires some rethinking and "getting used to" by designers. For example, designers now need to have an understanding of the abstract nature of their new audio system, a typical example being when executing an ATL-Trigger—this does not necessarily mean that sounds are being played. Even though the audio programmers try to "hide" the abstraction as much as possible from designers, it is still a system that allows for great extendibility and freedom. Furthermore, and depending on which audio middleware is used in production, audio designers have to define something that is completely new to them.

So where, and exactly how, do we make the handshake between the engine and the middleware? What system is responsible for updating what data? In the case of Wwise, this would be defining whether (for example) the footstep surface type is switched in CRYENGINE. In this case, this means that the dedicated ATL-Trigger is executed, or in the case of Wwise that CRYENGINE always executes the same ATL-Trigger, but additionally sets a switch to Wwise indicating the current surface type. Also, the way audio designers used to work with game programmers has changed. In the past, requests were often made to play/stop and update something from inside the game code. That work can now be done almost entirely by audio designers via setting hooks in the corresponding tools.

7.10 IMPACT ON PROGRAMMERS

Game and system programmers can also worry less about audio and with that micromanage less. Generally, all that is left for them to do is to inform and update game events and values that audio designers do not have access to. This also allows for simplification of game code, which in turn increases reliability and performance, and reduces debugging time because of a more straightforward design.

7.11 ATL HIGH LEVEL DESIGN

There are several items that are considered important for the ATL design. For instance, we wanted to present a clean and as slim as possible interface to the user. This way, we save coders from unnecessary headaches in trying to understand what "all those entry points" are good for and to minimize the possibility of misusing the system because of a confusing interface. For instance, there are currently really only six interface methods that programmers use to interact with the audio system.

```
GetAudioTriggerID(...);
GetAudioRtpcID(...);
GetAudioSwitchID(...);
GetAudioSwitchStateID(...);
```

```
GetFreeAudioProxy(...);
PushRequest(...);
```

You will find example code using the preceding methods in Section 7.14. We opted for having only a single method for requesting an action from the audio system, where the user fills out an "action execution request form" and sends that to the audio system. This is where the `PushRequest()` method was born.

It was explicitly decided to name it that way and not, for example, `PushOrder()` or `ProcessAction()`, because sometimes programmers can be falsely led by method naming. For example, `SetSomething()` could be understood as a sort of "order" to the underlying system and lead coders to subconsciously expect this "order" to be successfully carried out—this can then lead to parent code not properly handling failure states. Also, when using the word "request," the potential of an action failing seems more apparent and somewhat hints (even if it's subconsciously) to coders to prepare code so as to properly handle such cases.

Another main aim was to offload the program's main thread to ensure an even smoother program execution, and thus the audio system processes requests entirely on its own thread (i.e., the "MainAudioThread") and in this way the `Update()` method that an audio middleware implementation receives is called from that thread. As mentioned before, the `PushRequest()` method is used to leave a request with the ATL, which can be called from any thread and which executes by default asynchronously—this is useful for requests that do not need immediate processing. There are flags to customize how requests are handled internally, such as `eARF_EXECUTE_BLOCKING`, which indicates to the system to block the calling thread until the request has been processed. However, if the outcome of an action processing request is of importance, coders can conveniently register objects as listeners to specific requests.

7.12 ATL INTERNAL COMPOSITION

The audio system is split into three largely independent layers:

- `CAudioTranslationLayer` class

- `IAudioSystem` struct

- `IAudioSystemImplementation` struct

The `IAudioSystem` struct represents the interface game coders will use and holds methods for handling audio controls as well as the `PushRequest()` method. See Section 7.11 for a truncated list or Section 7.14 for code examples. The implementation of `IAudioSystem` contains the message queues, handles the scheduling and dispatching of incoming requests, and also houses the main audio thread. The type of message queue is also referred to as a multiproducer and single consumer queue. Additionally, it is the only object that holds and allows access to the `CAudioTranslationLayer` class via a member.

The `CAudioTranslationLayer` class keeps track of the audio system's current state: all of the registered audio objects, controls, listeners, and events. It also processes the requests submitted through the `PushRequest()` method. Among other manager type objects that it manages, it holds a pointer to the provided `IAudioSystemImplementation`.

The `IAudioSystemImplementation` struct represents an interface to an audio middleware. When processing the incoming requests, the `CAudioTranslationLayer` class calls the appropriate methods of `IAudioSystemImplementation` and records all of the resulting changes in the audio system state. Figure 7.3 illustrates this internal composition in a simplified way. At the time of writing, CRYENGINE provides implementations for FMOD Studio, SDL_mixer, and Wwise—currently, the source codes for these are publicly available.

7.13 HOW THE ABSTRACTION GENERALLY WORKS

In order for an audio middleware to be able to connect its own idea of a trigger, event, parameter, switch, or environment to a corresponding ATL control, we introduced ATL-Entities. These are in essence empty interfaces that define the data type to be connected. An audio middleware can derive from those types and create its specific implementation, which will then be used for registration with the ATL. For example, a Wwise or FMOD event can be connected to an ATL trigger via `IAudioSystemImplementation::NewAudioEventData`. This method is called during trigger creation, and for every event that is referenced by the trigger. Implementations must then return a pointer to the corresponding type for the ATL to store and handle in future requests. All of this parsing and creating is done during application boot and level loading, but not during game play for performance reasons.

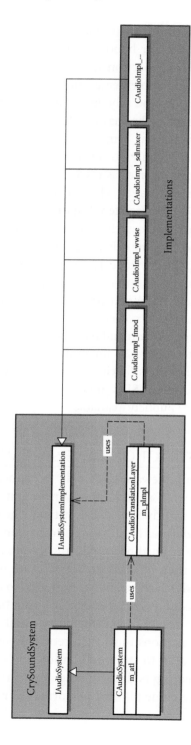

FIGURE 7.3   ATL internal composition (created using www.gliffy.com).

7.14 HOW TO WORK WITH ATL VIA CODE

There are three different ways of working with audio via code in CRYENGINE.

1. CAudioProxy

2. CEntityAudioProxy

3. PushRequest()

Before looking at any of the code involved, it is important to first explain, in CRYENGINE terms, what an AudioProxy and an EntityAudioProxy are.

7.14.1 What Is AudioProxy?

AudioProxies (sometimes referred to as AudioObjects) are simple code objects that provide combined and straightforward audio functionality such as executing triggers, setting states, or updating runtime parameters. This concept has been around since the early days of CRYENGINE and was, back then, called SoundProxies, as they were more about an actual sound instead of complex audio behavior. When an AudioProxy is initialized, the coder can supply a name for identification purposes, which is omitted in Release-type compilations. As AudioProxies can be positioned in the game world, they should ideally only execute 3D-type events. Even though they can also execute 2D events, doing so is not recommended because it is a waste of resources. In the case of 2D events, then you should rather use the PushRequest() method, which will be explained later in this chapter. Also, be aware that Audio Proxies have no affiliation to general game world entities.

7.14.2 What Is EntityAudioProxy?

Most of the objects in the game world are entities, and programmers have at their disposal the concept of proxies to extend an entity's functionality—in general, they are referred to as EntityProxies. Each of these proxies is named after the additional functionality they provide, such as EntityPhysicalProxy, EntityRenderProxy, or EntityAudioProxy. So, if a programmer wants, for example, to be able to handle audio specifics on an entity, they can instruct that entity to create an EntityAudioProxy, which will then be used to handle audio on this particular entity. This could be playing footstep sounds on a character, and at the same time updating some sort of surface type switch to adjust the footsteps accordingly depending on the surface type beneath the character's feet. As an animated character is naturally a rather complex entity, audio designers need to be able to describe several positions on the entity itself—for example, the feet, hands, mouth for voice playback, and the body for Foley-type sounds. Technically, an EntityAudioProxy is nothing more than a parent to and a wrapper around any number of AudioProxies.

7.15 USING AUDIO PROXIES

In order to work with a simple audio proxy, programmers first need to retrieve one from the AudioSystem. Those are usually pooled, and the pool size is determined by the s_AudioObjectPoolSize console variable.

```
// play a simple explosion sound somewhere in the game
// world without having to rely on a full blown entity

// get the IDs for all needed audio controls
pAudioSystem->GetAudioTriggerID("explosion", triggerID);

// retrieve a simple audio proxy from the pool
// note: might dynamically create one if the pool is
// empty
auto pAP = gEnv->pAudioSystem->GetFreeAudioProxy();

// initialize the audio proxy, will receive a unique
// audio object ID additionally registers with the
// audio middleware in case it makes use of this
// data
pAP->Initialize("ap_explosions");

// set the position
// note: can be matrix or simple 3 dimensional vector
pAP->SetPosition(pos);

// set the amount of ray casts for obstruction and
// occlusion calculations between emitter and
// listener to single ray
pAP->SetObstructionCalcType(eAOOCT_SingleRay);

// set the environments (reverbs) that the audio proxy
// has been positioned in
```

```
pAP->SetCurrentEnvironments();

// execute the audio trigger
pAP->ExecuteTrigger(triggerID, eLSM_None);

// return the audio proxy back to the pool
// note: might delete it if the pool is full
pAP->Release();
```

Be sure to `Release()` an AudioProxy when it is no longer required. This ensures that it is either returned to the pool or deleted from the system in case the pool is full. It should be noted that `ExecuteTrigger` should always be called last, because you could end up in a situation where the AudioProxy has not been positioned properly and is too far away from the listener. This might then instruct the audio middleware, depending on the event's particular setup, to not even start playing it. Think about it in this way: first describe exactly what you want the AudioProxy to do and where you want to do it, and only then tell it to execute. This is a general rule when working with the ATL via code.

7.16 USING ENTITY AUDIO PROXIES

To use an Audio Proxy, you will need to retrieve it from an Entity. Each Entity comes with a default audio proxy, which can be addressed explicitly via `DEFAULT_AUDIO_PROXY_ID` (which is the default parameter to all of the `CEntityAudioProxy` methods). The following code example does not provide an auxiliary audio proxy ID, so we assume the default auxiliary audio proxy.

```
// describing an exploding tiger tank
// this assumes that the audio events have been designed
// in the middleware to make use of below data

// retrieve the entity's audio proxy
auto pEAP = crycomponent_cast<IEntityAudioProxyPtr>(
    pEntity->CreateProxy(ENTITY_PROXY_AUDIO));

// get the IDs for all needed audio controls
// while still fast it is advised to do this
// in non-performance critical parts of the code
pAudioSystem->GetAudioTriggerID("explosion", triggerID);
```

```
pAudioSystem->GetAudioRtpcID("intensity", rtpcID);
pAudioSystem->GetAudioSwitchID("tank_type", switchID);
pAudioSystem->GetAudioSwitchStateID(
  switchID, "tiger", stateID);

// position the default auxiliary audio proxy
pEAP->SetAuxAudioProxyOffset(pos);

// set the explosion's intensity
pEAP->SetRtpcValue(rtpcID, fIntensity);

// set the type of tank that is exploding
pEAP->SetSwitchState(switchID, stateID);

// finally execute the audio trigger on the tank entity
// using the default auxiliary audio proxy
pEAP->ExecuteTrigger(triggerID, eLSM_None);

// same thing just more explicit and unnecessary
pEAP->SetAuxAudioProxyOffset(
   pos, DEFAULT_AUDIO_PROXY_ID);
pEAP->SetRtpcValue(
   rtpcID, fIntensity, DEFAULT_AUDIO_PROXY_ID);
pEAP->SetSwitchState(
   switchID, stateID, DEFAULT_AUDIO_PROXY_ID);
pEAP->ExecuteTrigger(
   triggerID, eLSM_None, DEFAULT_AUDIO_PROXY_ID);
```

To address an auxiliary audio proxy (one that is not the default), you must first create a proxy, then store the returned ID so that you can address it explicitly later on.

```
// play the fire ball sound at both of the magician's
// hands

// retrieve the entity's audio proxy
auto pEAP = crycomponent_cast<IEntityAudioProxyPtr>(
  pEntity->CreateProxy(ENTITY_PROXY_AUDIO));
// get the IDs for all needed audio controls
pAudioSystem->GetAudioTriggerID("fire_ball", triggerID);
pAudioSystem->GetAudioRtpcID("intensity", rtpcID);
```

```
pAudioSystem->GetAudioSwitchID(
    "magician_type", switchID);
pAudioSystem->GetAudioSwitchStateID(
    switchID, "master",stateID);

// create auxiliary audio proxies for both hands
// use the returned IDs to address them explicitly
auto leftHandID = pEAP->CreateAuxAudioProxy();
auto rightHandID = pEAP->CreateAuxAudioProxy();

// position each auxiliary audio proxy on a hand
pEAP->SetAuxAudioProxyOffset(leftHandPos, leftHandID);
pEAP->SetAuxAudioProxyOffset(
    rightHandPos, rightHandID);

// set the fire ball's intensity on each auxiliary
// audio proxy
pEAP->SetRtpcValue(
    rtpcID, fLeftIntensity, leftHandID);
pEAP->SetRtpcValue(
    rtpcID, fRightIntensity, rightHandID);

// set the type of magician
pEAP->SetSwitchState(switchID, stateID, leftHandID);
pEAP->SetSwitchState(switchID, stateID, rightHandID);

// finally execute both audio triggers
pEAP->ExecuteTrigger(triggerID, eLSM_None, leftHandID);
pEAP->ExecuteTrigger(triggerID, eLSM_None, rightHandID);
```

Once there is no further requirement for auxiliary audio proxies, you are free to remove them.

```
pEAP->RemoveAuxAudioProxy(leftHandID);
pEAP->RemoveAuxAudioProxy(rightHandID);
```

7.17 USING THE PushRequest INTERFACE METHOD

The PushRequest() method is used to request actions from the AudioSystem, but without the need to go through either an audio proxy or entity audio proxy. One simple example for this case is the updating of the listener transformation. In the case of CRYENGINE, this is done via its ViewSystem. `PushRequest()` internally creates a copy of the request data, so it is safe for users to create data on the stack.

```
// create a request with normal processing priority
SAudioRequest request;
request.nFlags = eARF_PRIORITY_NORMAL;

// create "set position" specific request data
// and pass in the transformation matrix
SAudioListenerRequestData<eALRT_SET_POSITION>
requestData(listenerTransformation);

// assign the specific data to the request
// and push it into the audio system
request.pData = &requestData;
pAudioSystem->PushRequest(request);
```

Many different actions can be requested, and they can be executed either globally or on a specific audio object. One example of a globally executed trigger is game menu music.

Note that all requests are processed in the order in which they were pushed in, but according to their priority. High-priority requests are processed before normal ones and normal ones before low priority ones.

```
pAudioSystem->GetAudioTriggerID(
    "menu_music", triggerID);
pAudioSystem->GetAudioSwitchID("menu_type", switchID);
pAudioSystem->GetAudioSwitchStateID(
    switchID, "ingame",stateID);

// first set the switch state
SAudioObjectRequestData<eAORT_SET_SWITCH_STATE>
setSwitchStateRequestData(switchID, stateID);

SAudioRequest request;
request.nFlags = eARF_PRIORITY_NORMAL;
request.pData = &setSwitchStateRequestData;
pAudioSystem->PushRequest(request);

// then execute the music trigger
SAudioObjectRequestData<eAORT_EXECUTE_TRIGGER>
executeTriggerRequestData(triggerID);
```

```
request.pData = &executeTriggerRequestData;
pAudioSystem->PushRequest(request);
```

If no explicit audio object ID is provided, the global audio object is assumed. You can also supply the GLOBAL_AUDIO_OBJECT_ID explicitly for clarity and for stating the intention.

```
request.nAudioObjectID = GLOBAL_AUDIO_OBJECT_ID;
```

7.18 CONCLUSION

Although an abstracting layer technology such as CRYENGINE's ATL is not rocket science or something entirely new in the field of general programming, it is, however, new to the audio programming field—a first achieved by Crytek. This rather different approach has been received with mixed feelings. Some view it rather critically, as different companies have different needs and requirements, whereas others find the approach intriguing and worth exploring further.

For Crytek, as a high-performance technology provider, this was the most feasible approach it could take so as to ensure customer satisfaction and future readiness. Furthermore, a number of games have now successfully shipped using this technology, and customers are really valuing the freedom of choice they now have and the ability to implement their own audio technology.

Of course it is impossible to cover every last detail in one book, let alone in just one section of a book. We therefore recommend to those who would like to know more about CRYENGINE to visit our documentation website, docs.cryengine.com. There is also a friendly and experienced community of developers at cryengine.com/community, which is also well frequented by Crytek staff.

III

Sound Designer Perspectives

CHAPTER 8

A Sound Designer's Perspective on Audio Tools

David Steinwedel

CONTENTS

8.1 INTRODUCTION

An audio programmer is the greatest blessing any audio department can have. You, the audio programmer, are a rare, prized, and special person. You may be a seasoned audio programmer who loves the work and would never do anything else, or you may be a first-time engineer who has been assigned to Audio because you're the new guy. If you're the second, I urge you to take this assignment as an opportunity and a blessing. If you do your job well, you will learn every system in the game extraordinarily quickly, because Audio touches everything. You will become a ninja that can delve into the Particle FX and Animation Systems, Combat Logic, AI, Pathing, Loading, Memory Management, etc. You will also never again in your career have a team of people that appreciate you as much as the Sound team does. Maybe, if you have children someday, they will love you almost as much, but probably not.

The systems you build and the tools that power them will literally be the difference in quality of life for a sound designer over the 2- to 4-year course of development of your game. They will allow your sound designers to work efficiently, leading to both a better game and a higher quality of life for those making it. Creating tools to accomplish this requires design for human efficiency, automation of as much as possible, and the ability to receive instantaneous feedback when making creative decisions. These are sometimes mundane tasks in the world of lens-flares, aliens, and explosions, but they make all the difference in the world.

8.2 HUMAN EFFICIENCY

Making your tools efficient for human time is a simple, low-cost way to improve the efficiency of your Audio team. It's also the fastest way to a bevy of free coffee, lunches, birthday presents, and a lifetime of gratitude. In many cases, only a little bit of planning and code are required to make a tool vastly more efficient.

8.2.1 The Keyboard Layout

Visit any postproduction house around the world, and you'll notice one object conspicuously absent: the mouse. A four-button trackball is the preferred input method of most sound editors, whereas others will use some other form of superior input device. Either way, if you watch a seasoned professional work for a while (especially on a mundane task) you'll come to appreciate the efficiency of movement. The monitor will dance as sound clips fly across the screen. The hands will barely move as a symphony of sound is built to single-frame precision in front of your eyes. At times, it looks like the editor is juggling audio clips on the screen. But how is this accomplished? And how can you provide such efficiency to your Sound team?

8.2.1.1 Minimize Hand Motion for Tools Requiring Pointer Input

In practical terms, neither hand should need to leave its primary position on the input device or keyboard. You can achieve this by choosing the most commonly used commands and applying them tactically on the keyboard. For a right-handed user (sorry, lefties), that layout is simple: stick to the left side of the keyboard.

8.2.1.2 Multiply Your Real Estate

Audio designers are used to learning a bevy of key commands. They are also used to a wide set of nontraditional modifier keys. Use this to your advantage. The first set of commands, which should also be the most used, can live under single keys. (You're making a game, treat your tools like one!) QWERT and ASDFG, and (to a lesser extent) ZXCVB and 12345 can all do *something* in your program. Don't forget about Space, Tab, Tilde, and Escape. What these commands do is up to you and your audio designer. Generally, these should be employed to replace the most often used functions that would otherwise require a mouse. For example, in ProTools, horizontal zooming is delegated to the R and T keys, and E will zoom a track vertically.

There are more valid modifier bindings than you might think. Control, Shift, Control-Shift, Alt, Alt-Shift, and even Control-Alt-Shift are all usable. The trick to expanding bindings is to reduce the radius used on the keyboard to maintain efficiency. For example, using the Control key (generally used by the pinky) makes reaching the 5 key a stretch. If you double modify with Control + Shift (pinky/ring finger), most index fingers cannot reach past the R key comfortably. See Figures 8.1 through 8.3 for an idea of modifier ranges.

8.2.2 Dealing with Forms: Tab Order and Control Selection

We've all seen it. We've all probably built it: the giant all-encompassing form of doom. Maybe yours has to do with the properties of each sound, or it may allow a sound designer to track assets and schedule voice sessions. Whatever it does, once your user gets to a form, their hands should never need to leave the keyboard.

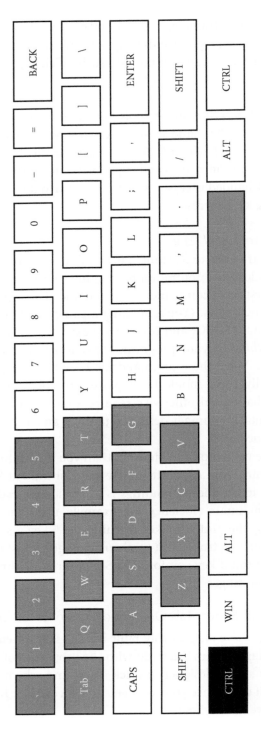

FIGURE 8.1 Key combos with Ctrl key pressed.

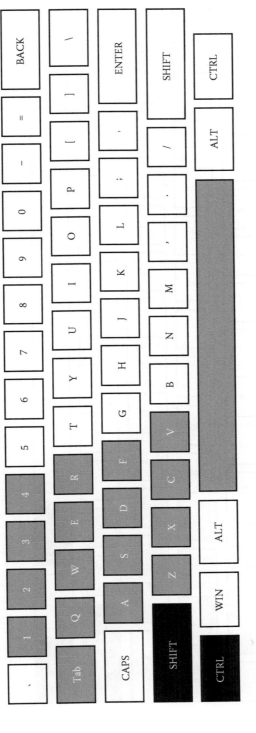

FIGURE 8.2 Key combos with Ctrl + Shift pressed.

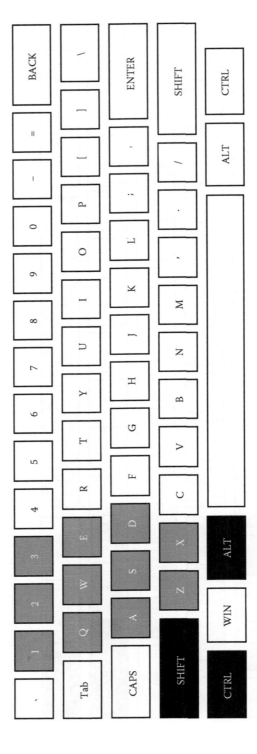

FIGURE 8.3   Key combos with Ctrl + Alt + Shift pressed.

Fortunately, this is an easily achievable goal. (Unfortunately, it's 2016 and I still have to write this section.) Without further ado, here are the commandments of user-friendly form building:

1. When opening a form, the first control should be in focus with its contents selected.

2. Tab order moves in the same direction and orientation as reading in the native language of your studio. For English, start at the top left, move across the form to the right, and start a new line when you reach the end.

3. When landing on a new control (by tabbing or otherwise), its contents are always to be selected by default to allow immediate input.

   a. If moving to a control with no value, then enable the cursor upon entering the control to allow immediate input.

4. All controls should allow full manipulation with only the keyboard.

5. If your form allows access to thousands of objects, create a fast, easy way to select among them.

6. Order controls so that the most-often used are near the beginning of your form.

There are some details that can be added to the preceding list for clarity.

Tab order (item #2 in this list) is important, but do note that grouped controls should follow this rule recursively. If your controls live together in a group box, then entering the first control in the group box should begin following the rules for the grouped controls from rule #1 as though it were the first control in the form. Once the cursor leaves the last control in the group, it continues on with the remainder of the controls in the form.

When ensuring that "All controls should allow full manipulation with only the keyboard" (item #4), there are a few controls to be aware of:

- Numeric Text Input should be editable with the arrow keys. In some frameworks, this means using a different control type (usually called a spin-box or a spin-button control). If your framework does not contain such a control, you should build it yourself out of a text-box and two buttons. Critically, the control should validate its input into the valid range, and allow input using just the arrow keys and modifiers. The minimum unit should move up and down with the arrow keys. Shift + Arrow keys should move the value by a factor of 10×, and Control + Shift + Arrow keys should move the value by a factor of 100×.

- For Combo Boxes, make sure your UI framework allows a user to select an entry using the tab, arrow, and enter keys. An important gotcha to watch out for is that many Combo Boxes will lose focus when making a selection with the keyboard, disallowing the user to tab to the next control, so be sure that your combo boxes retain focus. Once you have the basics in place, extra conveniences include partial-text filtering and selection. For a great example of a combo box, check out Excel's Data Validation style boxes.

- Radio Buttons were designed purely for pointer input, and some frameworks have no built-in method for keyboard manipulation, whereas others will require custom code to manipulate the control. In most cases, this control is used for items with three to six settings. If you have already solved the Combo Box, it may be easier to use that control instead of the Radio Button. If you do want to use it, make sure the arrow keys change the selected state while the control is in focus. For added ease of use, make sure the selection carousels around either end.

- Checkboxes will sometimes respond to the Enter key for state changes. The gotcha, as with Combo Boxes, is to make sure that focus is not lost when the state change happens. Another related problem is that the Enter key is also used to accept a form; if the Enter key is overloaded like this, it can lead to surprising results. If checkboxes in your framework have issues, you can always creatively work around them by using data validated text input with 0s and 1s.

There are a few ways to provide efficient filtering and access to many objects (item #5). One good example is the behavior of the Open File in Solution dialog in Whole Tomato Visual Assist, which is brought up by default using Alt-Shift-O within a solution. This control provides substring matches, path filters, multiple match strings, and negative filters in order to pare a potentially enormous list of files down to a manageable size. Study the details of this control as it is one of the most well designed interfaces for user efficiency in the history of the galaxy.

Finally, sit down with your sound designers from time to time and watch them use your tools. A few hours of watching them work will reveal inefficiencies that you can relieve in a few minutes.

8.2.3 Include Bulk Editing Controls

At some point, your sound designer is going to need to make broad changes to properties in your game. The sound designer might decide that everything is audible from just a bit too far away or that all the footstep sounds have too much random pitch applied. How you expose bulk editing functionality will depend on your tool chain, but you should always make sure they have the following abilities:

1. Ability to efficiently select multiple objects. This includes the use of Shift-Clicking to select a sequential series of objects as well as Control-Click to add one-off objects to the selected list. Being able to quickly filter and sort a list of objects will greatly help as well. In the use case listed above filtering would allow the sound designer to quickly find all objects with titles of "*_foot_*" to adjust her Footstep Objects.

2. Adjust values by an absolute input. $X += N$.

3. Apply a scalar to values. $X *= N$.

Don't forget to clamp output values based on the limits accepted by your engine.

8.3 AUTOMATE EVERYTHING

There are certain processes your sound designer will perform repeatedly. Find and automate those processes. Areas to focus on are import/export, auditing, and format conversion.

One example that saved a sound designer on Bioshock 2 weeks of work involved converting and compiling in-game sound banks, per character, per language, per platform, for localized sound files. The manual process involved exporting files from a digital audio workstation (DAW), naming them appropriately, applying per-character and platform settings, and generating a sound bank for each character and platform. Not only was this process tedious, parts of it were CPU intensive and error-prone. Because of this, the sound designer could not perform other work while the CPU was chugging along. Applying automation turned a multiday process every time a piece of dialog changed into an overnight task for the CPU to take care of.

Even the most experienced game developers will make implementation mistakes from time to time. Auditing scripts allow mistakes to be easily surfaced and fixed. For example, a long sound may have been accidentally marked to play as a sample when streaming is more memory efficient, or an Event's logic track may contain an unused marker that is an indicator that it is not set up correctly, or an Event may be assigned to the wrong bank. As development continues, you will find more and more ways in which the game can be broken. Although sound designers can certainly make the time to go through each sound one at a time and audit it for correctness, these sorts of correctness checks are exactly the place where automation tools shine. An auditing tool should be easily expandable so that new types of mistakes can be added and corrected as they are found.

8.3.1 Framework for Automation

For any automation process, you need to answer three key questions.

- What is the goal?
- What keys can we use to automate from?
- How far do we go?

Let's take a common example with audio, the importation of raw sound assets into your engine.

- Goal?
  - Allow anywhere from one to thousands of raw audio assets to be imported into the engine automatically.
- What keys can we use to automate from?
  - File naming schemes common to asset delivery. For example, player_male_footstep_01.wav, player_male_footstep_02.wav, etc., should all create the sound object player_male_footstep.
- How far do we go?
  - This is up to you and your audio team. The most basic implementation would take the raw files, package them up, and create sound objects based on the file naming system. Each object would have default values defined by the audio team (volume,

3D min/max distance, audio bus, etc.). A second-level script may parse the filename and apply various defaults based on common words. For example, objects with "foot" are applied to the footstep bus with a smaller min/max, whereas objects containing "weapon" go to the weapons bus and are audible at longer ranges. A completely thorough script would also apply compression settings based on the filename and build game ready sound banks so the sound designer could run the script and fire up the game immediately after to hear their work.

8.4 SPREADSHEETS AND OTHER TOOLS

Although it's fun and rewarding to create something from scratch, it's not always the best thing to do for your tools. It's important to evaluate existing tools and applications aside from the custom approach to find the best value.

8.4.1 Spreadsheets

Microsoft Excel has long been used in game development with great success. It is able to handle large volumes of data, has a refined user experience interface, and can perform some of the items called out above very well if the user is knowledgeable about the application (filtering, sorting, bulk editing).

The downsides of Excel also include issues to overcome and trade-offs to make.

The XLSX and XLS formats are not easily parsed, and no one wants to have to rewrite their parser because Microsoft decides to change their format. Also, these formats are binary, which makes for a lousy diffing experience when checking in data. The usual workaround is to use CSV or TSV files in the game engine while Excel becomes the host program for editing. Unfortunately, this means either of the following:

1. Export only: You lose the ability to bulk/auto import assets (see Section 8.2.1). It also limits you to VBA for scripts that operate on the data.

2. Import and Export means the end user must give up much of Excel's formatting (great for managing large asset volumes). It also means you lose the ability to organize through the use of tabs within the Excel worksheet.

Another problem is the 30,000-row spreadsheet of doom. At some point, a game simply has too many assets to comfortably manage in a spreadsheet format. It can quickly become too difficult for a sound designer to organize effectively and work quickly in such an environment.

Generally, Excel is a good tool for a small game with a few thousand assets or less. Beyond that, there are more robust tools to draw from for better workflows.

There are some absolute, "Do Not Evers" associated with spreadsheet programs I've seen applied in game studios.

1. Never use Google Docs or another online solution for hosting/editing your data. 99.9% uptime is a euphemism for *This service will fail the day before you ship.*

2. No lists inside a single cell. Spreadsheet programs were not built for this. Don't even think about it.

8.4.2 Spreadsheet Alternatives

Databases can fill in where spreadsheets break down. Databases are excellent tools that are fast and reliable, especially when dealing in tens- to hundreds-of-thousands of assets. In addition, there are some databases with front-end tools that allow easy manipulation of a GUI, allowing your sound designer to aid herself when tweaks are needed. The two immediate downsides to databases are source control interaction and required connection to the database to get any work done.

Finally, you can always go the fully custom route with original tools and a custom file system. This is by far the most expensive option, but it also provides the most flexibility. It is recommended only if your game has truly special needs that can't be achieved with any other manner of tools.

8.5 IN-ENGINE TOOLS

8.5.1 Mixing

Sound does not operate in a vacuum. To understand if one sound is too loud or soft, it must be heard in context with all other sounds. Additionally, the human brain only has a few seconds of recall when adjusting the balance between multiple sounds. Because of this, mixing can only be done well in real time. That means operating on assets in-engine is just as important as moving files around and setting up data for use by your game.

Some pieces of middleware allow direct connections between a running engine and the provided toolset. If your game is using one of these middlewares, be sure to setup and enable the capability—it's usually only a couple of lines of code. As the manipulation is done in the tool and heard in-engine, it allows the best of all worlds: real-time feedback for the person doing the mixing, plus the changes have already been recorded into the data set.

If you are using a custom engine or a piece of middleware that doesn't support live editing, you'll want to implement the ability to control your engine's runtime mixing technology. This is easily achieved through the use of console commands in engine. At the very least, your sound designers will need the ability to control a sound's volume, 3D min/mix distances, and reverb send, but you should talk with them about other properties useful to your game. Because these commands operate on in-data memory, be sure to create a way to push these changes back to the serialized data sources.

When new assets are added to the game, the first thing a sound designer will do is play with and listen to them in the context of the entire sound-scape. Because all sounds affect other sounds, it is very likely that tweaks to the current asset, or previously existing assets, will need to be made. Most game engines take a long, long time to load during the development cycle. Having the ability to hot-swap and add assets to the running engine is a huge win. Not only does avoiding the startup cycle save tons of time, it also allows your sound designer to make much better creative decisions about the final asset. If you can, use file system hooks to detect that the input files have changed and automatically reload them. Additionally, provide some sort of console command or menu item to completely shutdown and startup the audio engine with a reload of all sound data. This means that new data entries and assets come along for the ride.

8.5.2 Data Visualization

Most games are too complex, with too many things happening to debug audio and mix well with ears alone. Having the ability to visualize what your audio engine is doing is a big hammer in the toolset of a game audio team.

What sounds are playing now? A simple list of currently playing sounds has many benefits. Each sound in the list should include basic information including the sound object name, current volume, distance, and occluded state. Such a list can be used to pare down what sounds are playing (less is always more), identify when the 3D attenuation of a sound needs adjustment, and understand what playback prioritization should be between various sounds.

Where are sounds coming from? Seeing each sound at its currently playing position is also useful. Add a mode that adds a marker at the position of each sound showing its name, volume, and distance. This has overlapping but different benefits as a list of sounds. One huge benefit is when sounds are playing from too far away. Even if a sound is barely audible, it still adds clutter to the mix. Seeing lots of sound markers at large distances tells the sound designer to lower the max distance attenuation of a sound. It is also invaluable in debugging obstruction and occlusion issues by identifying sounds not playing when the sound designer knows they should be (e.g., that boss behind a wall should be making sound, so why isn't it?).

How is this level constructed? Give your team the ability to see a level as your obstruction and occlusion engine sees it. Additionally, let them see how reverb spaces are laid out, where different ambience zones are, etc. These should all be separate visualization modes. Mostly, this will ensure that all areas have appropriate coverage for obstruction and reverb. However, it also allows the audio team to identify when properties attached to these objects need to be adjusted.

What does the mix look like? Sound designers are very good about using their ears to mix a level, but particularly complex mixes can sometimes be vexing. Something as simple as a frequency spectrum graph, a VU meter, or a surround panning visualization can help to illuminate a complex mix.

8.6 KNOW YOUR CUSTOMER

Sit down with your sound designers from time to time and watch them work. Do this during different parts of development. Make sure you see them creating assets outside of your engine, moving those assets to your engine, creating and manipulating data for those assets, and finally mixing assets in game. When doing so, think about how you can make this process better, faster, more efficient, and give more creative control to your sound designer.

The reward you receive for efficient tooling is not immediately apparent. Your tools will allow a sound designer to focus as much creative energy as possible on making things sound awesome. A good toolset turns a computer and your game engine into an instrument used to compose a symphony of awesome. Great sound is consciously imperceptible to most people; however, it will manifest as players becoming more engrossed in your game, better reviews, greater MetaCritic scores, and ultimately a badge of honor for your resume.

CHAPTER 9

Working with Audio Designers

Florian Füsslin

CONTENTS

9.1 PREAMBLE

For the past 10 years, I have been working in the games industry and in every production during that time there has been one reoccurring question—is there enough prevision and a long-term plan? Development teams primarily think about their current project and the next step in the ongoing production. They rarely lift their heads and question their decisions with respect to whether they are sustainable and whether they will hold up in the years to come.

When developing software, finding a more generic solution to a problem takes time and manpower, which of course are considered a risk to production and are therefore avoided. This results in specially tailored solutions for the issues that arise in each product. For audio, this often ends up meaning completely different workflows, pipelines, procedures, and design tools—all of which require the audio designer to pretty much start from scratch with every new project. Furthermore, the game industry is undergoing constant change, and it is difficult to predict if "something" will be the next industry changing trend or if it is just a flash in the pan. The only solution to this unpredictable situation is granularity—that is, the goal to build a flexible set of tools that are constantly able to update, evolve, and adapt to the needs of various projects and in their different stages of production.

In the past, it was perfectly acceptable to write, build, or adjust a game engine for one product or one franchise. However, we now see this flexible and granular approach much more often in the modular structure of game engines, in audio middleware, or with audio plugins. The term often used is "convenience," and in the future the game engine with the best fidelity won't necessarily be the one of choice, but rather the one that provides the best workflow, most solid pipeline, and shortest turnaround for many iteration cycles. In such a solid granular audio framework, you then have the freedom to create the soundscape of the game you are imagining.

9.2 WHY SOUND DESIGNERS SHOULD RATHER BE NAMED AUDIO DESIGNERS

Historically in game audio, the soundscape was primarily used to provide acoustic feedback to the player, and rarely did the music stand out and be recognized as an iconic and creative element that could distinguish one product from another. While readability and feedback are still a big aspect, game audio is now often mentioned as a core pillar and unique selling point of a product.

Consumers also now expect an audio experience and to become fully immersed in an interactive game world regardless of the project scope or the target platform.

This expectation requires the previously separated elements of sound effects, music, and dialog to be understood as one cohesive audio vision. The goal, therefore, is to have an emotional impact on the consumer, a "theater of the mind" while establishing an immersive soundscape and teaching the acoustic language of the game mechanics. Such an audio vision requires careful thought as it can become complex, adaptive, and interactive. Hence, I prefer the term Audio Designer over Sound Designer as it reflects all the aspects of the role—architect, builder, narrator, psychologist, and sometimes magician.

9.3 ROLE OF AN AUDIO DESIGNER

The role of an audio designer has drastically changed over the past 20 years. The primary task has historically been to record and design a sound effect and deliver the uncompressed asset to a programmer. This person would then specify the playback behavior such as looping or positioned in the 3D game environment, as well as the appropriate sample rate and compression settings for the target platform.

The creation of these sound effects would have been achieved with audio production software on a digital audio workstation (which had been originally developed for linear media such as movies, commercials, or radio). Although this toolset is indeed powerful for the design of one specific sound and for a particular moment, it lacks the granularity and scalability to adapt for different game scenarios, especially the need for more variations of the very same sound that avoids repetition.

There was also a need to speed up production time and save valuable programming resources, while simultaneously increasing immersion and quality. So, to cater to both demands, a game-specialized audio toolset, production pipeline, and workflow needed to be developed.

This is where the providers of audio middleware software stepped in to deliver a backend via an application programming interface and a frontend in the form of an audio design tool. Programming is, of course, still necessary (primarily to expose audio trigger options in the game) while the actual audio is data driven and arrives with all the playback information it needs. However, with the establishment of audio middleware, the ownership and responsibility shifted toward the audio designer.

Today, an audio designer is responsible for all of the audio production steps—recording the raw asset, designing the content, then implementing and defining the playback parameters in the respective audio middleware and placing it in the game environment (often with very complex real-time behavior). While implementing the content and verifying quality, functionality, and consistency, the audio designer must meet the technical requirements of the target platform such as memory consumption, CPU load, and project disk space. Also, data management is now often part of the role and a full-blown AAA project can easily exceed 10,000 individual sound effects and 10+ hours of layered interactive music. Should the product be localized into different languages, then you could easily be dealing with 100,000+ individual dialog files—this requires a solid structure for asset management, a strict naming convention, and a plan for distribution and backup. Finally, this is especially important in those games with a service character, such as the free-to-play model, where the product is never finished, but is constantly being updated, extended, and adjusted.

Whereas other game development departments such as art, animation, and design have specialists for the technical aspects of production, audio is still often a one-man show and requires the audio designer to wear different hats all at the same time. The requirement to fill multiple roles at the same time while working on very different areas and aspects of the whole game can create a fair amount of pressure. It is a role with great power, but also great responsibility; despite being a generalist, every audio designer will have their strengths, weaknesses, and preferences. This is where an audio programmer can ensure that the technical part of game audio development is always understood, respected, and valued—the most awesome sound ever designed that does not play in the game and on the target platform is, unfortunately, not worth anything.

9.4 WHY AUDIO DESIGN SHOULD BE PART OF YOUR PRODUCTION FROM DAY ONE

Often, audio design is pushed to the end of production, and in some cases even outsourced. However, with growing expectations for higher quality audio and the requirements for a cohesive audio vision, it now demands that an audio designer is involved in a project right from the start. Ideally, this person is embedded in the production team from the initial concept, discovery phase, and beyond.

This early proof of concept has a very positive impact on audio engine feature requests. It is often the first anchor point for discussions about feasibility and priority. So having the audio pipeline thought through, laid out, and proven at the beginning of a project provides higher planning stability and a more reliable schedule without last-minute surprises. It also gives audio design and audio technology the time to build a trustworthy collaboration, which is important because both sides are working closely together to create the tools and the project structure, as well as determining the schedule and the delivery date for all of the required audio features.

As an audio programmer, you can ensure that the audio designer gets access to audio engine console variables for debugging and testing. You can also help to expose the correct checkboxes, dropdown menus, and trigger entries in the audio tools of your engine. Also, while enabling audio design to work independently don't forget to limit the access and functionality on core systems. Audio designers like to have "Swiss army knife" solutions—a single tool with access to every parameter possible. However, this can be counter-productive as they can get lost in all of the available options and settings, which often cause performance bugs in the product. Therefore, the rule of thumb should be—expose as much as is needed, but as little as is possible.

It is true that a great audio vision can be best achieved if the audio engine provides advanced real-time features, such as reverb, obstruction, occlusion, sound propagation, and the full palette of advanced plugin effects such as filters, synthesis, and dynamics known from postproduction. However, these features are often not necessary to ship a project successfully. In a worst-case scenario, the demand for a sophisticated "real-world" simulation can cause a loss of focus and occupy resources on nice-to-have details, rather than pushing the core pillars and values of the audio vision. Another advantage of early collaboration is the establishment of workflows whereby you can define the clear stages an audio feature or asset has to pass before it can enter the next phase. With this stage-gating, you ensure that no time is spent on asset design before the feature is ready or, vice versa, that a tool is developed without having all the required information and test assets available.

Many development tracking systems support this gated approach, and include time estimations and status progress with notification systems for all interdependent peers. These tracking tools also provide valuable data like how long it took to complete a task, whereas blocked tasks reveal dependencies that you might not have been aware of—you now have the ability to make well-informed decisions regarding how long the next feature will probably take. This leads to a more accurate planning method and improved communication between audio technology and audio design, which generates transparency and visibility toward other and often dependent project departments and project management areas. Finally, it creates traction toward the goal of meeting the project deadline and the quality expectation.

Figure 9.1 is an example of how to break down bigger tasks into stages:

INVESTIGATE:

The results can be presented in a document, PowerPoint presentation, or mockup video.

PROTOTYPE:

The results should support the game design prototype and presented in a controlled environment such as a test level in the Editor using the audio pipeline and middleware.

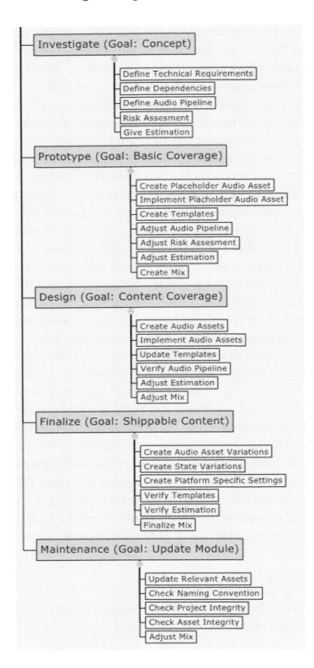

FIGURE 9.1   A graphical overview of the different development stages.

DESIGN:

The results should be presented in a production level that supports all aspects of the required game design and functionality and in full game including multiplayer (if applicable).

FINALIZE:

The results should be presented in full game mode and as to be experienced by the consumer.

MAINTENANCE:

The update should be functional and available in the upcoming build.

In addition, you can define steps to accommodate production dependencies, such as ready for audio, ready for audio technology, or just ready for review.

The stage-gating of tasks also helps you decide when to involve quality assurance to test your audio engine or feature for potential bugs. During the prototype stage, you are more interested in critical errors such as freezes or crashes while moving toward a fully functional feature. During the design stage, the focus shifts toward production speed and adjustments that cater to the scale of the project while maintaining and optimizing the feature. In the final stages, you will probably be most interested in optimization and polishing.

There are many obstacles, pitfalls, and hurdles to overcome during game production. Defining production steps and when they enter the next phase is crucial in keeping an overview. The earlier that audio design and audio technology work together, the better the tools, pipelines, and relationships will be. Because of its smaller size, audio also functions as a role model for other departments in terms of structure, collaboration, and trust.

9.5 WHY YOU NEED TO DEFINE THE AUDIO TERMINOLOGY

"I can't hear the sound!" is a common comment during game development. Although it is probably meant to communicate that the volume of a certain sound is too low, it can mean many different things to audio designers. Assuming it is not a hardware-related issue such as muted audio, inadequate speaker settings, or unplugged headphones, there are still many other possibilities—Is the sound not triggering? Is the sound triggering, but not loaded into memory? Is the sound triggering and playing, but attenuates too quickly? There could be any number of reasons why the particular sound is inaudible.

Precise audio terminology is the key to improving communication and achieving a more granular and detailed level of information, regardless of the target platform or development software used. Be it Event, Soundbank, Sound Definition, Parameter, RTPC, Preloading, Trigger, or Area Shape, reinforcing the precise usage of these terms will help to identify, debug, and resolve potential issues much faster. It also allows you to involve quality assurance testers because you can provide detailed information and user stories in regard to what they should be looking for if issues occur. In the best case, you receive a bug with all the relevant information in the form of log files, debug screenshots, and a detailed description of the steps to reproduce it, which will minimize the amount of time you need to spend on reproduction.

Of course, established terminology is also the foundation of any type of documentation and naming convention within the development team, as it assures that everybody is talking exactly about the same thing. Part of audio terminology also includes a rock-solid naming convention for every element in your game, be it folder, asset, game entity, or trigger. However, to keep the number of characters in check, the use of abbreviations helps to ensure readability while not blowing the character length limitations of some platforms. For example, this could be a one-letter indicator such as "w" for weapon, "v" for vehicle, or "l" for level; or a three-letter abbreviation such as "col" for collisions, "pro" for projectile, or "pfx" for particle effects.

Mimicking the folder structure of your development platform with the project structure also increases debugging speed and allows for easier packaging of the different game features and elements such as levels, characters, vehicles, weapons, patches, updates, or downloadable content. A continuous number at the end of the name can be used for variations of the same type, or, if you are working in a database structure, as a revision indicator. As file repositories can be case-sensitive, it can also prevent errors by establishing naming rules such as "lower case only," "underscore instead of a space," or "American spelling."

Figure 9.2 is an example how a naming convention for a vehicle sound effect could look like.

Following this convention, Figure 9.3 is an example of how a project structure in your middleware could look like.

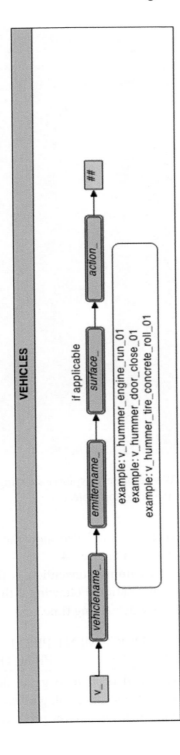

FIGURE 9.2 Visualization of naming convention theme showing an example for a vehicle sound effect.

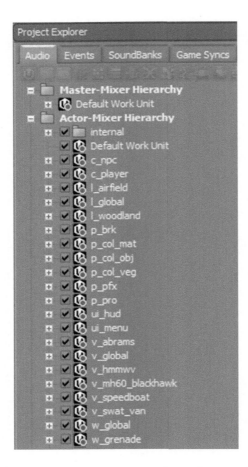

FIGURE 9.3 Audiokinetic Wwise project explorer showing the naming structure of the CRYENGINE Sandbox Editor project.

The Windows folder structure should also show the same hierarchy as for the original assets, as shown in Figure 9.4.

A solid audio lexicon and naming convention is the foundation for good interdisciplinary communication. Following it throughout all steps of production will save valuable debugging time.

9.6 WHY YOU NEED TO DOCUMENT PIPELINES, WORKFLOWS, TOOLS, AND BEST PRACTICES

Documentation is the abandoned orphan in game development. After all the energy that has been put into developing a feature, designing the assets, creating the tools, implementing into the product, and fixing all the

l_woodland
m_global
m_woodland
p_brk
p_col_mat
p_col_obj
p_col_veg
p_pfx
p_pro
p_ropes
ui_menu
v_abrams
v_global
v_hmmwv
v_mh60_blackhawk
v_speedboat

FIGURE 9.4   Windows folder structure.

small issues, then it's perfectly understandable why creating a wiki page, taking screenshots, formulating the feature, and creating use cases and examples in short and precise technical terms is not on everyone's agenda.

However, it should be! Good documentation saves a tremendous amount of time. Even if you are the only one who will ever work with your engine, it manifests your thoughts as to why you have designed and implemented the feature in the first place. It also functions as a snapshot or diary that can help you down the road should you ever pick on a particular feature again. This scenario can happen faster than you think—for example, your product gets ported to another platform, you end up working on a sequel, an update, additional content, or simply reusing the framework for a completely new product.

Furthermore, as soon as there is more than one person involved, documentation becomes an even bigger time-saver. Instead of explaining the same thing to each person you can point to the documentation, hence you only have to answer follow-up questions. Many of the web-based tools also allow commenting so people can share their thoughts, which can add a layer of brainstorming and feedback. It also creates a history as you can retrace the steps taken or decisions made during the different stages of production. In the case of outsourcing, then good documentation will reduce the amount of training time it requires to get a team up to speed.

As a further side effect, having good documentation prepares you for all sorts of eventualities—for example, having to explain or show your technology, pipelines, or workflows to third parties such as potential licensees, investors, or partners. Having good documentation can be just a couple of clicks to package and send. Finally, documentation does not always need to be detailed; often, a screenshot, a few bullet points, or short paragraphs are enough to convey key information.

9.7 WHY ORGANIZING AUDIO AS A CENTRALIZED DEPARTMENT IS BENEFICIAL

As the requirement for a cohesive audio vision needs audio designers to be embedded into the project, structuring the audio department in a central audio hub can increase your flexibility, particularly when working on multiple projects. While team-based structures have their place they do tend to vary much more in regards to their feature sets, tools, workflows, and pipelines. In a worst-case scenario, very similar features can end up being developed in each production team. It is not a case of cross-project synergy not working; rather, it's the inevitability that as team milestones approach then collaboration will slow down as each team strives for their own specific solutions for their assumed very special problem. A centralized department can minimize such feature duplication because they have an overview of all ongoing project developments.

Also, team-based structures are very focused on their production schedule, which normally causes an increased workload toward upcoming milestones. This often results in a roller-coaster ride, where there is a lot going on right up to the point of delivery, followed by a recovery phase shortly afterward. In a centralized department, resources can be shifted and be allocated to where they are most needed. This ability is useful as it helps to balance the increased demand for man-hours leading up to a demo or publisher milestone.

With a centralized audio department, workflows, pipelines, and procedures are established so as to cater to more than one project. It also has a positive impact on documentation and overall training as it allows for close collaboration and knowledge transfer among audio designers and/or audio technology. Related to that, a centralized audio department will be able to propagate a cohesive terminology: everything from loudness convention, naming conventions, templates, and building a central audio library to common rules for file repository usage, central backup servers, and project name tags for e-mail subject lines.

Therefore, a central audio department is not only more flexible and efficient, but people are also taking more pride in their work as they have an insight into all the projects the company is working on. This increased transparency increases morale as people feel empowered and a valuable part of a bigger entity. They also tend to be less stressed as they have a more constant workload and know that their colleagues will chip in if the workload requires it. They are therefore happier as they can focus on what every audio designer has in common—to make audio sound better.

9.8 CONCLUSION

Regardless of whether you are a small group of independent developers or part of a big production team, there is no excuse for not having a structure! At the end of the day, game development is a team effort where very specialized and passionate people come together to create a product. We need to use all the tools that are available to us to make production as simple and efficient as is possible. We need to build a solid production framework where we can maximize the time we spend on the creative part of the job. Finally, while growing in professionalism, we must not forget our inner child and to push the creative horizon. We need to be on our toes and to continue to focus on what made us join the game industry in the first place—make original games that are fun to play.

IV

Advanced Topics

CHAPTER 10

Open Sound Control

Jorge Garcia

CONTENTS

10.1 INTRODUCTION

Open Sound Control (OSC) is a data definition in a way similar to XML or JSON. It was specifically designed and optimized to address some of the challenges related with sending control data between audio applications in the same machine, or between machines over a network.[1] OSC was originally created in 2009 at the University of California–Berkeley Center for New Music and Audio Technology for providing flexibility in a wide range of possible applications, from gestural control devices to audio systems integration and music synthesizers. The popularity of the implementations of OSC as a communication protocol has also found applications in more general networking scenarios beyond audio, in part because of its ease of use and implementation in a wide range of programming languages and hardware.[2]

If you are familiar with some audio equipment and musical instruments, you may be wondering what the differences are between the musical instrument digital interface (MIDI) protocol and OSC, and why OSC exists at all since MIDI seems to be capable of similar functionality. The truth is that this has been an ongoing debate in the music technology circles for a while, but I would say that OSC is a more general solution to the problems that we can find in audio production, and more particularly in scenarios that involve networked devices, although it's also possible to stream MIDI data over a network (by using RTP-MIDI). It is true that recent proposals for a MIDI HD standard would overcome some of the limitations of MIDI, but OSC has been around for a while already and its maturity and simplicity makes it still ideal for some of the use cases that we can find in game audio development. One of the advantages of OSC is that it allows us to model any data format and meaning that we want, as we are not constrained with the typical musical notation and control change parameters that are found in the MIDI protocol. So the abstractions built with OSC can go beyond music terminology and are customizable for being easily human-readable, as we will see in this chapter.

I will start by explaining the value of integrating OSC in a game engine and a toolset, and the problems it can solve for both sound designers and audio programmers. Then we will go into some of the specifics and examples of a typical OSC implementation over UDP. I will also cover some of the possible optimizations that we may want to carry out for taking the most of the protocol. Some of the testing approaches and actual use cases are mentioned. This chapter then wraps up by mentioning some open source implementations of OSC that are freely available and that you can use straight from the box in case you don't need to roll out your own low-level implementation.

10.2 WHY INTEGRATE OSC IN A GAME ENGINE

So, we have a flexible networking protocol at our disposal—why should we be using it? There are some straightforward answers to this question if we think about it as a technical solution for communicating a toolset with the game runtime. But in the end, the reasons would depend on the flexibility of your in-house game audio engine (or the middleware you are using), and the design approach of the sound designers you are working with. If we think about the possibilities of real-time tweaking for game audio parameters, probably OSC can be a clear winner in order to reduce the iteration time spent from designers and for expanding their creativity.

And not only that: being able to easily integrate gestural controllers, EEG and VR headsets, networked musical equipment, or mobile devices with your game engine opens the doors for endless play and experimentation in the prototyping and incubation stages of a project. This would require a varying effort at the beginning depending on what you want to achieve, but as we will see, OSC is in the end a simple data definition and worth integrating as a protocol in your engine even if you have to roll out your own low-level implementation. This will allow you to "glue" different applications and devices easily by just using control messages. As an example, Guerrilla Games used it in their toolset.[3] Additional and upcoming uses of OSC also cover the control of Procedural Audio and synthesis models as well as collaboration in content creation scenarios.[4]

10.3 PROTOCOL IMPLEMENTATION

Before entering into any code details, it's good to have a bit of understanding of how networking protocols work. You have probably heard of UDP and TCP. The former is a popular protocol used in online games because it doesn't require checking the integrity of the data we are sending (usually in packets), so it inherently provides low latency, which is preferred for having a smooth and responsive communication stream. On the other hand, TCP is more popular in regular internet scenarios where the guarantee of receiving the data correctly (and in the correct order) is more important than latency. I'm not going to enter into the details of how UDP and TCP work since this goes beyond the scope of this chapter and this book, but you would be able to learn more about it from some standard computer networking literature. What we need to know is that for most of the scenarios, if we desire real-time low latency (within the range of 15 ms and below), we would initially want to start with UDP for generating a stream of data. This will also allow us to skip the hassle of dealing with some session setup and handling, and just start streaming messages from a sender (a "client" as defined in the OSC specification[5]) to a listener ("server" that digests and processes incoming messages).

10.3.1 Client and Server Models

So, we have this server and client model, but how does this correspond to my tools, to my game engine, or the mobile phone that I want to use for controlling the parameters in my game? Again, it depends on what we want to achieve (there are some use cases and scenarios mentioned later on in the chapter as an example), although what we basically need to define is where we want to send the data from as this will be our client, as well as where the part of our software or pipeline is where we are going to process the incoming messages as a server. If you plan to use a third-party OSC library, you may probably want to skip some of the details mentioned in this section. Nevertheless, I've found that having a better knowledge of how the protocol operates at a lower level can help to better design and scale your environment, as well as to help with tracking down issues.

For instance, let's think about a tool that has some audio faders we want to use for controlling the mix of our game in real-time. In this case, the tool will be a client that sends OSC messages over the network with the current values set within the minimum and maximum allowed for each fader. These messages then will be received and processed by our game (the "server"). This simple example already highlights several problems that we need to think about in a bit more detail. How do we format and send the data? What would be the rate for sending the control messages to the game? How do we process these messages? How many clients can connect to the game? Why would we need more than one server running in the game? Let's do some baby steps first in order to find out how the different pieces of the puzzle make all of this work.

First, we need a way for sending a stream of data from the client to the server. This can be easily achieved again by leveraging a networking primitive called a "socket." A socket is an abstraction for an endpoint within a network. We can think about it as a "sink," where the data can be sent from and received to. The socket is defined by an IP address that has ports, which are each of the paths that can be used by our data at a given time, like lanes on a road. The ports are identified by unsigned 16-bit numbers. Although it's also possible to set up a broadcast (sending data from one IP to a range of IPs) and multicast environment (sending data from more than one point to a list of IPs), we will only be covering one-to-one communication (unicast) over a local network (hence, not internet) for simplicity in this chapter, as it's probably the most typical case where we would be initially using OSC.

Luckily for us audio programmers, socket primitives (both for UDP and TCP communication) are widely implemented in the most common programming languages and frameworks. We can find implementations in C++ libraries like Boost's Asio or POSIX. The .NET framework also provides a sockets interface for C#. Since this programming language is commonly used for tools development in games, of the code examples for this chapter will be using it.

The basic calls for setting up a UDP socket in .NET with C# would look something like the following. We can now play with some code finally!

```csharp
using System;
using System.Net;
using System.Net.Sockets;

public class OSCClient
{
  private IPAddress _ipAddress;
  private int _port;
  private UdpClient _udpClient;

  public void Connect()
  {
    if(_udpClient ! = null) Close();
    _udpClient = new UdpClient();

    try
    {
      _udpClient.Connect(_ipAddress, _port);
    }
    catch
    {
      throw new Exception(String.Format(
        "Can't create client at IP address {0} and port
        {1}.",
        _ipAddress, _port));
    }
  }

  public void Close()
  {
    _udpClient.Close();
    _udpClient = null;
  }

  public void Send(OSCPacket packet)
  {
    byte[] data = packet.BinaryData;
    try
    {
      _udpClient.Send(data, data.Length);
    }
    catch
    {
```

```
      throw new Exception(String.Format(
        "Can't send OSC packet to client {0} : {1}",
        _ipAddress, _port));
    }
  }
}
```

This simple class allows us to connect and close a UDP client, as well as send OSC packets. If you are wondering what OSC packets are, we will cover the details shortly after this.

In the case of a UDP server, we can start by having some code as the following:

```
using System;
using System.Net;
using System.Net.Sockets;
using System.Threading;
using System.Collections.Generic;

public class OSCServer
{
  private UdpClient _udpClient;
  private int _localPort;
  private Thread _receiverThread;
  private OSCPacket _lastReceivedPacket;

  public void Connect()
  {
    if(this._udpClient != null) Close();

    try
    {
      _udpClient = new UdpClient(_localPort);
      _receiverThread = new Thread(
          new ThreadStart(this.ReceivePool));
      _receiverThread.Start();
    }
    catch
    {
        throw new Exception(String.Format(
          "Can't start server at port {0}", _localPort));
    }
  }
```

```
public void Close()
{
  if(_receiverThread != null)
  {
    _receiverThread.Abort();
  }
  _receiverThread = null;
  _udpClient.Close();
  _udpClient = null;
}

private void Receive()
{
  IPEndPoint ip = null;

  try
  {
    byte[] bytes = _udpClient.Receive(ref ip);
    if(bytes != null && bytes.Length > 0)
    {
      OSCPacket packet = OSCPacket.Unpack(bytes);
      _lastReceivedPacket = packet;
    }
  }
  catch
  {
      throw new Exception(String.Format(
        "Can't create server at port {0}", _localPort));
  }
}

private void ReceivePool()
{
  while(true)
  {
    Receive();
    Thread.Sleep(1);
  }
}
}
```

So this small class can already receive data asynchronously, which we can unpack and read in binary straight away. As we can see, our `ReceivePool()` function just polls data from the port the UDP server is bound to. Depending on our application and the bandwidth available, we may also want to have an event handler for performance reasons, but let's not worry about it for now. We will stick to this example and way of implementing a server for clarity and convenience.

10.3.2 OSC Addresses, Messages, Bundles, and Packets

Now that we have a way of sending and receiving streams of data over UDP, let's continue with implementing the OSC data definition. But first, we need to learn more about some terminology.

An OSC address is (as the name says) a way of expressing the location for our data. A valid address would be /fader/0 as an example. Note that any address always starts by a forward slash, and then any subaddresses are also separated by forward slashes. This is one of the reasons why OSC is so flexible, because it allows us to define and format the addresses for our data the way we want for our application. We could then define values for different faders (we started at index zero already) as /fader/1, /fader/2, and so on. After the address, we find the type tag, which is the information that hints about the type of data we will be sending for this address. The types of data supported by OSC include (not limited to):

- Integers: i
- Floating point values: f
- Strings: s
- Binary blobs: b

The data has to be 32-bit aligned for compatibility purposes. That is, we will need to pad our data with the corresponding number of zero-value bytes.[6] Then, after the type tag, we can append the data. For instance, in the case where we want to send a float value for our fader, the final data we will be sending and receiving is /fader/0 f 1.0. Simple and great, isn't it? We have just built our first OSC message. You may have also probably noticed that the address format in the message looks familiar: OSC was actually designed to resemble locations on the Internet (URLs!).

But we don't directly send OSC messages over the network, as it would be expensive and not very optimal if we think about it a bit: the granularity will be too small when we start sending large amounts of data. We will send them as "packets" of messages. Hence, an OSC packet can contain various OSC messages or OSC bundles. A bundle is another abstraction that allows us to "bundle" OSC messages that need to be sent together. It also allows us to define a time tag, or time stamp, which will be handy when we need to synchronize messages that represent actions occurring at the same time. One scenario that benefits from bundles is when we want to send data over a network using, e.g., UDP, as the order of arrival of the packets will not be guaranteed in this case.

Here is a possible minimal implementation for modeling an OSC packet that can pack and unpack float values. There are some generic methods used, so that we can add new types easily:

```
using System;
using System.Diagnostics;
using System.Collections.Generic;
using System.Text;

abstract public class OSCPacket
{
  protected List<object> _data;
  protected byte[] _binaryData;
  protected string _address;
  protected long _timeStamp;

  abstract public bool IsBundle();
  abstract public void Pack();
  abstract public void Append<T>(T msgvalue);

  public OSCPacket()
  {
    this._data = new List<object>();
  }
```

Here, we also take into account the endianness (byte ordering of the data) in order to be compatible with both big- and little-endian architectures. So, in this case, we swap the data in order to handle big-endian internally; but it could also be the other way around if we find it's more convenient for us.

```
protected static byte[] SwapEndian(byte[] data)
{
  byte[] swapped = new byte[data.Length];
  for(int i = data.Length - 1, j = 0 ;
      i >= 0 ;
      i--, j++)
  {
    swapped[j] = data[i];
  }
  return swapped;
}
```

Then, we can pack the values into binary as it follows:

```
protected static byte[] PackValue<T>(T value)
{
  object valueObject = value;
  Type type = value.GetType();
  byte[] data = null;

  switch(type.Name)
  {
    case "Single":
      data = BitConverter.GetBytes((float)valueObject);
      if(BitConverter.IsLittleEndian)
        data = SwapEndian(data);
      break;

    default:
      throw new Exception("Unsupported data type.");
  }

  return data;
}
```

And the other way round, for unpacking the values:

```
protected static T UnpackValue<T>(
  byte[] data, ref int start)
{
  object msgvalue;
  Type type = typeof(T);
  byte[] buffername;
```

```
switch (type.Name)
{
  case "Single":
    buffername = new byte[4];
    break;
  default:
      throw new Exception("Unsupported data type.");
}

Array.Copy(data, start, buffername,
            0, buffername.Length);
start += buffername.Length;

if (BitConverter.IsLittleEndian)
{
  buffername = SwapEndian(buffername);
}

switch (type.Name)
{
  case "Single":
    msgvalue = BitConverter.ToSingle(buffername, 0);
  break;

  default:
      throw new Exception("Unsupported data type.");
}

return (T)msgvalue;
}

public static OSCPacket Unpack(byte[] data)
{
  int start = 0;
  return Unpack(data, ref start, data.Length);
}
```

We also added some support for OSC bundles, as a bundle will start by the string #bundle when receiving it, so we need to handle it accordingly.

```
public static OSCPacket Unpack(
  byte[] data, ref int start, int  end)
{
  if (data[start] == '#')
  {
    return OSCBundle.Unpack(data, ref start, end);
  }
  else return OSCMessage.Unpack(data, ref start);
}

protected static void PadNull(List<byte> data)
{
  byte nullvalue = 0;
  int pad = 4 - (data.Count % 4);
  for(int i = 0; i < pad; i++)
  {
    data.Add(nullvalue);
  }
}
}
```

For completeness with the previous code blocks, a minimal OSC message and bundle implementations are also shown below:

```
public sealed class OSCMessage : OSCPacket
{
  public OSCMessage(string address)
  {
    _typeTag = DEFAULT.ToString();
    this.Address = address;
  }

  public OSCMessage(string address, object msgvalue)
  {
    _typeTag = DEFAULT.ToString();
    this.Address = address;
    Append(msgvalue);
  }

  private const char DEFAULT = ',';
  private const char FLOAT = 'f';

  private string _typeTag;
```

```
override public bool IsBundle() { return false; }

override public void Pack()
{
  List<byte> data = new List<byte>();

  data.AddRange(OSCPacket.PackValue(_address));
  OSCPacket.PadNull(data);

  data.AddRange(OSCPacket.PackValue(_typeTag));
  OSCPacket.PadNull(data);

  foreach (object value in _data)
  {
    data.AddRange(OSCPacket.PackValue(value));
  }

  this._binaryData = data.ToArray();
}

public new static OSCMessage Unpack(
  byte[] data, ref int start)
{
  string address =
    OSCPacket.UnpackValue<string>(data, ref start);
  OSCMessage message = new OSCMessage(address);

  char[] tags = OSCPacket.UnpackValue<string>(
                  data, ref start).ToCharArray();

  foreach (char tag in tags)
  {
    object value;
    switch (tag)
    {
      case DEFAULT:
      case FLOAT:
        value = OSCPacket.UnpackValue<float>(
                  data, ref start);
        break;
      default:
        continue;
    }
```

```
      message.Append(value);
    }

    if(message.TimeStamp == 0)
    {
      message.TimeStamp = DateTime.Now.Ticks;
    }

    return message;
  }

  public override void Append<T> (T value)
  {
    Type type = value.GetType();
    char typeTag = DEFAULT;

    switch (type.Name)
    {
      case "Single":
        typeTag = FLOAT;
        break;
      default:
        throw new Exception("Unsupported data type.");
    }

    _typeTag += typeTag;
    _data.Add(value);
  }
}
```

Again, we can expand this OSC message implementation for other data types. Before moving on to some timing and latency details, let's have a look into an OSC bundle implementation that allows unpacking bundles:

```
public sealed class OSCBundle : OSCPacket
{
  public OSCBundle()
  {
    _address = BUNDLE;
  }

  public OSCBundle(long timestamp)
```

```
{
  _address = BUNDLE;
  _timeStamp = timestamp;
}

private const string BUNDLE = "#bundle";

override public bool IsBundle() { return true; }

public new static OSCBundle Unpack(
  byte[] data, ref int start, int end)
{
  string address =
    OSCPacket.UnpackValue<string>(data, ref start);
  Trace.Assert(address == BUNDLE);

  long timeStamp =
    OSCPacket.UnpackValue<long>(data, ref start);
  OSCBundle bundle = new OSCBundle(timeStamp);

  while(start < end)
  {
    int length = OSCPacket.UnpackValue<int>(
               data, ref start);
    int packetEnd = start + length;
    bundle.Append(
      OSCPacket.Unpack(data, ref start,packetEnd));
  }

  return bundle;
}

public override void Append<T>(T msgvalue)
{
  Trace.Assert(msgvalue is OSCMessage);
  _data.Add(msgvalue);
}
}
```

10.4 DEALING WITH TIMING AND LATENCY

We have seen that the timing constraints are also important when dealing with real-time streams of OSC data. As mentioned previously, bundles can be used as a way of synchronizing OSC packets that are meant to be processed together. By using time tags or time stamps, we can mark a packet with some timing information that would be of help for our application. In the previous example, `message.TimeStamp = DateTime.Now.Ticks` is used for retrieving the ticks elapsed. We can also use a 64-bit fixed-point time tag as mentioned in the specification.[7] It's worth mentioning though that bundles are optional, and they aren't a requirement for starting a simple OSC communication.

In addition to this, being a communication over a network, we will be dealing with some common issues such as packet losses, bandwidth limitations, and latency. In terms of latency, UDP communication is usually good enough for the real-time scenarios we will be dealing with (below 20 ms in local networks), but we have to keep in mind that the way we deal with incoming data will define in part the behavior of our application, be it the game or the tool side. So, in the case of sending and receiving messages, this will obviously lead us to think about the number of OSC messages we are sending and/or receiving every game frame update. Although we can be receiving OSC messages asynchronously in a separate thread, we still need to take into account the processing of the addresses and the mapping to the functions or events in our game. Luckily, OSC is lightweight enough, but we can also carry out different optimization strategies for handling large volumes of data.

10.5 OPTIMIZATIONS AND BEST PRACTICES

Probably one of the most straightforward but not so obvious optimizations we can do is hashing the addresses, so that we don't send the entire address string but a hash of it.[8] This requires a bit of additional work for keeping track of the hashes and for carrying out the conversions (which would unavoidably add a bit of extra processing overhead), but we may find it handy in environments where we have tight bandwidth constraints.

On the other hand, we can take advantage of some data redundancy when the same OSC message is sent all the time. A state can be cached in our receiving end so that we only need to update this state every time we receive a different value for the same OSC address.[9]

10.6 TESTING APPROACHES

No OSC library or implementation will be complete and useful in a game audio production without having some testing strategies. I've found that having a way to verify correct connection of OSC clients and servers is fundamental to know that the data will be received or will arrive as expected before sending any data over a network. For instance, having a test Pure Data or Max MSP patch listening to the messages that are being received, or a patch that sends tests OSC message data is useful for an initial sanity check. We saw already that connections over a local network will usually be more reliable if compared with connections over the Internet. We can also create different test cases for the data types we can send using OSC, as well as different sizes for stressing the bandwidth available. In cases where we need to dig a bit deeper, tools such as Wireshark[10] for analyzing network traffic are also useful to us.

10.7 AVAILABLE OPEN SOURCE OSC LIBRARIES

In previous sections we covered some low-level details for implementing our own OSC protocol variation from the specification. In case you don't have the time, skills, or resources for implementing OSC from the ground up, there are a number of available online implementations released under Open Source licenses that can help us.[11] You will still need to spend some time integrating them with your engine, but most of the lower level details will be handled for you. The majority of the APIs out there provide a common interface for creating a connection by specifying an IP address and port, and for sending OSC messages in different ways, while still maintaining the specification terminology that we covered in previous sections. What is not offered in most of them is a way of handling and parsing OSC data, as it may be application-specific (again, because of, e.g., bandwidth, timing constraints, or the application design). So, the logic for handling OSC data is usually left to the client code that uses the library.

As mentioned previously in this chapter, we can easily find OSC implementations for pretty much any mainstream programming language. Perhaps one of the most known OSC implementations in C++ is oscpack from Ross Bencina.[12] For C# to be integrated with desktop applications, the Bespoke OSC implementation from Paul Varcholik is also popular.[13]

10.8 CONCLUSION

In this chapter we reviewed the data definition and protocol implementation, as well as some code examples and use cases, so that we can integrate OSC in our game engine and tools. Although it may seem like a complex endeavor at first, having a basic OSC implementation up and running can be even easier if we leverage some third-party libraries. Bridging the gap between a tool and a game engine (be it in-house or third-party) with a flexible language such as OSC opens the doors for better integration between all of the software pieces in game audio development, as well as experimentation while prototyping novel features and technology.

NOTES

1. http://opensoundcontrol.org/introduction-osc
2. Freed, A., DeFilippo, D., Gottfried, R., MacCallum, J., Lubow, J., Razo, D., Rostovtsev, I., Wessel, D. 'o.io: A unified communications framework for music, intermedia and cloud interaction'. ICMC 2014, Athens, Greece.
3. https://www.youtube.com/watch?v=s123eCd0RUY
4. http://opensoundcontrol.org/files/OSC-Demo.pdf
5. http://opensoundcontrol.org/spec-1_0
6. http://opensoundcontrol.org/spec-1_0-examples#typetagstrings
7. http://opensoundcontrol.org/node/3/#timetags
8. http://research.spa.aalto.fi/publications/papers/smc2011-osc/
9. http://opensoundcontrol.org/files/osc-best-practices-final.pdf
10. https://www.wireshark.org/
11. http://opensoundcontrol.org/implementations
12. http://www.rossbencina.com/code/oscpack
13. https://bitbucket.org/pvarcholik/bespoke.osc

CHAPTER 11

Listeners for Third-Person Cameras

Guy Somberg

CONTENTS

11.1 3D LISTENER BASICS

One of the fun features in *Hellgate: London* was the ability for most weapons to switch between first-person and third-person modes. While this feature provided some interesting challenges for the sound designers, none were more daunting than the problem of attenuation. We got complaint after complaint that the mix sounded really good in first-person, but that all of the sounds were too quiet in third-person. We needed to figure out a location to place the listener such that the third-person mix would sound as good as the first-person mix.

The audio engine listener is typically placed at the same location and orientation as the camera. This ensures that what you're seeing and what you're hearing match up. You'll use code something like this:

```
void GameEngine::Update()
{
  // ...
  mAudioEngine.Set3dListener(
    mpCamera->getPosition(),
    mpCamera->GetOrientation());
  // ...
}

void AudioEngine::Set3dListener(
  const Vector3& vPosition,
  const Quaternion& qOrientation)
{
  mvListenerPosition = vPosition;

  FMOD_VECTOR pos, fwd, up;
  pos = VectorToFmod(vPosition);
  // Y Forward, Z up in this case, but use whatever
  // 3D orientation your engine uses...
  fwd = VectorToFmod(qOrientation * Vector3::YAxis);
  up = VectorToFmod(qOrientation * Vector3::ZAxis);
  mpSystem->set3DListenerAttributes(0,
    &pos,
    nullptr, // Velocity
    &fwd,
    &up);
}
```

This code will work for many games, particularly first-person shooters. It is tried and tested and true, and will give you good results most of the time.

But it's also fundamentally broken for a large class of games. Let's take a look at why.

11.2 THE THIRD-PERSON CAMERA SYSTEM

If the camera isn't in the player's head, then it is typically placed in the air somewhere so that we can see the player, or at least see the action on the screen that we're interested in. In Figure 11.1, we have an example of such a system. The player is in the center, the camera is up above her, and the three sound sources (labeled A, B, and C) are in the world around the player. (Although you can't see it in this diagram, we're going to assume that the player is facing left.)

FIGURE 11.1   Our situation.

11.3 THE DESIRED RESULT

Before we begin looking at the various options of where to place the listener, let's first determine what we expect the results to be, and then we can try to achieve them. In our diagram, channels A and B are roughly equidistant from the player's location, so we want to make sure that they're attenuated at the same volume. Channel C is further away, so it should be attenuated more than A and B. At the same time, what the player sees should match what she hears, and, since all of the sounds are placed physically in front of the camera, all three should be panned to the front speakers. Table 11.1 summarizes our desired results.

Now that we know what we expect the pan and the attenuation to look like, we can compare a number of different options of where to place the listener. In the next few sections, we'll try putting the listener in a few different places and see how well the results match up with the expected results from Table 11.1.

TABLE 11.1   Desired Panning and Attenuation Results

Channel	Panning	Attenuation
A	In front	Loudest
B	In front	Same as A
C	In front	Quietest

11.4 LISTENER IN THE CAMERA

Let's put the listener into the camera, as shown in Figure 11.2. All of the channels are in front of the listener, so they're all panned to the front speakers, which is great! It's exactly what we're trying to achieve. But what about the attenuation? Well, channel C is closest to the camera, so it's going to get the loudest, followed by B, then A. You can see the results summarized in Table 11.2.

Well, that's no good! The panning is all correct: all three channels are panned in front, which matches up with our desired result from Table 11.1. But the attenuation is all wrong: the channels that are supposed to be loudest end up being quieter, and the ones that are supposed to be quiet end up being loud. Let's try something else.

FIGURE 11.2   Listener in the camera.

TABLE 11.2   Results with Listener in the Camera

Channel	Panning	Attenuation
A	In front	Quietest
B	In front	Middle
C	In front	Loudest

11.5 LISTENER IN THE PLAYER CHARACTER'S HEAD

What if we place the listener inside of the player character's head? After all, that's really what we're trying to model, right? What could possibly go wrong? Let's try it, just like in Figure 11.3. What happens now?

Well, now the attenuation is all correct. Channels A and B are equidistant from the listener, and C is further away, so they all get appropriately attenuated for distance. But this time, the panning falls apart. Since our player character is facing left, channel A will be panned in front, but channels B and C will both be panned to the rear speakers! Oh, dear. We can see this option summarized in Table 11.3.

Once again, we get half of the equation correct, but mess up the other half. This time the attenuation is all correct, but the panning is messed up.

FIGURE 11.3   Listener in the player's head.

TABLE 11.3   Results with Listener in the Player's Head

Channel	Panning	Attenuation
A	In front	Loudest
B	Behind	Same as A
C	Behind	Quietest

11.6 LISTENER PARTWAY BETWEEN PLAYER CHARACTER AND CAMERA

One option that I have heard being tried (anecdotally, although the game will remain anonymous to protect the guilty—and hopefully very ashamed—parties) is to place the listener halfway (or partway) between the camera and the player character, as shown in Figure 11.4. Let's run our thought experiment once more.

In this example, channels A and B will be panned in front, which is correct, but channel C is still behind the listener, and so it's going to get panned to the rear. For attenuation, channel C is the closest to the listener, so it's going to be the loudest. Next farthest away is channel B, followed by channel A. Table 11.4 summarizes these results.

This is so horrible that it is, in the words of physicist Wolfgang Pauli, "not even wrong." I can't even express the depths to which this idea is wrong. In fact, let's forget that we ever even thought of this idea, and banish it from the world entirely.

FIGURE 11.4 Listener partway between.

TABLE 11.4 Results with Listener Partway

Channel	Panning	Attenuation
A	In front	Quietest
B	In front	Middle
C	Behind	Loudest

11.7 THE CORRECT SOLUTION

Our solutions so far have moved the listener to various positions in an attempt to find a solution that gives us correct behavior for the attenuation and the panning. I think it's pretty safe to say that there is no single position that will give the correct attenuation and panning. So how do we get to where we need to go?

If we look at all of the (valid) solutions described above, each one either solves the attenuation or the panning, but not both. What if there were a way to solve each half of the problem independently? It turns out that there is a relatively simple solution, but we will have to break the standard model of the listener.

First, put the listener into the camera. This rule is inviolate, and there's not really any excuse not to do so. Next, we will fabricate a new position that we will call the Attenuation position, which will be placed (in this example) in the player character's head. This setup is demonstrated in Figure 11.5.

For each nonvirtual playing channel, find the distance from the channel's 3D position to the Attenuation position, as shown in Figure 11.6. Then we find the normalized vector from each channel to the listener position, as shown in Figure 11.7. Finally, place each channel along the normalized vector at the distances calculated from the attenuation position, as shown in Figure 11.8.

FIGURE 11.5   Listener and attenuation position.

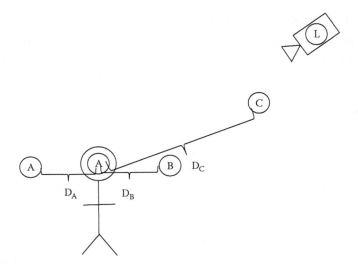

FIGURE 11.6   Calculating distances to attenuation position.

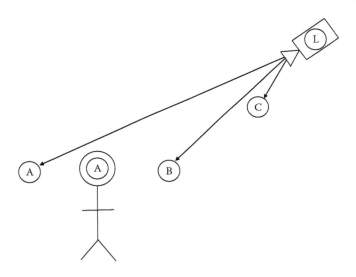

FIGURE 11.7   Vectors from listener to sound sources.

Let's examine the attenuation and panning results for the final positions for the channels after this algorithm, which we are calling A′, B′, and C′. First, for panning, each sound is panned in front. This makes sense, because we haven't changed the orientation of each channel relative to the listener position. For attenuation, channels A and B have each been moved closer to the listener, but channel C has actually been moved farther away!

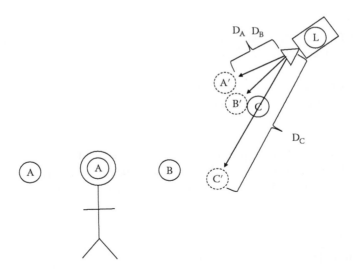

FIGURE 11.8   Repositioned sound sources.

TABLE 11.5   Results with Split Listener and Attenuation Position

Channel	Panning	Attenuation
A′	In front	Loudest
B′	In front	Same as A
C′	In front	Quietest

The attenuation of each channel is, *by construction*, exactly what we need it to be. Table 11.5 summarizes these results.

That's it! Table 11.5 is identical to Table 11.1. We have found a solution. To review, the algorithm for each channel is as follows:

- Calculate the distance (d) from the Channel's position to the Attenuation position.

- Find the normalized vector ($\hat{N}$) from the Listener position (L) to the Channel's position.

- Place the underlying playing channel at $L + d\hat{N}$.

In code:

```
Vector3 Channel::GetVirtualPosition() const
{
  float fDistance = Vector3::Distance(
    mSystem->GetAttenutationPosition(), mPosition);
```

```
Vector3 vDirection =
    (mPosition - mSystem->GetListenerPosition());
vDirection.Normalize();
return
    mSystem->GetListenerPosition() +
        fDistance * vDirection;
}
```

That code has two square roots—one for the distance calculation and one for the vector normalize. Therefore, you should take care to call it only once, and to cache the result if the position hasn't changed since the last frame.

11.8 EXCEPTIONS

The system described in Section 11.7 will give you correct attenuation and panning for sounds when your game has a third-person listener. But there are some situations in which you would actively want to disable this functionality and simply use the channel's position for both attenuation and panning.

The canonical example of this is footsteps. Let us imagine a situation in which the camera is in a fixed position, and is watching the main character move around the screen. We want to experience the game world through the character's viewpoint, so most sounds in this situation should use the algorithm described above. However, as our character moves around

Position 2

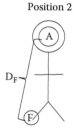

Position 1

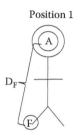

FIGURE 11.9 Footsteps.

and gets closer and further away from the camera, her footsteps should attenuate.

Figure 11.9 demonstrates this situation. The camera is in a fixed location, and the player moves from Position 1 to Position 2. But if we follow the algorithm, each footstep is exactly the same distance from the player's head (where the Attenuation position is) which means that the footsteps won't get quieter as the player moves further away.

One could argue that it is more consistent with the rest of the sounds in the world to position the footsteps sounds that way, but the fact is that in most situations, it *sounds* better and more natural to have the footsteps get quieter as the player moves away—at least, in third-person games where the camera is in a fixed location and not attached to the player's feet.

It is tempting to simply attach an exception to the piece of code that is playing the footsteps, but a better solution is to allow the sound designers the freedom to hook this exception to any sound, at the sound level. Or, even better, at the instance level.

11.9 OBSTRUCTION AND POSITIONAL CALCULATIONS

There is one more caveat to implementing this technology: it can mess up implementations of features that depend on the position of the playing channel. One example of this is obstruction calculations.

If you're performing obstruction calculations yourself, you have to make sure to use the position of the channel as reported by the game, rather than the virtual position calculated by the algorithm. If you don't, then the occlusion will almost certainly be incorrect. Sounds can get moved around radically, including to areas that you were not expecting.

Sometimes, your audio middleware will provide automated obstruction calculation functionality. For example, FMOD provides a Geometry API that allows you to create Geometry objects that automatically perform obstruction and occlusion effects for you. However, you must be very careful with this, because FMOD will use the location that you provide, which must (by necessity) be the virtual position, which will give you incorrect results.

For FMOD, in particular, you will need to set the FMOD_3D_IGNOREGEOMETRY flag on your channels (and be sure to reset it any time that you call Channel::setMode() or Sound::setMode()). Then call System::getGeometryOcclusion() for each Channel and set the occlusion using Channel::set3DOcclusion(). For the Studio API, call

`EventInstance::getChannelGroup()` and use the same calls on the resulting `ChannelGroup`.

This sort of issue exists for any other position-based calculation. Whatever problem you're trying to solve using the channel's position, you need to make sure that you're using the proper position value for it. This may necessitate a bit of finagling, as with the FMOD occlusion system described above, but it is something to be aware of when implementing your own systems.

11.10 CONCLUSION

Once we implemented this feature into *Hellgate: London*, all of the complaints disappeared. It was a beautifully simple design that satisfied everyone—the sound designers did not have to do any extra work to mix for third-person attenuation, and the game sounded markedly better as a result.

Getting proper 3D panning and attenuation is more than simply attaching the listener to the camera—there is a small but important chunk of code that will eliminate your panning and attenuation woes. Although you do have to be aware of exceptions such as footsteps, and be careful that any systems that are operating on the position of the sound are operating correctly, the results are worth the extra time.

CHAPTER 12

Interactive Music Systems for Games

Aaron McLeran

CONTENTS

12.1 INTRODUCTION

Music is a vital part of the landscape of our lives. In the context of story-telling, music drives a narrative and provides powerful emotional cues to the listener. Narrative tension and release are quite literally represented in the abstractions of a musical composition. In the case of games, where the narrative and experience is fundamentally interactive, music becomes no less important. Therefore, designing interactive music systems is an important aspect of game audio programming.

At a high level, game audio engines can be described as a feature-rich software sampler that manages and organizes thousands of audio files, which play synchronized to game events and are driven by many more thousands of complex real-time parameters. For many successful games and game audio engines, music is treated as simply another audio file. It is only differentiated by the fact that it is played back at a higher priority (usually with reserved voices) so that it is guaranteed to have resources to play, is nonspatialized (i.e., 2D), often looping, and—because of its usually longer duration (and thus larger memory requirements)—is streamed from disk rather than loaded into resident memory. This approach is not sufficient because many other games require music to more closely match and respond to the game's dynamic environment. In these cases, where interactive music systems need to be designed, music systems require their own complex state machines, logic controls, timing mechanism, and implementation tools and potentially other techniques.

This chapter will discuss a variety of technical issues involved with implementing these more complex interactive music systems and present a number of approaches and techniques. These are by no means the only possible implementation strategies, nor are they necessarily the best: there are about as many different approaches to interactive music as there are audio engines and audio programmers. I have chosen those described in this chapter as they represent the basics of interactive music as implemented by most game audio engines today and can stand as the ingredients for any more unique approaches required for any particular game.

12.2 PREREQUISITES

Before getting into the more exciting details of interactive music systems, we should first briefly describe a few issues that are important when simply playing music in a game audio engine. The first issue with music is that music files are typically large. This means that you'll first want to choose an appropriate music compression format and design a system for streaming audio from disk. For many interactive music systems, music files need to be able to loop without any clicks or pops on loop boundaries; however, not all audio file formats support seamless looping (e.g., most MP3 encoder/decoder schemes).

Another issue is that you need to compensate for the fact that playing streaming audio files often results in a noticeable latency between the request to play the audio file and when the audio file is actually audible. This delay is caused by the inherent latency in seeking files on disk and then loading those files into memory. Therefore, it is important to implement a mechanism to prime or preload chunks of audio in the stream before the sound is triggered, or to provide ways to force the synchronization of other systems to audio streams.

The details of audio compression and audio streaming are not within the scope of this chapter, but I feel they should be mentioned before getting into the specifics of interactive music systems.

12.3 SIMPLE MUSIC SYSTEMS

Many games simply play music for discrete states of a game: different menus, parts of a level or map, win/lose states, etc. Although I wouldn't exactly characterize music systems like this as strictly interactive, such systems serve as a useful foundation to the more complex systems and utilize many of the same basic components. Figure 12.1 shows the states that might exist in a basic 2D platformer game and labels the music for various states.

12.3.1 Looping Music

Because players can be, in some game state, modes for an undetermined amount of time, and because music needs to play for the entire time the player is in that state, music is often looped while in these states. Examples of game states that may require looping music states are called out in Figure 12.1. If music is intended to be played back looping, it's important that the composition itself is written such that the loop point is disguised and makes sense compositionally. One downside to looping music, especially if the loop is short (which may be because of a memory constraint), is that the music can become monotonous and repetitive. Instead of looping, some games instead play a given music file to its completion then simply restart the music after a period of silence.

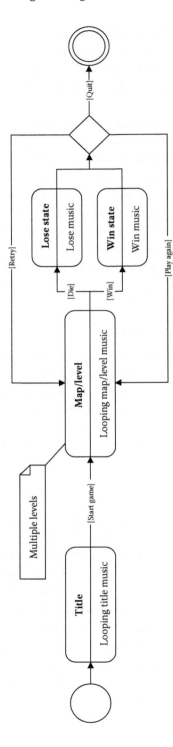

FIGURE 12.1 State diagram of a simple game and music states.

12.3.2 Music Variation

One way to combat the monotony of looping music for indeterminate game states is to create musical variations that randomize when the music repeats itself. Instead of simply returning to the beginning of the same music file, the music can instead select another piece of music that is similarly composed and play that. With enough variations, it's possible to significantly reduce fatigue.

12.4 INTERMEDIATE MUSIC SYSTEMS

The simple music systems described earlier suffer from a number of drawbacks. They aren't able to intimately respond to a player's actions as each state is triggered from a more global, coarse-grained state change. Each state change is accompanied by a totally different and discrete piece of music; there is no continuity of composition between each state. Transitions between states are abrupt (even if crossfaded), and repetition can cause significant listener fatigue. Variations are entirely different pieces of music rather than varied components within a single composition. In this section, I'll present various improvements to the basic music systems described earlier that will help compensate for their various shortcomings.

12.4.1 Finer-Grained Game States and Parameter-Driven Music Choices

One immediate improvement to interactive music is to create more nuanced and finer-grained game states. Figure 12.2 builds on Figure 12.1's states. For example, instead of defining a game state at the map level, one can create game states that reflect player choice, player state, AI state, past choices, or even time. In an RPG that changes the story based on the morality of their choices, the music can reflect those choices. To avoid listener fatigue, the music may change to a more ambient or subdued composition if the player spends more than 10 minutes in the same mode.

In order to select music compositions that more accurately reflect and/ or drive the emotional context of a player's experience, music systems can also play music or change state based on dynamic game parameters. Always playing intense combat music when a player enters combat might not be a wise choice. Instead, choosing what music to play based on the player's level versus the enemy's level, or the number of enemy involved, or the players status (e.g., low health) might result in more appropriate

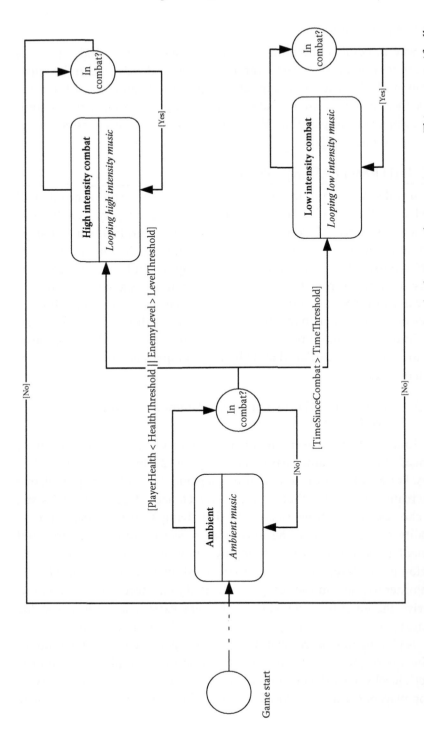

FIGURE 12.2 More complex state diagram using more game parameters to make decisions about music states. This case specifically demonstrates transitioning from ambient music to varying levels of combat music depending on game state.

musical choices. Music not only drives player emotion, but it should also represent the emotions that the player ought to feel. The same intense combat music for a nonintense battle can break game immersion.

12.4.2 Crossfading with Stingers

Crossfading at arbitrary points in a given piece of music to a different piece of music can be aesthetically and compositionally abrupt. For example, a given music file might have established a musical expectation rhythmically (defining a musical pulse and phrase). Changing at a random point in that musical phrase to a different piece of music might result in an awkward missed beat or pulse. One simple way to disguise musical transitions is to play musical sound effects or musical stingers (i.e., not large streamed pieces of music) that are intended to sound like part of the music stream but introduce some noisy or disguising musical component that can play during the abrupt transition. A stinger might be a large cymbal crash, a dramatic chord, a bunch of timpani playing something loud and dramatic, a percussion roll, etc.

12.4.3 Crossfading Using Synchronization Constraints

Although more complex, another way to avoid the issue of abrupt musical transitions is to provide metadata about the playing music file that indicates when an appropriate time to transition to a new piece of music is. These synchronization points are analogous to animation key frames. There are two common ways to generate the synchronization points: either a composer defines them explicitly in a tool, or the composer provides metadata about the composition that defines the musical meter and tempo (i.e., BPM) and restrictions on when to allow music transitions (e.g., every N bars). When a musical state change is determined and made by the audio engine, it will wait for the next synchronization point (or point within the current musical phrase) before performing the crossfade to the new music. This scheme is shown in Figure 12.3. This way, the underlying tempo and pulse of the music can be maintained between different musical states and thus achieve a more cinematic and cohesive musical experience.

12.4.4 Synchronization Constraints and Special Transition Music

Even with synchronization points and stingers to mask musical state transitions, it can still sound too abrupt when switching between different musical states and loops. This is especially true if the two pieces of

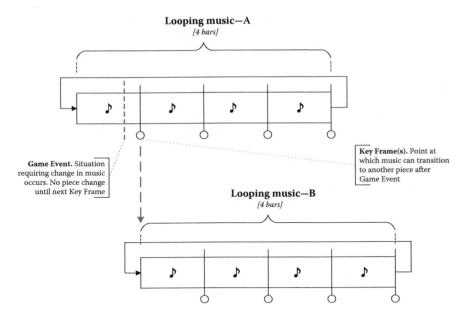

FIGURE 12.3 Key-framed looping music transitions between two looping pieces of music.

music are in different musical key signatures, time signatures, or tempos, or if they have totally different themes or phrasing. Instead of immediately switching to the new piece of music, the composer can provide special fragments of "glue" music that transition from piece to piece (and state to state) using appropriate compositional techniques such as key and tempo modulations, and dramatic pauses or crescendos. Figure 12.4 illustrates this additional transitional music to the synchronized state change.

12.4.5 Multilayered Music

An alternative approach to creating totally different pieces of music for different game states is to create musical loops with multiple layers of composition that are intended to be played back simultaneously. This is a particularly useful approach for game states that are only differentiated by a single parameter. For example, combat music might be characterized by intensity. Low-intensity combat music might just have a few extra bits of percussion. High-intensity combat might introduce shrieking trumpets, pounding bass, and complex percussion. If they're all fundamentally the same composition but with different layered components, the music transitions can occur more quickly and seamlessly, without synchronization

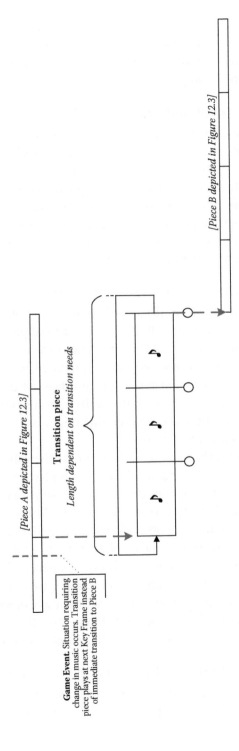

FIGURE 12.4 Key-framed looping music transitions using specifically composed transition music. Note that the bar-lines remain synchronized between the musical pieces.

points or transition music, and thus respond to the action more immediately and more intimately. When combined with musical stingers, this approach can produce the illusion of instantaneous musical reaction to gameplay with minimal compositional complexity.

12.4.6 Multilayered Music with Stingers and Musical Events

Another approach to creating layered interactive music is to separate out the percussion and rhythmic components of a music track from the nonpercussive components. This way, the rhythmic elements can be triggered independently and thus more immediately respond to gameplay. If timed appropriately, percussive sounds can more quickly start, stop, and transition to different parts than nonpercussion parts. Thus, it's possible to create the feeling of more responsiveness while still maintaining the musical integrity of the orchestral and melodic components.

12.4.7 Multilayered Music Implementation Strategy

One technical limitation with multilayered music is that playing multiple pieces of music simultaneously will likely require multiple simultaneous music streams, a requirement that on some platforms might prove prohibitive. This problem is exacerbated when combined with the need to transition (crossfade) to different pieces of multilayered music. If using four layers of music, for example, with the desire to transition to a second four-layer music composition, an audio engine might be required to support eight simultaneous audio streams!

A clever way to avoid this issue is to incorporate the different layers of music into the same music file. Since music is typically played back in stereo, a multichannel audio file could be considered multiple layers of the same piece of music. For example, if four layers of an audio music file were exported into a single eight-channel audio file, you could write code that turns on different channels based on a game parameter. Normally, an eight-channel file is intended to be back on a 7.1 surround sound system, where each channel corresponds to a different speaker in a surround sound system. Because music is usually played back in stereo, you can instead use each stereo-pair in the single eight-channel audio file as a separate layer. With this trick, you can actually get four layers of music streaming with a single music stream.

12.4.8 Randomized Crossfading Layers and Musical Tracks

For some game states, where players may spend hundreds of hours and many months or years playing, the primary musical and technical goal is to maximize variation possibility and minimize listener fatigue. An example of this might be an open world in an MMO game where players may spend hundreds of hours listening to game's ambient music. One approach to solving this problem would be to simply compose enough different music and hope that players don't get tired of listening to the same pieces of music getting played over and over again. However, with hundreds of potential gameplay hours, this is not only impractical compositionally, but would require way too much disk space to store all the music.

Alternatively, the composer could instead compose a "palette" of ambient music fragments and loops that could sound good when randomly played together in various layers and in various sequences. Then, during the open world gameplay, these fragments would randomly and slowly crossfade between them and randomly sequence one from the next.

12.5 NOTE-BASED MUSIC AND REAL-TIME INSTRUMENTS

So far, we've discussed the problem of music in games from the perspective of prerecorded files of music in large files. An alternative approach to game music is to "perform" the music in real-time with software instruments: either performed through synthesis or via sampled instruments. In addition to the memory benefits of removing the need for large audio music files (and the associated complexities of streaming, compression, etc.), music is now performed "on-the-fly" and can be driven more intimately by game-state and game parameters.

There are numerous downsides to this approach as well. For example, the audio engine will need to deal with music taking up a larger percentage of active voices (each note would be a "voice") and therefore require more CPU processing, and the music itself will potentially sound less "cinematic" as sampled instrument playback will not have the benefit of nuance a human performer can bring. Although not widely used in games today, real-time synthesis can be used instead of sampled instruments and may provide the potential for a more nuanced performance. The technical issues with real-time synthesis are CPU resource requirements and managing a potentially large number of synthesis parameters automatically (for nuanced performance).

12.5.1 Composition and Performance Metadata

One approach to note-based music is to drive the real-time instruments via a metadata file that represents the composition. MIDI, MusicXML, Mod Trackers, or your own custom music format could serve as the music composition and performance representation. Once in this format, the previously described techniques for interactive music and streams also apply to this: state management, synchronization points, transition music, etc.—all apply to music played back in this format. The added benefits to this method are numerous: the instrumentation itself can change owing to game-state and player choice, individual parts are easily muted or varied, and music can be stopped or started instantly with no need for crossfading.

12.5.2 Player-Created and Player-Performed Music

Once an audio engine supports instruments, it's only a matter of extending the ability to perform the instrument from automatic playback systems to players themselves. When dealing with player-created and performed music, the key technical issues become instrument control via keyboard input (computer or MIDI keyboard), input latency management, and network latency in multiplayer games. There are many game types and game modes where musical performance from players can provide exciting possibilities and musical immersion.

12.6 GENERATED MUSIC

The next step beyond driving precomposed music with real-time instruments is to actually generate the composition itself "on-the-fly." The details of creating this type of music, called variously generative music, procedural music, or algorithmic music, is beyond the scope of this chapter to describe. There are a number of approaches to generating music: Markov techniques that analyze existing compositions to build a table of note and/or chord transition probabilities, probabilistic techniques that make musical decisions from handcrafted probability distribution tables, constraint-based generative grammars, and any number of hybrid approaches. Nevertheless, the same techniques described above also generally apply to generated music with the additional benefit of the composition itself being capable of being affected by game state, parameters, and player interactivity. Assuming that an implementation for creating generated music exists, this section will briefly review some applications of generative music for games.

12.6.1 Layered Generative Components
      with Traditionally Composed Music

Because some styles of music are exceedingly difficult to generate algorithmically, it's possible to get the benefits of generated music by layering generated music alongside precomposed music. A perfect application of this is to combine a generative percussion system with a prerecorded music system (using techniques described previously). The generated percussion can instantly and intimately respond to gameplay events, creating fills, grooves, etc., on-the-fly, while the higher-quality, handcrafted orchestral system is playing alongside it.

Another example is to transition between generative systems and non-generative systems depending on the need for the game. Cinematic sequences and gameplay events might require careful composition while open-world background ambience could use some generative music technique.

12.6.2 Using Generative Techniques for Better Player-Created Music

As mentioned previously, real-time instruments can provide players the ability to express themselves in a game. However, most players will likely not have any musical training and will not really have the knowledge or skill to produce music that they (let alone others) might enjoy. You could potentially design a system where a player "feels" like they are performing a prerendered or preauthored piece of music, but then you'd likely take away the sense of creativity and spontaneity that you'd hopefully want to be able to provide with such a system.

One solution to this problem is to apply generative music techniques and constraints so that the player can feel like they are being creative and expressive while the music itself is compositionally sound and enjoyable to listen to. For example, a well-tuned melody or rhythm generator might be customizable to player preference. Player input could be responded to in a "musical" way that will always make their expression "sound good" while also giving them the sense that they're injecting their own personal taste.

Another possible application of generative techniques and player-created music is a means to compensate for input and network lag for multiplayer group performances. If players are not creating note-for-note compositions but instead interacting with an algorithm "on-the-fly," it's possible for the various input parameters to be synchronized and interpreted for each client so that each player's playback sounds musically enjoyable from their perspective.

Obviously, the details of a such system are where the devil lies. Nevertheless, the point remains that generative techniques can enable better player expressivity and musical gameplay.

12.7 CONCLUSION

We've only barely scratched the surface of the various issues involved in designing and writing interactive music systems for games. I hope this chapter has given a sufficient introduction so as to spark ideas on how you might approach supporting interactive music for your own game projects. Even though I presented the material at a surface level with a clear demarcation between various approaches, many successful interactive music systems use hybridization, combining different aspects of the various approaches described, sometimes utilizing different techniques within the same game.

CHAPTER 13

Granular Vehicle Engines

Dave Stevenson

CONTENTS

13.1 WHAT IS GRANULAR SYNTHESIS?

Granular synthesis is a method of playing a sound source where the source is split into small sections of wave source called "grains." These grains can then be organized and played back in a randomized sequence in order to be able to create the illusion of a single sound playing, which can be parameterized based on game inputs.

There are many ways to use granular synthesis.

- **Dynamic One-Shot Sounds**: Each one-shot sound is broken up into sections start/main/end, where each section can be shuffled with a number of variations, creating a greater mix of sounds. For example, by splitting a sound into three sections, each with two variations, you can achieve eight unique sounds.

- **Dynamic Looping Sounds**: A loop is split into multiple sections. Then, by playing each section randomly together, you can create a looping sound with less noticeable loop points.

- **Dynamic Sound Synthesis**: The resulting sound is created by replaying grains from a small section of the original source, where the grains match or closely match a parameter, i.e., RPMs.

The last one is the method used to replicate the sound of a vehicle engine, usually replacing a Revband system. A Revband system consists of a number of loops that are pitched together to match tone, and where only one or two loops can be heard at a time.

For Engine Granular Synthesis, you need to start with a source recording of the engine, going from low revs (or idle) and rising to full revs/rev limiter. This one sample can be used to represent an aspect of the engine, usually one for engine and one for exhaust, and possibly another two for off load of each.

In the Revband system described earlier, we would use only a few small sections of this same sample, adjusting their pitch to cover the RPM range. The Granular Synthesis system will use most (if not all) of the data, to make a stream of useable data. To make a full engine, you would probably use at least one source for the engine and one source for the exhaust, to give a good mix of what the vehicle sounds like. For an improved system, you may wish to have two sources and streams for each engine and two for the exhaust as well, where one covers the on-throttle version of the engine, and one covering the off-throttle. This would produce a dynamic engine that captures all of the sound characteristics of the vehicle's engine. However, going this far will result in a trade-off as the more data is used, the more it will affect the memory constraints that may be applied to your system.

13.2 GRAIN CUTTING

For a granular engine, you need to generate the grains from your original source. The source needs to be analyzed so that we can see where to cut our grains and what size they should be.

The first step is to calculate the RPMs of the engine run as this will connect the sections of the source with the RPMs of the source engine and each grain, allowing us to cut the grains. Also, when playing the sound back in the game, the RPMs will be the connection from the game engine to the sound, so this connection is important. To establish this connection, we first run the source through a series of fast Fourier transform calculations that will give us the frequencies that are in the source.

13.2.1 FFT

To analyze the source data, we want to find the frequencies that are present in the signal, and in particular, we want to note the dominant (loudest) frequencies. We run the data through a series of FFTs with sections of the source. The FFT returns a collection of frequencies and volumes of those frequencies. The following C# code function returns an array where the index is the frequency and the value is the volume.

The inputs to this function are as follows:

data: source data.

number_of_samples: number of samples passed to function, this needs to be a power of two. If there is not enough data, the data can be filled with zeroes.

sample_rate: sample rate of the source data.

freq: the array of data that will be filled with the volume frequency data.

```
public void FastFourierTransform(
  float[] data,  Int32 number_of_samples,
  Int32 sample_rate,
  ref double[] freq)
{
  double pi = Math.PI;

  //variables for the fft
  Int32 n, mmax, m, j, istep, i;
  double wtemp, wr, wpr, wpi, wi, theta, tempr, tempi;

  //new complex array of size n=2*sample_rate
  float[] vector = new float[2 * sample_rate];

  //put the real array in a complex array
  for (n = 0; n < sample_rate; n++)
  {
    if (n < number_of_samples)
    {
```

```
      vector[2 * n] = (data[n] / 32768.0f) * 8.0f;
    }
    else
    {
      vector[2 * n] = 0;
    }
    vector[2 * n + 1] = 0;
}

n = sample_rate * 2;
j = 0;
for (i = 0; i < n / 2; i += 2)
{
  if (j > i)
  {
    SWAP(ref vector[j], ref vector[i]);
    SWAP(ref vector[j + 1], ref vector[i + 1]);
    if ((j / 2) < (n / 4))
    {
      SWAP(ref vector[(n - (i + 2))],
           ref vector[(n - (j + 2))]);
      SWAP(ref vector[(n - (i + 2)) + 1],
           ref vector[(n - (j + 2)) + 1]);
    }
  }
  m = n >> 1;
  while (m >= 2 && j >= m)
  {
    j -= m;
    m >>= 1;
  }
  j += m;
}

//Danielson-Lanzcos routine
mmax = 2;
while (n > mmax)
{
  istep = mmax << 1;
  theta = (2 * pi) / mmax;
  wtemp = Math.Sin(0.5 * theta);
  wpi = Math.Sin(theta);
  wpr = -2.0 * wtemp * wtemp;
```

```
wr = 1.0;
wi = 0.0;
for (m = 1; m < mmax; m += 2)
{
  for (i = m; i <= n; i += istep)
  {
    j = i + mmax;
    tempr = wr * vector[j - 1] - wi * vector[j];
    tempi = wr * vector[j] + wi * vector[j - 1];
    vector[j - 1] = (float)(vector[i - 1] - tempr);
    vector[j] = (float)(vector[i] - tempi);
    vector[i - 1] += (float)tempr;
    vector[i] += (float)tempi;
  }
  wr = (wtemp = wr) * wpr - wi * wpi + wr;
  wi = wi * wpr + wtemp * wpi + wi;
}
mmax = istep;
}

//calculate the volume values for the frequencies
//from the complex array
Array.Resize(ref freq, (sample_rate / 2) + 1);
for (i = 2; i <= sample_rate; i += 2)
{
  double value =
    Math.Sqrt((Math.Pow(vector[i], 2) +
               Math.Pow(vector[i + 1], 2)));
  freq[i/2] = value;
}
}
```

The last provision with this code is that indices of the array are relative, and need to be multiplied by the ratio of (number_of_samples/sample_rate). This gives us the actual frequencies that we can use. Once we have the frequency data we can graph this, so we can see the dominant frequencies that we want to use to cut the source into our grains.

13.2.2 Graphing FFT

The first aim is to figure out the fundamental frequency, for each sample set, over the whole source run. The best way to do this is to run the FFT analysis in sections over the source wave. The best way to visualize this is to graph the data results. There are various ways to show the data:

Heat map—a graph showing frequency mapped over time, and using a color scale that maps to the volume, as shown in Figure 13.1.

Frequency map—a graph that shows frequency and time (like the heat map); however, this graph shows peak frequencies that match (or closely match) from section to section, by the highest volume, as shown in Figure 13.2.

With these graphs, we are looking for a clear section that shows the dominant frequencies through the whole graph—so we are looking for a band of frequencies that match the rise of the RPMs of the source. It may be helpful to generate an indicator that maps the dominant frequency per time slice, or even develop an automatic algorithm that can detect the strongest line through the graph/source. For our system, we could draw a line on top of the graph, and then use the values from the line to match the correct frequency band when cutting our grains.

Now going through the source, we take the dominant frequency, which usually equates to the frequency of a cylinder firing of the engine. Sometimes the main frequency isn't easy to pick out on the graph, usually because it is broken up owing to other dominant frequencies. The nature

FIGURE 13.1   Heat map of exhaust run.

FIGURE 13.2   Frequency map showing frequency matches.

of the FFT results and frequencies is that multiples of the frequency will also show up in the FFT. This needs to be taken into account, as the calculation will be based on the main (base) frequency, so this multiplication will be required in the grain size calculation.

When calculating the grain length, the base frequency will indicate the engine cylinder fire length: one pop of the engine. For a grain, we will try to capture a sequence of firings that match the engine cycle, which will vary depending on the engine type. A straight 4 or 6 will have a sequence that equates to the number of cylinders—that is, you can capture each cylinder in the firing sequence in order. A V6 or V8 will have a sequence the same as the number of cylinders, but as these grains will be bigger, you can achieve a more varied sound by capturing half of the cycle (three or four cylinders) in each grain. For example, for a V6, capture 1, 2, and 3 in one grain and 4, 5, and 6 in another. Then, when playing back you can keep the odd (first half) and even (second half) grains in sequence, but mixing which ones are used together.

The grain length now equates to ((1/base frequency) × number of cylinders). This calculation gives the length of the grain, but now we need to figure out where we apply this. When originally working on this, the target was to start and end grains at a point where the source values cross zero, going above zero from below. However, during the process of developing the system, we decided to change this because extra frequencies were produced when playing the two grains. These extra frequencies were caused by the starting and ending frequencies being so different. To combat this, we decided to cut the grains during the first peak of the grain, and used the same techniques to match between the two grains. The most important discovery we made during this process was to always cut the length dictated by the dominant frequency; otherwise, every extra sample in a grain will generate a buzzing noise.

So, the basic formula for cutting the grain becomes:

- (First iteration only) find ideal grain start.

- FFT (*n* samples, where *n* is a power of 2).

- Find the loudest frequency closest to our indicated frequency band.

- Calculate the grain length.

- Locate the start and end points of the grain.

- Copy/mark the grain.

- Move to the end of the grain and repeat until all of the source in consumed.

You may also want to store a value with each grain that indicates the RPM of the grain, or at least the percentage through the RPM range, which allows us to select grains according to the game's engine. If it's possible that the engine sound you are using won't match the engine characteristics of the in-game engine, then it's probably best to save this value as a percentage between the lowest frequency and the highest frequency that you indicated. This way, if the RPM ranges don't match you can interpolate between the minimum and maximum to match with the values that have already been stored with the grains.

13.3 PLAYBACK

There are two different playback-related issues that we need to deal with: what grains to play and how to play them.

13.3.1 What Grains to Play

The first issue that the system requires is knowing which grains should be played. With each grain, we should have the equivalent RPM value of the grain. The engine system will have an RPM value that is required for playback, and we can match this value with the grain data that we have. Once we have our target grain, it can be played in the system output; however, playing the same grain over and over again won't sound good, or be even close to convincing enough to sound like an engine. One of the problems is that playing back the same grain, such as a small waveform, will cause a buzzing sound.

To eradicate this buzzing, we need to ensure that the same grain isn't played too often. To do this, we create a window around the "target" grain, usually around 6–10 grains. This now gives us a clearer sound that is closer to the sound of an engine, but only randomly picking grains can still cause the same grain to play too many times. We need to track the previously played grains so that we can keep a big enough space around multiple playbacks of the same grain. Figure 13.3 shows the target grain and window of grains.

The best method to conquer this buzzing issue is to use a shuffle method, which makes sure that all of the grains in your window are used before moving on to repeat a grain.

FIGURE 13.3　Target grain and window of grains.

13.3.2　Shuffling Grains

Once we have a target grain and a window of grains, we can generate a play-list of grains, but to do so we need to have a list of the previously played grains (which would be empty, if it's just starting). Now the playlist can be generated.

The first grain when creating a new list should always be the target grain, and we fill the playlist with randomly picked grains from the window. Each time we randomly pick a grain, we must ensure that it has not been played in the last $n/2$ grains, where n is the size of the grain window. This is done until we have a play list of n grains. When $n/2$ grains have been played, we can then generate another $n/2$ grains in the same fashion. Once the target grain changes (usually because of engine RPM changes), the whole list will require regenerating from scratch. Figure 13.4 shows the grains after they have been shuffled.

13.3.3　How to Play the Grains

Once we have the grains that we want to play, we now need to play these grains. The usual way to play back our source is to use an input source plugin, usually through a middleware engine. If you are using a propriety system, you will probably be able to play sound from a buffer, or more accurately a ring buffer.

With a middleware solution, or from my own recent experience with Wwise, the system will request more data to be played, and the main task is to fill this buffer with enough data to play continuously.

13.3.4　Stitching Grains Together

The next issue to tackle is how to transition cleanly from one grain to the next. With our grains that we have harvested from our original source,

FIGURE 13.4　The grains shuffled.

we now have discrete sections of audio that we want to play, along with a working order to play the grains. Because the grains are coming from different sections of the original source and different fundamental frequencies, the starts and ends of the grains probably won't match up, in value or even gradient, which in the time domain can cause additional frequencies to creep in.

There are various methods to go from one grain to the other, some of which will depend on how the grains are generated.

The first method is to crossfade between the grains. This method requires extra data for each grain, as each grain will need the grain length + the length of the crossfade, which can increase the memory requirement of a single engine. This method can also duplicate a huge amount of data if you don't manage it carefully. If you are including all of the sources cut into your grains, you already have the extra data there, so you just need to pull it from the appropriate location.

To crossfade from one grain to the next, we place the grain data into the buffer, as per a normal grain sample. After the last sample of the grain, we will mix the fade data with the next grain samples. Figure 13.5 shows a crossfade from one grain to the next.

The second method I have used was to fade between the grains, but because of memory constraints, I didn't have enough space for all of the grain sources, not to mention extra samples for crossfading. I created a way to fade from one grain to the next by calculating a "virtual crossfade." This "virtual crossfade" is generated by taking the difference between the last value from the first grain and the first sample of the next one. This value buffer was reduced so that eventually we were only using values from the second grain. Figure 13.6 demonstrates a crossfade using just the next grain source.

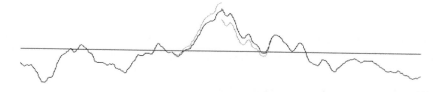

FIGURE 13.5   Crossfade from one grain to the next.

FIGURE 13.6 Crossfade using next grain source only.

13.4 CONCLUSION

With all of these steps put together, you should be able to take a source sample of engine noise, generate grains, and play back the engine noise at your chosen RPM. More than this, hopefully you have the inspiration to use this technique in different ways to add a little variation to your projects. The only limitation is your imagination...well and maybe memory.

CHAPTER 14

Debugging Features for Middleware-Based Games

Jon Mitchell

CONTENTS

14.1 INTRODUCTION

Modern game audio middleware like Wwise and FMOD are increasingly powerful and take most of the heavy low-level lifting off the audio programmer. Most also come with powerful profilers, remote logging, and game state inspection tools that can make the task of debugging complex projects much more manageable. However, once your project reaches a certain level of complexity, these tools by themselves often aren't quite enough, or in the worst-case scenario are simply not available in the build that is displaying the bug you're hunting. In this chapter, I'll describe an easily built set of tools and debugging approaches that complement the middleware remote-debugging features, and can make working on the audio of a large-scale game a little easier for both programmers and designers. This chapter is written from the perspective of a long-time Wwise user, so although some techniques are Wwise-specific, I have seen many of these ideas independently implemented in game engines using all sorts of combinations of in-house audio code and middleware, so I'd urge you to read on even if Wwise isn't your middleware of choice—much of this will likely be easily extensible to whichever codebase you are using.

14.2 MIDDLEWARE UIDs

Wwise allows the use of a hashing algorithm to turn all of its string-based identifiers for events, RTPCs, state names, and so on, into 32-bit integer UIDs. Although using strings can often be quick and convenient at the start of a project, it's best to switch to using hashes as soon as possible.

In modern PC-based games, the CPU and memory cost of using strings is manageable, even when dealing with large numbers of events and RTPC settings per frame. However, if you are working with Unity and C#, passing strings to Wwise can very quickly result in poor garbage collection performance. Using UIDs solves these problems effectively, at the cost of increased difficulty in debugging. We can no longer easily see which text identifier a method is referencing, just an inscrutable number. If we have game code that performs operations on strings, or debugging features that display the strings onscreen, these will no longer work. Ideally, we want to keep the performance advantages of IDs and the debugging ease of strings.

14.2.1 AudioSymbols

The solution I use is to create a class specifically for Wwise symbols containing both the UID and, in debug builds, the human readable string. If we load the list of valid strings into memory when the game is initialized, we can create a hash map of the UIDs to the Wwise strings, and still see readable strings in the debugger. It also allows us to access the string for display in onscreen and logged debug text. In addition to runtime use, having access to the set of valid strings can be helpful for in-game tools. I use the same code in our game editor to provide an autocomplete box for Wwise symbols, and to color-code Wwise symbols that are misnamed or no longer exist.

14.2.1.1 Listing: AudioSymbol.h

```
#define READABLE_SYMBOLS_IN_DEBUGGER

class AudioSymbol{
public:
  AudioSymbol(const char* name);
  ~AudioSymbol();

  const uint32_t GetID() const {return id;}
  const char*    GetDebugName() const {return debugName;}

private:
  uint32_t id;

  #ifdef READABLE_SYMBOLS_IN_DEBUGGER
  const char* debugName;
  #endif

  //prevent assignment between AudioSymbols
  AudioSymbol& operator=(const AudioSymbol& source){}
};
```

14.2.1.2 Listing: AudioSymbol.cpp

```
#include "AudioSymbol.h"

typedef std::map<uint32_t, RegistryEntry* >::iterator
  it_type;
typedef std::pair<uint32_t, RegistryEntry*> pair_type;

SymbolRegistry* SymbolRegistry::instance = nullptr;
```

```cpp
SymbolRegistry* SymbolRegistry::Instance(){
  if (!instance){instance = new SymbolRegistry();}
}

const char* SymbolRegistry::Add(
  uint32_t id,const char* name ){
  it_type i = symbols.find( id );

  RegistryEntry* entry = nullptr;

  if ( i == symbols.end() ){
    entry = new RegistryEntry(name);
    symbols.insert( pair_type( id, entry));
  }
  else{ entry = i->second; entry->AddRef();}

  return entry->GetName();
}

void SymbolRegistry::Remove( uint32_t id ){
  it_type i = symbols.find( id );

  if (i == symbols.end())
    return;

  i->second->ReleaseRef();

  if (entry->GetRefCount() == 0){
    delete i->second; symbols.erase(i);
  }
}

const char* SymbolRegistry::Find(uint32_t id){
  it_type i = symbols.find(id);

  if (i == symbols.end())return nullptr;

  return i->second->GetName();
}

void SymbolRegistry::DebugDump(){/*omitted for brevity*/}
```

```cpp
RegistryEntry::RegistryEntry(const char* _name):
refCount(1),
name(nullptr){
#ifdef READABLE_SYMBOLS_IN_DEBUGGER
  int stringLength = strlen(_name);
  name = (char*)malloc(stringLength + 1);
  strcpy(name, _name);
#endif
}

RegistryEntry::~RegistryEntry(){
#ifdef READABLE_SYMBOLS_IN_DEBUGGER
  free((void*)name);
  name = nullptr;
#endif
}

AudioSymbol::AudioSymbol( const char* name ){
  FNVHash<32> hasher; //wwise hashing algorithm
  id = hasher.Compute((const unsigned char*)name,
    strlen(name) );

  const char* registryName =
    SymbolRegistry::Instance()->Add(id, name);

  #ifdef READABLE_SYMBOLS_IN_DEBUGGER
  debugName = registryName;
  #endif
}

AudioSymbol::~AudioSymbol(){
  SymbolRegistry::Instance()->Remove(id);
}

const char* AudioSymbol::GetDebugName() const{
  #ifdef READABLE_SYMBOLS_IN_DEBUGGER
  return debugName;
  #else
  return "<none>";
  #endif
}
```

14.2.2 Loading the Strings

Wwise doesn't expose its string table directly, but if you enable "Generate Header file" in the Project Settings, it will create a C header file with named constant values for each of its UIDs.

It's easy enough to process this file as text into a format suitable for loading into your game engine.

14.2.3 Wrapping the API

To ensure all Wwise calls use our AudioSymbol class, it's a good idea to wrap at least the portions of the Wwise application program interface (API) you use. Although this is a bit of a chore, it also gives us a good framework to start instrumenting API calls with our own custom debug functionality.

In our engine, we also created wrappers for GameObjects and Events. Although the Wwise Query API gives you access to lists of active GameObjects, and the Events playing on those GameObjects, we found the Query API to be too slow for our purposes. Most, if not all, of the Query methods lock the Wwise thread, so calling this every frame can introduce significant delays, especially on older consoles such as the PS3 and Xbox 360. Instead, when creating a GameObject or playing an Event, we keep lists of our wrapper objects on the game thread, which are updated by callbacks passed into PostEvent.

14.3 VISUAL DEBUGGING INFORMATION

Often, when working on a large-scale project, I'll be assigned to make feature improvements or bug fixes on an area of the game where I have little to no idea how the feature is implemented. If you're lucky, you'll still be able to talk to the people who implemented the feature—but if you're working on an external code base with minimal support, or the feature author is no longer at your company, or even if they're just on vacation— you're on your own! Adding visualization to the game audio can help you familiarize yourself with how GameObjects and Events are used for a specific feature, and put you quickly on the path to fixing it.

14.3.1 Sound Radius Spheres

Wwise has its own GameObject viewer built into the Authoring tool, but it can sometimes be difficult to see how the view of the naked GameObjects correlates with the game geometry.

Luckily, it's an easy task to replicate this view in your game itself. If you're not keeping track of GameObjects and their positions yourself, you can use the Query methods to give you a list of active GameObjects, their positions, and maximum radius.

```
AK::SoundEngine::Query::GetActiveGameObjects
AK::SoundEngine::Query::GetPosition
```

14.3.2 World Coordinate Positioned Text

I've found it extremely useful to be able to see a quick summary of the following information on a given GameObject onscreen:

- GameObject name

- World position

- Distance from the Listener

- Maximum attenuation radius of the playing Events

- A list of playing Events

- RTPC and Switch values

All of this information is also available using the Query methods:

```
AK::SoundEngine::Query::GetPlayingIDsFromGameObject
AK::SoundEngine::Query::GetEventIDFromPlayingID
```

14.3.3 Filtering the Debugging Information

Figure 14.1 shows a typical game scene with all GameObject audio debugging information displayed. Visual debugging information is great, but if there is too much of it onscreen at once, it can be difficult to tell what is going on. To solve this problem, we use two search filters: one that filters by GameObject name, and one that filters by Event name. In addition, each of the individual debug information elements for a GameObject can be toggled on/off with a debug menu option. Figure 14.2 shows this dialog. In Figure 14.3, we can see that the debugging information is much easier to interpret with the filter on.

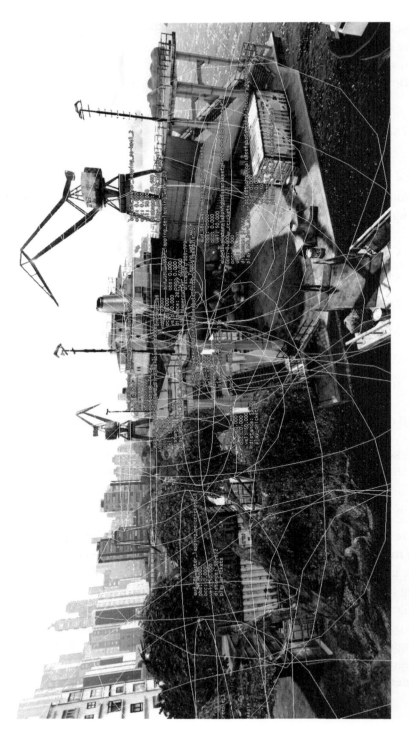

FIGURE 14.1 A typical game scene with all GameObject audio debugging information shown. Useful, but hard to tell what's going on!

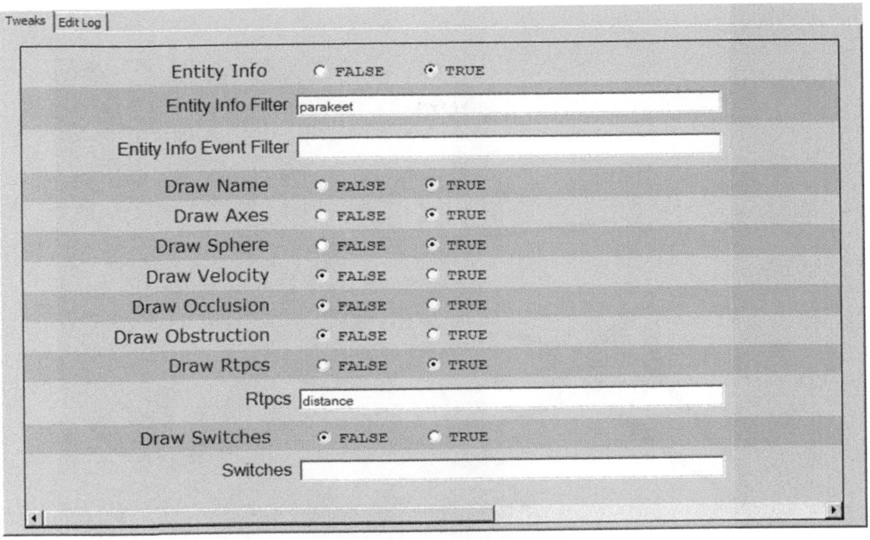

FIGURE 14.2   Options to filter and control the debugging information.

14.4 UNDER-THE-HOOD DEBUGGING FEATURES

14.4.1 Breaking Execution on Specific Events

This is a simple idea that has saved me many hours of feature implementation and debugging time. In a large-scale game, audio events may come from a large variety of sources. In UFG's engine, audio events can come from any of the following:

- Direct calls from C++ code

- *Skookum*, our script language

- *Freeman Action Tree*, our animation blending and animation state tree

- *Freeman AI Tree*, our AI behavior and logic tree

- *Audio Emitters*, our system to manage playback of positional ambient sound

- *Trigger Volumes*, 3D spheres or volumes that trigger events when a player or game object enters or exits them.

Most large-scale games will have a similarly large set of subsystems where audio calls can come from. Often, debugging a game audio feature will

FIGURE 14.3   After filtering, the debugging information is much easier to interpret.

require diving into at least two or three of these subsystems. The Profiler logs and our in-game debug tools tell us *which* events are happening, but don't tell us anything about *where* exactly the calls are coming from. Being able to quickly identify which subsystems are involved in an audio feature is crucial to quickly understanding and debugging it. If we can break program execution when a specific event is posted, we can then inspect the call stack to determine which subsystem an event is coming from, and inspect our game objects and game data in the debugger at the precise instant an event occurs, which is often useful for tracking down a bug or verifying a feature.

Implementing this is easy enough—as all the game's calls to `AK::SoundEngine::PostEvent` are within our API wrapper, we can either compare the posted event IDs with the one we want to break on directly, or use our AudioSymbol lookup table to match all or part of a string. In Win32 programs, we can programmatically break using `__debugbreak()`, but almost all compilers will have an equivalent. In the very unlikely case that your compiler doesn't, you can manually set a breakpoint on a line that outputs a debug message. In addition to trapping posted Events, it can also be useful to be able to set breakpoints when an RTPC is set via code, rather than as part of a Wwise event, and when a sound bank is loaded or unloaded.

14.4.2 Event Filtering

When you're debugging, it can sometimes be useful to reduce the events triggered in the game to the subset of events relating to the feature you're working on. This means the Capture Log in Wwise will only show you events and objects that you're interested in, and you'll only hear sounds that are relevant. Although you can achieve much the same effect by soloing objects in Wwise, and using the filter boxes in the Capture Log, doing this in game code can still be a useful tool in your debugging arsenal, for several reasons:

- If you suspect that a particular event being fired off is contributing to the issue you're debugging, you can temporarily suppress that event and its effects by filtering it out.

- I have encountered numerous bugs where connecting to Wwise prevents the bug from occurring or otherwise changes the bug's behavior.

To filter the playing Events, I pass a comma-separated list of values to either filter out or include. The audio engine pauses any events playing on

GameObjects that don't pass the filter tests, and doesn't play any new ones. If the filters are changed or removed, any paused events are restarted.

14.4.3 Custom Event Properties

Filtering by event name lets you filter out categories of sound very quickly and reasonably well *if* your Wwise event names are carefully organized and consistent. Although I'd strongly recommend that all large Wwise projects adhere to some sort of naming standard, this still won't always map neatly to categories of sound that you'd like to enable/disable. Wwise allows you to attach Custom Properties to Sounds and Audio Objects, but not, sadly, to Events. UFG's audio engine has an `AudioEventProperties` class, to allow us to optionally associate a set of properties with Events. This allows us to categorize events into groups or channels so they can be turned off and on while debugging an issue. We've also used the same grouping system for runtime optimizations, such as reducing the frequency of RTPC updates for less time-sensitive sounds.

14.5 TEAM DEBUGGING PRACTICES AND PROCESSES

In a large-scale game with a big audio team, debugging audio features, and keeping them debugged, is everyone's responsibility. We came up with several collaborative debugging techniques that made the most of everyone's skills. Designers who worked on an audio feature are (not surprisingly) often better at spotting bugs and flaws in a feature than the audio programmer, who may be better at fixing them. It's not always immediately obvious to either the designers or the programmers what is causing a feature to break. Game code? Game data? Audio engine code? Audio engine data? Missing Wwise events? Badly set up Wwise objects? Least likely, but worst of all, you might encounter a bug in the middleware itself. There are many points at which a game feature can break, and the better the team can work together to identify the likely point(s) of failure, the faster they can work out who is best equipped to fix it.

14.5.1 Using Fraps with the Profiler

One simple but very powerful technique we use for debugging our games is a combination of time-stamped game footage capture and Profiler capture. Using `AK::Monitor::GetTimeStamp`, you can embed the time code used by the Profiler into the game footage, which we captured using Fraps,[1] a freeware video capture program. When designers noticed errant behavior when testing the game, they would take a Fraps capture of the offending portion of the game, and save the Wwise capture log as a *.prof* file. This way, team members could see and hear the bug in action, and cross-reference it with the Profiler session. This allowed us to diagnose the cause of many bugs without us each having to individually spend the time reproducing it, and to get multiple eyes and ears on especially worrisome problems quickly.

14.5.2 Checklists to Diagnose Missing Sounds

A large portion of the audio bugs that are reported from QA on our games were variations of "The $THINGY doesn't make any sound." In fact, the sound of various $THINGYs being missing has made up a large portion of the audio bugs on *all* the projects that I've worked on. Either I am especially unlucky, or finding out why sounds aren't sounding is a large part of every game audio programmer's lot in life. I'm going to assume the latter. As it turns out, the root causes of missing sounds often turned out to be the same things, over and over again. So much so, we ended up making a checklist that could be used by designers and programmers alike.

- Does the event to trigger the sound actually happen? If not,
  - Has the event been added to a sound bank?
  - Is the sound bank containing the event loaded?
  - Does the event actually exist? Is there a typo in the event name?
  - Is the game's *.pck file up to date?
  - Is the sound bank containing the event loaded? If not,
    - Does the game have enough memory left to load the bank?
    - Is the audio pool used by the sound bank fragmented?
    - Is there a typo in the sound bank name?
    - Is the sound bank included in the game's *.pck file?
- The sound loaded and started playing correctly, but still isn't audible.
  - Is it stopping immediately? If so,
    - Check your virtual voice settings and bus limit settings.

- If not,

    - Check your mixer settings—is a mix state making the object inaudible?

    - Check your falloff settings—is the game attenuated by distance falloff?

    - Check your RTPC curves—is the sound attenuated by the RTPCs?

Some of these issues are automatically flagged as errors in the Wwise Profiler, but others require manual inspection of the capture log, or the data in the Wwise Authoring Tool.

14.6 DATA VALIDATION AND WORKFLOW TOOLS

Checklists are great, but the bug that takes the least time to fix is one that *never happens in the first place.* Since our checklist is a list of What Usually Goes Wrong, it's also a great place to start when trying to think of ways to improve your workflows to reduce the problem, or better yet—to aggressively automate it out of existence.

14.6.1 Make Use of Wwise's Own Validation Checks

Wwise has a powerful set of project integrity and error checks—although not all of the errors it reports are necessarily issues on all projects, it is worth making as many of these errors fatal errors as possible.

14.6.2 ID Search Tool

At least a couple of the common issues in the checklist are caused by simple typos in the input data. Everyone makes mistakes, but verifying that a string exists in a large list is a job for your friendly neighborhood computer, not a sleep-deprived and groggy game developer. Before we implemented AudioSymbols, the first way we looked up which ID mapped to which string was by manually searching in the Wwise_IDs.h file exported by the build. This got old pretty quickly, so I created a quick GUI tool to parse the header, and return the string that matched a specific ID, or the string/ID pairs that matched a given string. I extended this tool to also search our code, script, and data directories, creating a list of all of the references to AudioSymbols in our project. This proved invaluable for catching typos, references to IDs that no longer existed, and for tracking down from where in the project a sound was triggered without having to run the game itself. Figure 14.4 shows the ID search tool.

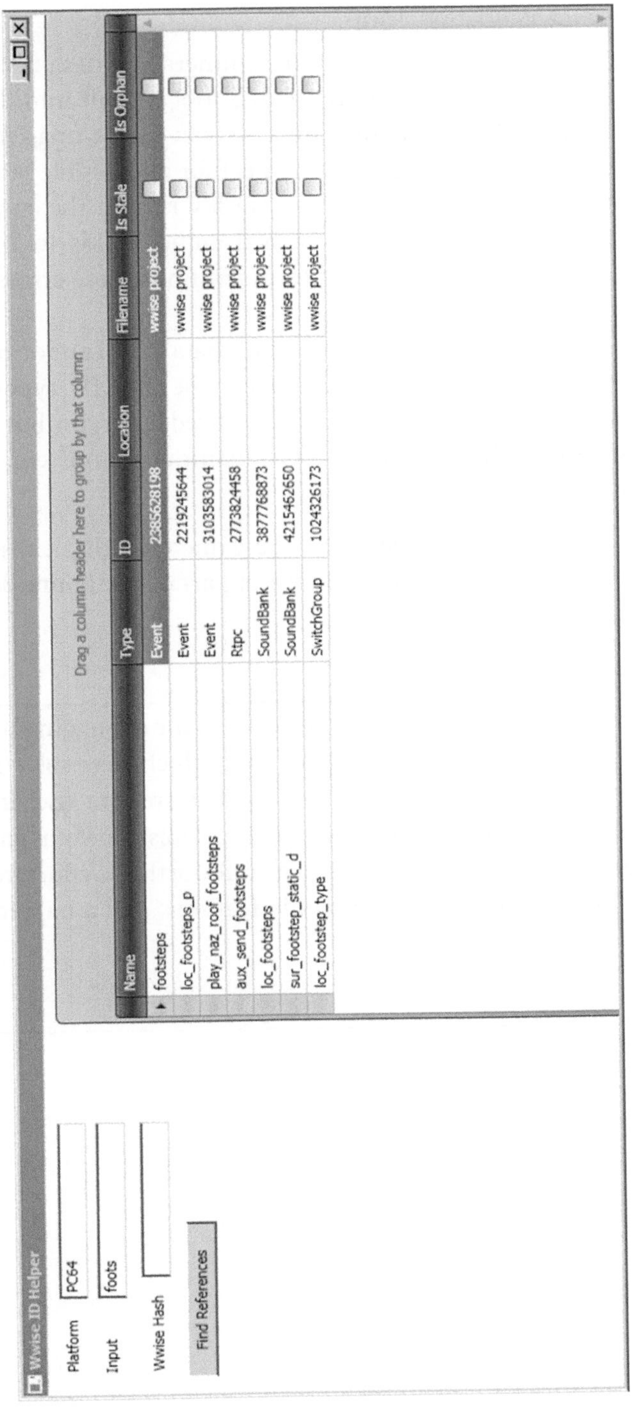

FIGURE 14.4 The ID search tool.

14.6.3 Wwise ID Validation Tool

In addition to a GUI tool for use by programmers and designers as part of debugging, the back end of the ID search tool is built into the audio pipeline for use as a data validation step. As you might imagine, doing a search in all the files of a large game project for all possible Wwise IDs isn't practical at every build step, so this is only run on the audio build machines responsible for providing cached audio builds to the team, which automatically e-mails the audio team if it finds these errors:

- A Wwise ID is referenced in the game data that cannot be found in the Wwise project. This symbol can be any ID type—Event, SoundBank, RTPC, etc. This is usually caused by a typo, but can also be caused by a deliberate deletion or renaming of an Event, without updating all of the game data.

- A Wwise symbol is referenced in the game data that exists in the project as an Event, but this Event is not part of any SoundBank.

14.7 CONCLUSION

Hopefully, this chapter has given you some ideas for debugging tools and approaches you may not have considered, but which may solve some of your problems. No matter which audio middleware you use, investing some time into developing custom debugging tools for your particular engine and project's needs is almost always well worth the effort, resulting in decreased debugging time, better audio features, and a happier audio team.

NOTE

1. http://www.fraps.com/

CHAPTER 15

Open World Game Optimizations and Limiter Systems

Matthieu Dirrenberger

CONTENTS

15.1 INTRODUCTION

Open world games give to the player a freedom of movement and action that is incredible for the immersion aspect. However, this often comes with a counterpart—complexity. It is far more complicated to create a game without loading screens that has free roaming possibilities than a linear game. Most linear games offer better graphics and better sounds than open world games because they have good knowledge of what assets they will need at any point in time. But, by thinking further and optimizing, we can reach and even surpass linear games, and reach the top quality of other AAA games on the market. That is what we do on the brand I am working on: *Far Cry*.

This chapter will focus on the CPU overload aspect that happens in the case of event spamming. In this open world game context, the CPU is easily busted by the audio middleware trying to process too many game requests.

This common problem can be solved in many ways; I will reveal a few methods I used in the past. The first one, called "bus limitation," which is based on a dynamic bus priority limitation, was a fallback method I used at the end of production. However, the method was surprisingly good and really efficient, so I continued to iterate on it with different methods named "gameplay limiter" and "event limiter." I continued until I improved the system enough to finally have my own game sound engine priority system named "in game event limiter" using sound metadata and player focus, taking care of the sound event priorities before sending them to the audio middleware.

15.2 OPEN WORLD LIMITATIONS

The *Far Cry* games are focused on giving a wide open world sandbox that has a diversity that allows the game to be (and stay) entertaining for hours, and that always pushes the player to dig deeper into the open world. This diversity has a cost. The sheer number of encounters, animals, vehicles, weapons, and biomes, leads to a frustrating fact that is always there for open world game creators: you can't reach a high quality level for every single element in your game. The quality of the real gameplay elements will always be lower than a linear game following a corridor or using closed portals.

Even having some constraints applied by game designers, the expectations are so high that we need to decrease some resource quality. This is not only the case for the sound, but also for graphics and animations. Typically, you are using a loading ring around the player that uses entities to load. So, any resource in your game is an entity coming with its graphics, animations, AI (almost nothing scripted is in the open world), and, of course, sounds. So the more diversity there is, the more you need memory and CPU to be able to manage everything.

But even with these limitations, we wanted and we definitely managed to reach the top of the quality that can be expected from an AAA game. Every single part of the code has optimization systems, from AI to graphics, and we could probably write an entire book about open world game optimizations/limitation systems.

I will cover only a few of these limitations and explain how we handled the problems concerning the CPU usage related to the sound event processing.

Note: Some of these aspects were more important with the early-generation consoles such as PS3 and XBox 360, and could be rightly seen as obsolete on next-generation consoles, but they are good general practice, so I think it is still interesting to discuss them.

15.3 GENERAL CPU OVERLOAD PROBLEM

I need to define my words. I will use the term "sound engine" to speak about the internal part of the games' sound system that sends requests. I will use the term "audio middleware" to speak about the third-party code that processes requests and actually does the sound rendering.

The biggest audio problem that showed up on the games I worked on was the CPU overload caused by the sound engine. Usually, it is possible to squeeze data in memory by using aggressive compression or by removing variations, but you can't really squeeze the CPU time; there is only one way to reduce it: process fewer operations.

Basically, the CPU time used by the sound is divided into three parts:

1. The game's main thread processing the sound system through the game engine updated each frame, with all related subsystems, such as ambiance, music, weapons, dialogs, and cinematics.

2. The command executor thread that processes the requests sent by the game sound engine to the audio middleware.

3. The sound renderer that processes mixing and effects, and plays all the sounds.

You can reduce the time taken by the game sound engine by optimizing; you can reduce the time taken by the sound renderer by having rules restraining CPU usage by defining a max polyphony and a limited number of effects. But you can't really reduce the time consumed by the command executor that processes the event queue filled by the game sound engine.

The problem to understand here is that any sound request is processed, even if the sound is not in an audible roll-off, and even if many sounds are playing and this sound will be virtualized. It costs the entire event processing, with volume computation, tree search, etc., before it is dropped and passed to the next one. Naturally, this cost will depend on the audio middleware you are using, and usually, the more complete your audio middleware is, the more costly your event processing becomes. If your audio middleware is a big black box, you will have no power to optimize, but if you are using an intermediate layer you can do some beautiful optimizations here.

Depending on the way your threading is done with synchronous/ asynchronous threads, single- or multi-threaded, with the game controlling or not the task's start of the command queue executor and/or audio renderer, it can create various issues such as the sound lagging/cutting, or even worse, the entire game stalling.

It is common to have the main thread with the game sound engine executed on the main core and the two other processes on another core, so you only risk losing your sound, but the game will continue to run. In this case, if you have too many messages to process within a single frame, it will make your sound stall, because the renderer will wait for the command queue executor to be entirely processed.

Without going deeper into the engine aspect of this very classic problem, you can easily understand that the problem is to limit the number of events sent to the audio middleware in each frame.

15.4 EVENTS SPAMMING

The systemic nature of open world games doesn't help much with event spamming, because you can't easily control how many events the game will send. You have random entities everywhere spamming events all the time, and since the player can take a driving vehicle, helicopter, or a glider and can basically jump anywhere in the world at anytime, you can't predict what will happen.

Examples of game elements triggering events:

- Random encounter will have a weapon such as an AK-47 that triggers four sounds each time the NPC shoots. There are footsteps, Foley for NPC gear, the clothes, dialog/barks, animations that are playing sounds from AI, or markups in animations; you often have up to 20 of them in your loading ring radius.

- Animals with footsteps, Foley, barks, and animations that are playing sounds from markups.

- Vehicles having a sound for each wheel, suspension, frame, animations, multiple loops for the engine, and fake wind sound.

- Ambiances are playing one to three streamed pads plus one to three random FX playing sounds randomly depending on frequency.

- Sound point systems and virtual sound point systems that are playing loops with orientations on trees for the leaf sounds, waterfalls, wind on cliffs, radio systems, etc.

- Sound lines, sound shapes, or sound volumes playing ambiance followers on the player, loops, single shot, or positioned random FX.

- Multitracks for the wind and different weather systems.

- UI triggering sounds for the player feedback information.

This list is just to show you the numerous elements in a game that can trigger sounds and eventually burst the event queue. For the vast majority of these sounds, you can add information such as position updates, and a few real-time parameter controls (RTPCs) coming from the game.

With an open world game having dozens of NPCs shooting at you, and multiple ambiance and environment systems, it can easily burst your event queue, which buffers them each frame then tries to process every single event/RTPC update before the end of the frame.

In the same vein, the polyphony can explode and cost too much for the renderer. Usually, a priority system exists to prevent this kind of problem, so the user sets a priority for each sound in the audio tool, and these priorities should, in case of problems, cut the lowest priority sounds or at least prevent them from playing again, when the polyphony limit is reached.

The reality is, this doesn't work. This is a fallback system that prevents the system from crashing or lagging, but if you hit the polyphony limit and you need the sound engine priority system to sort your game sounds, then you have a bigger problem.

Usually, these systems are based on distance or roll off (audibility factor). So, coupled with the priority, it can find a way to sort out what can play or not. But in my case this was not good enough, because even using roll off I had audible artifacts and the mix was horrible. These artifacts were happening when a voice was cut in the middle of playing, sadly on transient peaks of the waves (a "pass by zero" fade out system should be implemented first in any audio middleware to avoid any click).

A basic mixing problem: the game being a shooter, the guns have the highest priority and are loud because they are guns. Naturally, because this is exactly that kind of game, the guns were always playing, while ambiances and SFX were always shut down by the audio middleware priority system. It was not that bad during the fight's action phase, but it really became noticeable when the player was passing from this phase to an exploration phase, where you need to correctly hear the ambiances between shots.

The two main problems are now defined. First, sending too many events leads to a lag in the event queue processing; and second, it pushes the audio middleware to the max polyphony all the time, creating a bad-sounding mix because only the highest priority events were playing. So in a shooter game, I ended up with almost only the sound of guns playing, plus eventually rendering lags, because even by respecting the polyphony, it was playing only sounds with more costly effects (guns), and the original design was not taking all of these effects into the CPU cost calculus.

15.5 THE BUS LIMITER IDEA

The designs we have in our engine imply using the gameplay systems to manage most of the audio logic, and the sound system itself is only used at a pretty low level. This is a design choice that pushed me in the direction I chose to solve the problem. There are other and definitely better ways to fix the problem, such as managing each gameplay system individually by adding some audio information to them, or simply by moving the audio logic in the sound system. But I had to ship a game within a short time frame, so a refactoring of every single gameplay system was not really an option.

Concept explanations:

- Synchro sound: The synchro sound is a value saying how many audio rendering passes were stacked during the previous frame. This value should be "1" all the time, meaning that it only prepared the data for the next frame. So if it stacks more than 1, it means that it is receiving too many events, and it is not able to process the event queue and/or compute all the audio rendering the sound engine is asking for. This creates situations where the sound is cutting/lagging.

- Sound Type: In the Dunia engine, I have an abstraction of the main audio busses, named Sound Type, which is set with every single sound in the game. The main purpose of this object is to help gameplay features and mixing, but it is also a very useful tool to debug and analyze what sounds are playing.

15.5.1 Information and Tools Available

The following is a list of information that was accessible for determining and preventing the event spamming issue:

- Callbacks giving real-time polyphony by chosen busses
- Playing sound count based on the sound types
- Callback giving real-time status of the command queue executor, by setting threshold percentage for the command queue usage and a threshold limit for the synchro sound

```
static void QueueWarning(
  SND_CommandQueueNotificationReason reason,
  sndHandle userData)
{
    CSoundSystem* s =
      reinterpret_cast<CSoundSystem*>(userData);
    switch(reason)
    {
    case SND_COMMAND_QUEUE_USAGE_ABOVE_THRESHOLD:
        s->LimitSound();
        break;

    case SND_COMMAND_QUEUE_USAGE_BELOW_THRESHOLD:
        s->StopLimitSound();
        break;

    case SND_QUEUED_SYNCHROSOUND_ABOVE_THRESHOLD:
        s->LimitSound();
        s->SynchroSoundLimit();
        break;
```

```
case SND_QUEUED_SYNCHROSOUND_BELOW_THRESHOLD:
    s->StopLimitSound();
    s->StopSynchroSoundLimit();
    break;

default:
    ASSERTSOUND(false, "Unsupported value!");
    break;
    }
}
```

There is another thing I need to add—in the audio middleware I used, I had a bus system that had an optional priority system that was not derivative and used the sound volume (audibility factor) coupled with the priority for determining which sound to cut. So, if you set 16 voices of polyphony on a bus, it doesn't affect the parents or children bus's polyphony. At this point, I had only one limitation set at 64 voices on the master bus.

15.5.2 CPU Performance Analysis

You always need to figure out what consumes the most CPU, etc. Most engines offer profiling tools. You can also use tools such as PIX from Microsoft. You only need to add some CPU time tracing into the audio middleware, both in the command executor and in the renderer.

Using these tools, you can determine an approximate cost for each effect used, and you can deduce interesting facts by cross-referencing numbers. In my case, I saw that the CPU cost had a little offset and that it was linear with the number of voices processed. As I said earlier, it was almost only guns playing. These sounds had tons of effects such as low pass filter and EQ varying by roll off. So I tried to reduce the gunshot bus limit by more than 50%.

Before, I had up to 45 voices playing for guns and I reduced the max gunshot bus polyphony to 20. As I said earlier, you can't really cut off a looping gun sound playing, but after multiple tests, I determined that with a limitation between 15 and 20 voices, I very rarely saw a gun firing without sound. Also don't forget that the priority system used the audibility factor as a sorting factor, so only the loudest gunshots were playing, which was covering any other limited sound. At this point, compared to before, I was able to reach my full polyphony without any

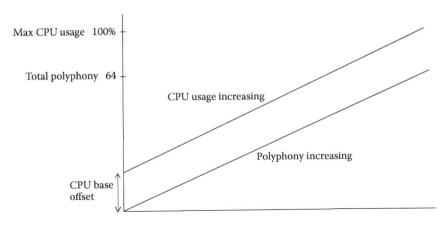

FIGURE 15.1   Graph of polyphony versus CPU usage.

CPU lag due to the sound renderer, thanks to the other sounds that were less costly.

In conclusion, limit all your main busses with a high limit that should never be exceeded (in my case, 20 voices for the third-person gunshot bus). Choose a value by thinking what is required to keep the CPU usage from ever reaching this value, plus the rest of the sounds until you hit the polyphony limit (Figure 15.1).

15.5.3 Dynamic Busses Limits

Even with a nice first result, too many voices were still allowed. It was not possible to set a fixed number for each main bus, because if you take the worst-case scenario for each main bus you end up with a system needing 256 voices.

For example, the ambiances were taking around 35 voices alone just doing nothing in the game being alone in the middle of a field, so when I went at any point of interest I had up to 50 voices in the category "ambiance." It was easily busting our polyphony because of this polyphony "offset" always taking half of our resources. I could have been tempted to set a limit of around 24 or something similar, but by doing that it was sometimes cutting one or two of the three main ambiance pads (they were multitrack quads with a day and night version of the quad; so they were able to take 24 tracks only for pads). If any other ambiance sound was playing at the same moment I could have lost a pad, which was not an option. You want good ambiance quality with 50 voices when you are in exploration mode.

Having all this information and having a priority system in the audio middleware, I thought that a first solution to try was simple. The problem was the static bus limit and the fact that it had to be used at the end of the chain. The solution was to add something that was permitted to change dynamically the bus limit on each bus, depending on the gameplay action. It was simple to add it in the code. A few other third-party audio middleware are offering this kind of feature, too. Now, I had a tool, but I still needed to find a smart way of using it to be able to keep a good mix quality in the game.

15.6 THE LIMITATION SCHEME

The approach to define how to set the bus limit is simple. The scheme is defined by the following parameters:

- Single player/multiplayer

- Platform

- Gameplay state: exploring/mission/combat

- Player driving a vehicle or not

- Sound engine state: event queue/synchro sound

- Polyphony for each main bus

Then, you choose the best busses to work with. In my case, it was almost all the subbusses at one level under the master bus, plus a few specifics such as explosion bus and vehicle bus.

You will have to balance how many voices of each bus can be played simultaneously, and determine a model for each gameplay case you encounter. Here are a few examples:

- Outpost capture: many gunshots, less ambiance, few vehicles, few animals

- Driving a vehicle: many vehicles, few shots

- Exploring: tons of ambiances, many animals, few shots, few vehicles

- Mission: many barks/dialogs, many guns, few ambiances, few animals

Another important step is to define the number of levels that you want to use in your scheme to limit your sounds. In my case, five levels were enough:

- Loose limitation, meaning almost no limitation, with only big values for each bus

- Forced limitation triggered by a few gameplay states setting the system with specific settings (in my case, more adapted to gunfights)

- Warning limitation triggered when the system was hitting a high polyphony or synchro sound lag

- Hard limitation triggered by warning limitation, plus a few gameplay states

- Critical limitations triggered by max polyphony or event queue processing lag

```
class LimiterClass
{
public:
   virtual ndF32  GetFootstepsDistanceLimit(
                     ndU8 sizeIndex);
   virtual ndBool IsSystemReducingAmbiance();

private:
///Limiter system variables
enum BussesLimitTyp
{
 LimitTyp_LooseLimit,
 LimitTyp_ForcedLimit,
 LimitTyp_WarningLimit,
 LimitTyp_HardLimit,
 LimitTyp_CriticalLimit,
 LimitTyp_NumLimit
};

enum BussesIndex
{
   BussesIdx_AmbianceBus,
   BussesIdx_3rdPersonFoleyBus,
```

```
  BussesIdx_3rdPersonFoleyWeapon,
  BussesIdx_3rdPersonWeapon,
  BussesIdx_Wind,
  BussesIdx_OutdoorPad,
  BussesIdx_AmbLocal,
  BussesIdx_AmbRandom,
  BussesIdx_AnimalFoley,
  BussesIdx_BulletImpact,
  BussesIdx_Explosion,
  BussesIdx_DestructibleObj,
  BussesIdx_InteractiveObj,
  BussesIdx_MovableObj,
  BussesIdx_Vehicule,
  BussesIdx_ArenaAmb,
  BussesIdx_NumValues,
};

enum BussesLimitIndex
{
  BussesLimitSP,
  BussesLimitMP,
  BussesLimitNumClasses,
};

BussesLimiterSchemeClassIndex m_activeSchemeClass;
BussesLimitTyp m_currentLimitType;

//General limiter info used everywhere
U32 m_nbLimitedBusses;
ISoundSystem::busInfo m_masterBus;
Vector<U8> m_warningLimits;
Vector<U8> m_overloadLimits;

//Footstep distances used for animals
ndVector<float> m_footstepsDistanceLimit;

//Audio Middleware limitation states
bool m_synchroSoundLimit;
bool m_eventQueueLimit;

//Gameplay limitation states
bool m_combatState;
bool m_combatStateChanged;
```

```
bool m_drivingState;
bool m_drivingStateChanged;

//Ambiance limiter
bool m_soundSystemReduceAmbiance;

float m_timeSinceLastBusUpdate;
bool m_isMPBusLimitationSchemeActive;
};
```

This function will determine the limitation state to apply:

```
void BussesLimiterFunction(float deltaTime)
{
  m_timeSinceLastBusUpdate += deltaTime;

  if ( snd_deactivate_bus_limiter != 1
&& (IsSystemReceivingAudioEngineWarning()
|| m_combatStateChanged
|| (m_timeSinceLastBusUpdate >=
     BUS_VOICES_LIMIT_UPDATE_LATENCY ||
     deltaTime == 0.0f))
  {
    m_combatStateChanged = false;
    m_activeSchemeClass =
      GetMPBusLimit() ? BussesLimitMP :
                        BussesLimitSP;

    m_limitTyp = LimitTyp_NumLimitations;

    //General limitation based on total polyphony used on
    //master bus

    bool isWarningState =
      m_masterBus.totalPolyCount > m_warningLimit ||
      m_synchroSoundLimit;

    bool isCriticalState =
       (m_audioEngineEventQueueLimit ||
        m_masterBus.totalPolyCount >= m_overloadLimit);

     if ( m_combatState || m_drivingState ||
   ( m_activeSchemeClass ==
```

```
            BussesLimiterSchemeClassIdx_MP) )
       {
            m_limitTyp = isCriticalState ?
              LimitTyp_CriticalLimit :
                 isWarningState ?
                    LimitTyp_HardLimit :
                    LimitTyp_ForcedLimit
       }
       else
       {
            m_limitTyp = (isWarningState || isCriticalState) ?
LimitTyp_WarningLimit : LimitTyp_LooseLimit;
       }

       for (ndUInt i = 0; i < m_nbLimitedBusses; i++)
       {
          UInt busId = m_limitInfo[i].m_busId;
          UInt maxPoly = m_limitInfo[i].m_busLimits[m_
          limitTyp];

          if( !SND_SetBusLimit(busId,maxPoly) )
          {
             Error("Failed to set bus limit on %ld\n", busId);
          }
       }
       m_timeSinceLastBusUpdate=0.0f;
    }
}
```

With this information, it is simple to do a limitation matrix that is applied to each frame on the *n* busses I choose to limit. This works like a state machine defining the current value to set for each bus depending on the other parameters using a macro.

```
///Limiter macro
#define LIMITER_VALUE( schemeType, busName, \
                      limitationScheme ) \
  m_limiter[BussesLimit_##schemeType].m_limitInfo \
    [BussesIdx_##busName].m_busLimits \
      [LimitTyp_##limitationScheme]
```

15.7 OPTIMIZE GAMEPLAY CODE BASED ON BUS LIMITER STATE

This previous section described an empirical method that permits discriminating problematic data and limits it at the renderer level. This is one of the three bottlenecks for the CPU. The next one to optimize is in the game code itself. Fewer events sent and fewer voices requested to play equals less CPU usage.

Once your dynamic bus limiter is done, you can use it as a general bias, which will drive any other gameplay system playing sounds.

For example, I extended the system to the footsteps using the limiter state as a general value applied on a footsteps limiter that was adding a more subtle approach for its own limiter.

The footstep system uses the NPC/animal size to let the footstep play or not, by checking the limiter state and the entity size, and comparing two squared distances.

```
struct FootstepsLimits
{
    F32 FootstepsLimitsLength[
        FootstepsLimitsValueIdx_NumValues]
};

///Footsteps limiter based on distance
static FootstepsLimits
FootstepsLimitsSchemes[LimitTyp_NumLimitations] =
{
  // LimitationStateIdx_LooseLimitation
  {15.f, 30.f, 70.f},
  // LimitationStateIdx_ForcedLimitation
  {10.f, 20.f, 50.f},
  // LimitationStateIdx_WarningLimitation
  {5.f, 20.f, 40.f},
  // LimitationStateIdx_HardLimitation
  {5.f, 10.f, 30.f},
  // LimitationStateIdx_CriticalLimitation
  {1.f, 5.f, 20.f}
};
```

```
ndF32 * selectFootstepsLimitsLength =
  FootstepsLimitsSchemes[m_limitTyp].
  FootstepsLimitsLength;

ndF32 FootstepsLimitLengths[
        FootstepsLimitsValueIdx_NumValues] =
{
  selectFootstepsLimitsLength[
    FootstepsLimitsValueIdx_Small],
  selectFootstepsLimitsLength[
    FootstepsLimitsValueIdx_Medium],
  selectFootstepsLimitsLength[
    FootstepsLimitsValueIdx_Big]
};

for(ndU8 i = 0;
    i < FootstepsLimitsValueIdx_NumValues;
    ++i)
{
  m_footstepsDistanceLimit[i] =
    FootstepsLimitLengths[i];
}

// the function called by the gameplay code will return
// depending on the current limiter state, the max roll
// off value allowed for the requested entity size
ndF32 GetFootstepsDistanceLimit(
        FootstepsLimitLengthssizeIndex)
{
  return m_footstepsDistanceLimit[sizeIndex];
}
```

More systems were driven by the limiter in the same way; for example, the ambiance manager dynamically allowed more or less streamed ambiance pads depending on the platform, the fighting, or the driving states.

Here's an interesting anecdote. On *Far Cry 3*, I even shipped the game with a trick permitting us to save one stream when you drive a vehicle. In the XBox360 DVD-Only version in particular, because the vehicles were able to go up to 60 km/h, it was really near the limit for streaming the world and had too many sounds playing from the disk. So, I did a fade out on the ambiance pads synched with the vehicle engine initialization sound fade in. The engine was covering the ambiance pads, so nobody ever noticed that no ambiances were playing when you are in a vehicle.

15.8 EVENT LIMITATION APPROACH

Even with all these systems, you will need a better approach. As I said earlier, the bus limiter system is more a production quick fix than a perfect solution. So, on the next game (*Far Cry 4*), I created a new system that acts before sending any event. I called it the Event Limiter.

The purpose of this limiter is for each entity in the game to only allow a number of limited voices. It was mainly used for NPCs, animals, and vehicles.

15.8.1 Information about Sound Modules Sending Sounds

You will have to define your code modules triggering sounds, then list and explicitly tag them in the code. In *Far Cry 4*, we had the following modules able to trigger sounds: NPC, Gun, Animation, AI, Footsteps, Feedback, Foley, Gear, and Script.

15.8.2 Filtering Class

Create a class that will filter any event sent to the sound system. At the same time, you will also register the related entity/object in your class. You will also be able to specify the module tag for the sound/entity couple. So, you have the information on the number of sounds (and how many from each module are) playing on every entity in your world. You push in a per-system list on each sound playing that will later be removed when ending.

Once you have this system in place, you will have the possibility to create your own rules.

For example, I can take an NPC that has multiple sounds playing on it, coming from any system, such as gameplay code, animation, script, or AI. These sounds include footsteps, Foley for the clothes, weapons, ammo, gear, barks, gunshots, dialogs, and animation sounds. You will get the NPC entity reference from any system trying to play a sound for him. Then you define your NPC rule: the polyphony you will allow for one NPC in the game (say, six sounds per NPC) and the priorities between each module playing the sound. Then you will also prioritize sounds depending on what's happening to this NPC. If his AI state is "chasing," you will prioritize footsteps and barks over gears and Foley sounds, because you need to hear the NPC moving around you.

So, here you get the idea. I limit the event by having better granularity, which is based on game objects and not only on a bunch of sounds that have the same sound type. Here, you need to be careful not to be too brutal with limitations; but with this—coupled with gameplay information such as NPC AI state (shooting or exploring), bus limiter general information, and distance to the player—you can adapt the rule values and end up with a really fine-tuned event limiter system.

Code example:

```cpp
class CEventLimiter{

  public:

  // You can have a specific list for each module, but
  // I choose to compute and update the numbers each
  // time I play a sound.

  struct SSoundEvent
  {
    U32SoundId     mySoundId;
    CEntity*       myRelatedEntity;
    ESoundModule   myRelatedModuleEnumValue;
  };

  bool CEventLimiter::CanPlay(SSoundEvent myEvent)
  {
    if(!IsDiscarded(myEvent))
    {
      PushNewSoundIntoList(myEvent);
      return true;
    }
    return false;
  }

  // This is called each frame at the end of the
  // sound system process

  void CEventLimiter::UpdatePlayingSoundList(
    SoundList myPlayingSoundList);

  private:

  struct SSoundEntity
  {
```

```
    CEntity* myEntity;
    Vector<SSoundEvent> myPlayingSoundList;
  };
  Vector<SSoundEntity> m_registeredEntities;

  bool CEventLimiter::IsDiscarded(SSoundEvent myEvent)
  {
    //rules here

    if(/*...MAGIC HAPPENS HERE...*/)
    {
      return true;
    }
    return false;
  }

  void CEventLimiter::PushNewSoundIntoList(
                       SSoundEvent myEvent)
  {
    //will add the sound
  }
};
```

Then, you will have a test function called by your generic play sound function:

```
if( !m_eventLimiterInstance::CanPlay(myNewSound) )
{
  return false;
}
```

15.9 IN-GAME LIMITER USING SOUND METADATA AND PLAYER FOCUS

Now, it is the future with next-generation consoles, with more than 300 MB memory allowed for sound and a little bit better CPU performance. All of this CPU and memory have afforded us some new possible approaches. You can create a system that loads your entire sound tree plus the metadata related to each sound ID.

Your sound engine knows the sound hierarchy, priorities, max rolloff, or any useful information.

At this point, you can route your old bus limiter system to your in-game limiter and use a decision tree based on both gameplay states and sound properties. In fact, you will be able to do the priority computation that was previously done in the audio middleware, in your game sound engine. So, you will save the cost of an event sent each time you can discriminate one.

The system will act like the audio middleware priority system, but this one will be yours and you will have the possibility to tune it at runtime as I tried to do before using the bus limiter. It will be able to discriminate play events when it knows that I already have too many sounds playing in each category, and eventually compute the rolloff distance and some threshold algorithm to send the event or not depending on gameplay states.

The main difference with the audio middleware system is the fact that I don't have the sound volume at this point. So, I can't evaluate two similar sounds with the same priority based on volume.

15.9.1 Have a Clear View of Your System

As I did before for the event limiter, you need to register any playing sound and identify it by bus and priority, so you can see what happens and make decisions based on that. You still have the information used by the initial bus limiter. You will know the audio middleware state and you will be able to evaluate and set your tuning based on these parameters. But now, having the bus and the priority information for each playing sound, you can apply the priority algorithm before sending the event.

A good approach to consider is to create profiling tools first. You create all the systems that allow you to have a clear view of what is requested, what is playing, and what is discarded in real time on the screen and with logs for statistics. Then, it will be easier to create the rules and the decision trees you will use for sorting your events.

The only problem I still encounter is, as I have said before, I don't have real-time volume information for playing sounds and new events. That is what differs from sorting these events in the audio middleware. Also, the audio middleware is able to stop a sound that is playing, to let an event with a higher volume play. Our system will only discard play events. It could be possible to override the stop event, but in my case it was not relevant. And, don't forget that the original goal is to reduce the number of events I send.

15.9.2 Player Focus and Rolloff

You need to find a way to sort events having no audibility factor. I propose an approach that is related to a game design/creative point of view and that could fit for any game. I think that it will reinforce the open world immersion to have visually oriented sounds playing. So, taking that into account, you can create an algorithm that prioritizes sounds playing in front of the player. Taking the depth of field and the angle of the player view, I can use a simple algorithm. If the sound plays in front of the player at a short to medium distance, it is a very high priority. If it is on the side it is medium priority. If it is behind, it is low priority. The distances are also used as sorting parameters. As shown in Figure 15.2, the weight for each

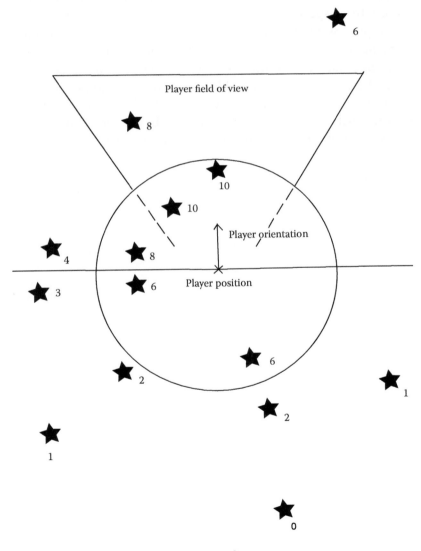

FIGURE 15.2   Panning visualization at 180°.

priority is directly related to the player orientation. This is, of course, only used on one shots and random sounds.

Orientation, distance, priority, bus, sound type—these factors let us create very simple rules to sort in an efficient way the events triggered by the game.

15.10 CONCLUSION

Through this chapter, I tried to give you some idea about how to manage these three specific CPU problems, but I also tried to show you an iterative process for managing a problem that can happen in production. Sometimes, the best solution is not the most beautiful, but the more efficient in a short time frame. Fortunately, there are also preproduction phases where you can take a problem from its roots and definitely fix it using a smarter and cleaner method. Naturally, this is not a problem that every game will encounter, but even so, it can be good to think about a few systems to maintain the creative craving in a smart way.

CHAPTER 16

Vector-Based Amplitude Panning

Guy Somberg

CONTENTS

16.1 A BRIEF INTRODUCTION TO PANNING

Panning is one of the fundamental properties of an audio engine. Most middleware takes care of the details for you, but, if you're writing your own low-level mixer or have some custom panning needs, you can still end up in situations when you need to implement it yourself. So, what do we mean when we talk about "panning" in the context of this chapter? Ultimately, what we are going to build up here is a description of a formula that takes a number of parameters as inputs, and outputs a set of values indicating how loudly to play a sound out of each available speaker.

On the surface, you would think that panning is relatively simple. On a two-speaker system, you take the input value (how far apart to put the sound in between the speakers) and scale your sound by that much onto each speaker. You could even extend that principle to use a simple angle-based formula for surround-sound systems. The end result would even sound halfway decent.

But it would be wrong. You would end up with strange artifacts. The simplest way to hear them is to write a simple program that moves the sound around the listener in a circle, then listen for dead spots, volume changes, or other artifacts. If you don't do your panning properly, you'll end up with all sorts of badness.

16.2 VECTOR-BASED AMPLITUDE PANNING

Rather than build up a solution from first principles, I'm going to jump right into the proper way of implementing a panner. Vector-Based Amplitude Panning (VBAP) was developed by Ville Pulkki in 1997 at the Laboratory of Acoustics and Audio Signal Processing at Helsinki University of Technology.[1] The original paper[2] is a valuable read for understanding the underlying mathematics of what it is and why it works. I highly encourage you to read the paper and understand it. However, in this chapter, we will be looking at it from a more pragmatic perspective: the math is there, but how do we actually put it into practice?

Ultimately, what our algorithm is going to do is give us the algorithm for the following function:

$$f(\vec{S}, D, E) \overset{\text{VBAP}}{\Longrightarrow} \vec{V}$$

In other words, given information about each of the speakers, the direction of the input, and its extent, we apply VBAP to get a vector of volumes for each speaker.

16.3 ALGORITHM INPUTS

Let's examine the inputs to the function in more detail.

16.3.1 Speaker Information

In general, the information about the speakers won't change in the middle of gameplay. This is the sort of data that you can collect at startup, and then keep around as static inputs to your panning function. Of course, you may have a strange environment where your speakers are moving around as the game plays. In that case, you'll have to acquire this information at the beginning of the update.

So, what information are we interested in for each speaker?

- **Position**—In VBAP, we need to flatten speaker positions into their relative locations along the unit circle. So, we need 2D coordinates for the speaker's location along the circle.

- **Angle**—We also need the angle from the forward vector (the vector {0, 1}) that this speaker occupies. You can calculate this from the position. Or, contrariwise, if you're given the angle, you can calculate the position from that. We will need both values for this algorithm.

- **Neighboring Speakers**—VBAP works on pairs of speakers at a time, so we'll need to know which speakers are next to this one. Technically, you only need one neighboring speaker for the algorithm, but you may want to have both.

- **Friendly Name**—For debugging purposes.

16.3.2 Source Direction

This is the direction that the sound is coming from along the unit circle. Its value ranges from −180° to +180°. For the purposes of this algorithm, we are only interested in the angle that the sound source is coming from. As with all angles in this algorithm, we treat forward as the vector {0,1}. To find this angle, project the sound source's 3D position onto the listener's plane, then you can find the angle to the listener's Forward vector.

Alternatively, you can expose this value directly to your sound designers as a value that they can adjust, irrespective of the 3D position.

16.3.3 Source Extent

The extent is how much of the speaker field is taken up by this sound. Its value ranges from 0° to 360°. It is also expressed as an angle, but rather than being an angle relative to another angle, it is used as a quantity. If the extent is 180°, then your sound takes up half of the speaker field. If it is 1°, it takes up just a sliver. Figures 16.1 through 16.3 show a visualization of what the extent looks like at 180°, 90°, and 30°, respectively. Effectively, the extent is how localized your sound source is.

You can calculate extent from 3D position based on the distance from the listener. The further away a sound source is, the smaller its extent will be. As it gets closer, the extent will reach its maximum when the listener is basically on top of the sound source. And, as before, you can always expose this value to the sound designers directly.

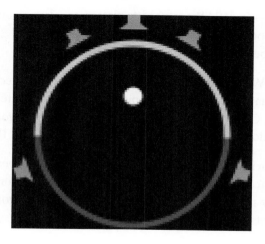

FIGURE 16.1 Panning visualization at 180°.

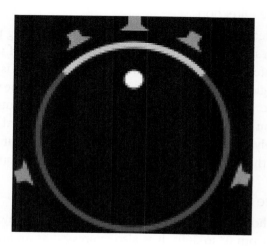

FIGURE 16.2 Panning visualization at 90°.

FIGURE 16.3   Panning visualization at 30°.

16.4 ALGORITHM OUTPUTS

Ultimately, we want to take all of these inputs and perform some algorithm on them to get a volume that we can apply to each speaker for this particular sound. So, if we have N speakers, then we want N values from 0 to 1, which we will use to scale our output signal to each speaker.

16.5 THE ALGORITHM

The VBAP algorithm operates on speaker pairs. For each pair of speakers, we find an angle between those two speakers that the sound is perceived to be coming from, as well as a gain for the sound. The angle is, effectively, the midpoint of the amount that the sound fills in the space between the speakers, and the gain is the percentage of the space between the speakers that the sound takes up. Once we have the angle and gain, we generate a scaled point source and figure out the gain that it would apply to each speaker. Finally, we divide the resulting volume by the root sum square (RSS) of the two contributions in order to normalize the result.

This contribution is calculated for each pair of speakers, so each speaker will be visited twice: one for each neighbor. As a final step, we once again divide the resulting contribution for each speaker by the RSS of all of the contributions in order to normalize the results.

I'm purposefully being vague about some of the calculations in the above summary—we'll come to the details as we build up the code.

16.5.1 RSS

Let's start by writing out a helper function to calculate the RSS of a sequence. The RSS is exactly what it describes: the square root of the sum of the squares of the inputs:

$$RSS = \sqrt{\sum_{i=0}^{N} x_i^2}$$

You can think of it as the length of the vector formed by the components of the input.

16.5.2 Calculating the Speaker Gains

All of the relevant calculations are described in Section 1.2 of the original Pulkki paper, but we will summarize it here. Figure 16.4 describes the situation that we are in. We have two speakers at some angle apart, and a virtual sound source between them. We need to project the sound source (p) onto the speaker vectors (I_1 and I_2) in order to find the respective gains (g_1 and g_2). Basically, we have the relation that

$$p = g_1 I_1 + g_2 I_2$$

It seems as though we have one equation now with two unknowns (g_1 and g_2), but the fact that it's a vector equation means that we can trivially split

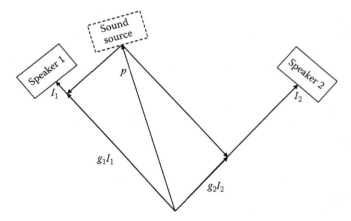

FIGURE 16.4 Calculating speaker gains.

it out into two equations and two unknowns. By writing this in matrix form, we can solve it a bit more cleanly:

$$p^{\mathrm{T}} = gI_{12}$$

Here, g is just a 2D vector containing $[g_1\ g_2]$ and I_{12} is $[I_1\ I_2]^{\mathrm{T}}$. To solve this, we must multiply both sides by I_{12}^{-1}, the inverse of I_{12}. We calculate the inverse by dividing by the determinant and shuffling the values.[3] The determinant may not exist, though, if the speakers are directly across from each other. In that case, we use a different algorithm to find the projection. Regardless, assuming that the inverse exists, the resulting formula is:

$$g = p^{\mathrm{T}}I_{12}^{-1}$$

If the inverse does not exist, we can project the sound source onto the vector and use the percentage along the path to calculate the panning.

16.6 THE CODE

16.6.1 RSS

Let's jump right into the code with a function to calculate the RSS over its inputs. There are all sorts of fancy C++ that we could use to make this happen, but we'll go with a simple templated function:

```
template<class T>
float RootSumSquare(const T& t)
{
  float fSumOfSqures =
    accumulate(begin(t), end(t), 0.0f,
    [](float fSum, float fEntry)
      { return fSum + fEntry * fEntry; });
  return sqrt(fSumOfSquares);
}
```

This way, we can simply pass in our structure, and whether it is a built-in array, a std::array, a std::vector, or any other data structure, it'll accumulate properly. (So long as the elements are convertible to float.)

16.6.2 VBAP Function

Now, we can move on to actually calculating the VBAP function. First, we'll have the function declaration and the edge-cases:

```
array<float, MAX_SPEAKERS> VBAP(
  float fSourceDirection, float fSourceExtent)
{
  array<float, MAX_SPEAKERS> pOutput;
  pOutput.fill(0.0f);

  if(pSpeakerInfos.size() == 1)
  {
    // The VBAP algorithm operates on pairs of
    // speakers.  If you are in mono output mode, then
    // there is no work to be done.  You can take this
    // check out of the VBAP function so that you
    // don't have to do it over again every time you
    // run through this.
    pOutput[0] = 1.0f;
    return pOutput;
  }

  float fHalfExtent = fSourceExtent / 2.0f;
  float fMinAngle = fSourceDirection - fHalfExtent;
  float fMaxAngle = fSourceDirection + fHalfExtent;
```

Now that we're set up, we can go ahead and iterate over all of the speaker pairs. We're assuming that they're in some externally accessible location: either a member variable of your audio engine class or a global location. We're just calling it gSpeakerInfos here.

```
  for(const auto& tSpeaker : gSpeakerInfos)
  {
    float fThisAngle = tSpeaker.fAngle;
    float fLeftAngle = tSpeaker.
    pLeftNeighborSpeaker->fAngle;

    if(fThisAngle >= 0.0f || fLeftAngle <= 0.0f)
    {
      // We're in the normal case here
```

```
    UpdateSpeakerPanning(tSpeaker, pOutput,
      fMinAngle, fMaxAngle, fLeftAngle, fThisAngle);
  }
  else
  {
    // We're wrapping around, so we want to make sure
    // that we get the appropriate calculation.
    // Only one of these two will actually do
    // anything, so we just do them both.
UpdateSpeakerPanning(tSpeaker, pOutput,
        fMinAngle, fMaxAngle,
        fLeftAngle, fThisAngle + 2.0f * kPi);
    UpdateSpeakerPanning(tSpeaker, pOutput,
        fMinAngle, fMaxAngle,
        fLeftAngle - 2.0f * kPi, fThisAngle);
  }
}
```

That conditional in the middle of the loop bears some explanation. Each speaker is assigned a single angle relative to the forward vector, but this means that the speaker to the left of this speaker may cross over the zero line. If that happens, then the math starts to break down because the difference between the angles of the speaker on the left is not actually on the left. To resolve this, we rotate around the circle, either by adding 2π radians to this speaker, or subtracting 2π radians from the left speaker. This will bring the angles into alignment relative to each other. We then call UpdateSpeakerPanning() both ways, because the first thing that it will do is exit early if the angles aren't right.

We'll come back to UpdateSpeakerPanning() in a moment. First, let's finish the VBAP() function off by scaling all of the values by the RSS of the outputs.

```
  float fRss = RootSumSquare(pOutput);
  if(fRss != 0.0f)
  {
    for_each(pOutput.begin(), pOutput.end(),
      [=](float& v) { v /= fRss; });
  }

  return pOutput;
}
```

So that's the core of the functionality: we've iterated over each speaker. Let's see how we actually calculate the panning.

16.6.3 Updating Speaker Panning

First, let's see the declaration.

```
void UpdateSpeakerPanning(
  const SpeakerInfo& tSpeaker,
  array<float, MAX_SPEAKERS>& pOutput,
  float fMinAngle, float fMaxAngle,
  float fLeftAngle, float fThisAngle)
{
  // Early exit if the sound is not audible between
  // these speakers.
  if((fThisAngle < fMinAngle) ||
      (fLeftAngle > fMaxAngle)
    return;
```

So far, it's pretty simple: just a function declaration with an early exit. Next, we need to calculate the gain (percentage of the angle range) and direction (midpoint of the angle range).

```
  // Find the angle range that this sound occupies
  // within this range.
  float fFromAngle = max(fLeftAngle, fMinAngle);
  float fToAngle = min(fThisAngle, fMaxAngle);
  if(fFromAngle > fToAngle)
    { swap(fFromAngle, fToAngle); }

  // The direction is the midpoint of the angle range.
  float fDirection = fFromAngle +
                    (fToAngle - fFromAngle) / 2.0f;

  // The gain is the percentage of the angle range
  // that the sound occupies.
  float fGain = (fToAngle - fFromAngle) /
                (fThisAngle - fLeftAngle);

  // If the sound is a point source, then go ahead and
  // let it play
  if(fGain == 0.0f && fMinAngle == fMaxAngle)
    fGain = 1.0f;
```

Now that we have the inputs, we can perform the actual calculations.

```
Matrix2x2 tSpeakerMatrix {
  tSpeaker.vPosition,
  tSpeaker.pLeftNeighborSpeaker->vPosition };
Vector2 vContributions{ 0.0f, 0.0f };

if(tSpeakerMatrix.InverseExists())
{
  // The speakers are some angle apart
  Vector2 vScaledSource{
    fGain * sin(fDirection),
    fGain * cos(fDirection) };
  vContributions =
    vScaledSource * tSpeakerMatrix.Inverse();
}
else
{
  // The speakers are 180 degrees apart, which is
  // the common case in stereo setups, but can also
  // appear in esoteric multi-speaker
  // configurations. The math is slightly
  // different here.
  Vector2 vScaledSource{ sin(fDirection),
  cos(fDirection) };

  float fSpeakerDistance =
    tSpeaker.vPosition.Distance(
      tSpeaker.pLeftNeighborSpeaker->vPosition);
  vContributions.x =
    CalculateStereoPanning(tSpeaker, vScaledSource,
                           fSpeakerDistance, fGain);
  vContributions.y =
    CalculateStereoPanning(
    *tSpeaker.pLeftNeighborSpeaker,
    vScaledSource,
    fSpeakerDistance,
    fGain);
}
```

If the inverse exists, then it means that we can use the vector math described above to find the gain. If it doesn't exist, then the speakers are directly across from each other, and we need to do some different math, which we'll see momentarily.

Before that, though, we need to normalize the output for these two speakers by dividing by the RSS.

```
auto tContributions =
  { vContributions.x, vContributions.y };
float fMultiplier = 1.0f;

float fRss = RootSumSquare(tContributions);
if(fRss != 0.0f)
{
  fMultiplier = fGain / fRss;
}

pOutput[tSpeaker.nIndex] +=
  vContributions.x * fMultiplier;
pOutput[tSpeaker.pLeftNeighborSpeaker->nIndex] +=
  vContributions.y * fMultiplier;
}
```

That's it! It looks a bit complicated, but it's exactly the math that we described in Section 16.5.2. The only missing piece is the CalculateStereoPanning() function.

16.6.4 Calculating Stereo Panning

To calculate stereo panning, we project the sound onto the line formed by the speakers. This ends up being a two-line function, if you're willing to accept one very long line.

```
float CalculateStereoPanning(
  const SpeakerInfo& tSpeaker,
  const Vector2& vScaledSource,
  float fSpeakerDistance, float fGain)
{
  float fContribution =
    1.0f - (tSpeaker.vPosition.Distance(
            tSpeaker.vPosition +
            tSpeaker.vPosition.Dot(
              vScaledSource - tSpeaker.vPosition) *
```

```
        tSpeaker.vPosition) / fSpeakerDistance);
  return fContribution * fGain;
}
```

16.6.5 Summary

The whole algorithm is a framework for the vector–matrix product. Ultimately, it's a loop over the speakers, where we perform some simple math over each speaker pair and sum it up.

16.7 OPTIMIZATIONS

There are a couple of places where the code can be made faster:

- Because the speaker pair matrices are always the same, the result and the inverse can be cached.

- In order to determine whether a matrix inverse exists, you have to calculate the determinant. Precalculating the determinant to use in the inverse will make that calculation more efficient.

16.8 CONCLUSION

The VBAP algorithm creates a very natural-sounding effect. As sounds move around and get closer and further away, they'll fill the speaker field very cleanly, and you won't get pops as the sound moves. Some middlewares actually already implement this algorithm internally for their regular 3D panning. However, if you are implementing your own mixer, or if you want to create some customized panning solution, it can be very valuable to understand what is happening under the hood.

NOTES

1. http://legacy.spa.aalto.fi/research/cat/vbap/
2. https://ccrma.stanford.edu/workshops/gaffta2010/spatialsound/topics/amplitude_panning/materials/vbap.pdf
3. The precise details of the matrix math are not important to this discussion. Most game engines will have a 2D matrix library available. If your engine doesn't, then there are plenty of books and online references that explain the mathematics very clearly.

CHAPTER 17

Dynamic Game Data

Tomas Neumann

CONTENTS

17.1 INTRODUCTION: GAME DATA IS THE DRIVING FORCE FOR AUDIO

In the past 10 years, the concept of sound integration has undergone a dramatic paradigm shift. Instead of providing lots of properties on how to play a sound the moment the game triggers it, sounds nowadays are data-driven and hold all important information within their authoring data. This has caused an important shift in responsibility toward the sound designers to design, author, debug, and implement sounds. This includes picking up dynamic changes from the game and manipulating sounds accordingly.

Imagine a racing game with a perfect recording of the engine sound, but regardless of how much the player is pushing the pedal onto the floor, the playback is locked at a static RPM. Not only would the player receive no feedback on how fast the car is going, this boring sound would drive (pun intended) everyone crazy within minutes. It seems natural that in some way the state of the engine is driving the pitch of the engine sound, which may even be dependent on the selected gear, the incline of the street, or the current position in the race. Players expect game data to dynamically change sounds and although some of these changes might be subtle, they can provide experienced players helpful information to learn how to master the game over time.

It is trivial to come up with a wealth of examples of game data that the sound engine would want to query:

- Is this a friendly or enemy footstep?

- Is the damage buff on the selected weapon active?

- What level is the fireball spell?

- How many rounds of ammunition are left in the magazine?

- Was another wood resource harvested within the last 5 s?

- Is the cat's health under 50 health points?

- What is the traction of the tire?

- What is the angle between the character's look-at vector and the local player?

- What is the current time scale of the game world?

Which of the many game data end up changing the sounds are usually decided by the sound designers. Different games often have very different needs when it comes to what is important information for the player. In modern video games, most sounds are dynamic and change according to the state of the player or the game world. But even music or voice properties can change depending on certain game values. These dynamic game data can be used to drive changes within sound middleware or in-house sound solutions. Typical sound systems can react to changes through real-time parameter control (RTPC), logical switches, or states. Sound designers can use this extra information to blend between sound variations, pick completely different sounds, or change the mix of the whole game.

This chapter offers an efficient approach for individual sounds to ask for and consume ever-changing values from the game domain to create dynamic sound effects, which provide the player with valuable feedback. We will develop a system that only requires an initial implementation to provide certain game data, while the authoring side is easy for sound designers to access and to pipe information into their sounds in a way they need them.

17.2 GAME DATA—THE BASICS

When I explained the game data system to our sound designers, I asked them to think back to when they were a child. You have hundreds of questions to ask, but the real challenge is to find the right person to ask. If you ask your classmate how old she is, you will get a different answer than asking your teacher.

Often, these types of game data information are published on concepts such as hierarchical scene entity components. For example, we could ask the front left tire of a racing car for its spin, which gets resolved on the tire game entity. Asking the same tire for its speed, might not be resolved by the tire, but by the parent entity, the car itself.

Other approaches might be implemented as a huge global dictionary, which resolves similar queries. For our example implementation in this chapter, it is not critical how you decide to develop such a system in your game engine. Additionally, you can also decide if it is better to pull the values on demand, or have the game push every value blindly, regardless of if there is a consumer or not. In any case, it is important that a sound knows whom to ask for what information. In this implementation, we will have a hierarchical structure with a global resolver on top as a fallback.

For instance, it could be possible for any sound to ask its entity what the time scale of the world currently is. Although this is information no entity can answer directly, eventually the game itself can answer this question in the global resolver by going up the hierarchy.

I want to clarify the terms I will use across the chapter.

- **Authoring**: To define static properties and links in the game editor or middleware

- **Implementation**: To write code for the framework of game data for the game client

- **Publishing/Querying**: To set and ask for game data value at runtime of the game client

17.3 AUTHORING GAME DATA

We use `GameData` in our game editor or the database to identify and describe "questions" we want to ask later. We start authoring some `GameData` entries into the game databank by matching a unique ID with a description and a default value. It depends on your implementation on storing and exposing game data, if this is a raw xml file, a database table,

TABLE 17.1 Authoring of Three Examples for GameData, Their IDs and Default Values

GameData ID	Default	Description
1001	0.0f	AngularVelocity
1002	1.0f	HealthRatio
1003	Max	TimeSinceDiedInSec
1004	0.0f	Velocity

or binary data, which can be manipulated with your game editor. Let's create a few in Table 17.1.

This data is usually accessed by programmers every time they implement a new GameData, and it can be statically loaded by the game because it does not change at runtime. In our case, we only define a default value, but you can add extra properties for blending over time, how to treat unresolved queries, or other scenarios.

17.4 IMPLEMENTING THE GAME DATA SYSTEM

We need a system that can query dynamic values from the game or store them so we can ask for these values. This is the basic framework you can ask your questions to. For the sake of keeping this example short, some common concepts were removed from the following sample code. If you want to implement this on multiple threads, you need to take care of locks, which guard read and write access. Also, to keep things simple, we assume that the type of every game data value is a float. It would be easy to extend the example with templated value types in order to store bool values, integers, or even colors or identifiers.

The GameDataValue class holds the default value defined in the editor and the current value populated by the game at runtime. For simplicity, we define a bool that toggles if we have a new value set or should retrieve the default. Here, you could add concepts for target values and blending timing behavior if you want.

```
class GameDataValue
{
  float m_default;
  float m_current;
  bool m_set;
}
```

The GameDataResolver is a component or similar structure that stores and queries GameDataValues in a hashmap sorted by the GameDataID.

A resolver can either resolve a query, reply with the default, or bail if the
GameDataID is unknown.

```
class GameDataResolver
{
  [...]
public:
  enum GameDataReturn
  {
    GameDataOK,
    GameDataDefault,
    GameDataUnknown
  }
  void SetValue( const u32 GameDataID,
                 const float InValue )
  {
    m_mapGameDataValues[GameDataID].m_current =
      InValue;
    m_mapGameDataValues[GameDataID].m_set = true;
  }
  GameDataReturn QueryGameData( const u32 GameDataID,
                                float &outValue );
private:
  std::map<u32, GameDataValue> m_mapGameDataValues;
}
```

If a GameDataResolver is asked for a value, first we check if this
GameDataID is known in this scope. If we have an entry, we either return
the current value or the default value. If this GameDataResolver does
not know about the GameDataID, then we ask the parent.

```
GameDataReturn GameDataResolver::QueryGameData(
  const u32 GameDataID,
  float &outValue )
{
  GameDataValue* data =
    m_mapGameDataValues[GameDataID];
  if (data != NULL)
  {
    if (data->m_set == true)
    {
      outValue = data->m_current;
```

```
      return  GameDataOK;
    }
    else
    {
      outValue = data->m_default;
      return  GameDataDefault;
    }
  }

  if ( __GetParent() != NULL)
    return __GetParent->QueryGameData( GameDataID,
                                        outValue );
  else
    return GameDataUnknown;
}
```

The GameEntity is often an object that is associated with something in the game world, such as a character, a light, a model, or a weapon. Our GameDataValues will be published into a GameDataResolver by the game, and then they will be available when we query them. For instance, the individual spin for our four tires gets published on the GameDataResolver on each tire. Often, a GameEntity holds basic properties such as a position and transformation matrix. For our example, I included two types of velocity on the level of the GameEntity.

```
cclass GameEnity
{
public:
  GameDataResolver* GetGameDataResolver()
  { return &m_gameDataResolver; }
private:
  GameDataResolver m_gameDataResolver;
  float m_velocity;
  float m_angularVelocity;
}
```

17.5 PUBLISHING DYNAMIC GAME DATA VALUES

With our framework in place, we can now start publishing changing values into the resolver. Let's say the angular velocity is something we can easily compute per update, and then we add the value to every

GameDataResolver in the GameEntity by setting the current value into the resolver.

```
#define ANGULARVELOCITY 1001
#define VELOCITY 1004
void GameEntity::Update()
{
  computeAngularVelocity();
  m_gameDataResolver->SetValue( ANGULARVELOCITY,
                                 m_angularVelocity );
  m_gameDataResolver->SetValue( VELOCITY, m_velocity );
}
```

For the other two GameDatas, let's say we have a class for a living thing. Alternatively, this could be a health component within the GameEntity.

```
#define HEALTHRATIO 1002
#define TIMESINCEDIEDINSEC 1003
class LivingThing : public GameEntity
{
private:
  float m_health, m_healthMax, m_timeSinceDiedInSec;
  float __GetHealthRatio()
    { return m_health/m_healthMax; }
}
void LivingThing::Update()
{
  m_gameDataResolver->SetValue(HEALTHRATIO,
                                __GetHealthRatio() );
  m_gameDataResolver->SetValue(TIMESINCEDIEDINSEC,
                                m_timeSinceDiedInSec);
}
```

17.6 GAME DATA AND RTPC PAIRS

Now that we have the game pumping in the values, we need to match the correct GameData to our sounds. First, we need to author some RTPCs that will be used by the sounds. This usually happens in the middleware tools by the sound designers, or the list ends up being available in your editor. I intentionally choose a different order for our RTPCs in Table 17.2.

TABLE 17.2   Authoring of Three Examples for RTPCs

RTPC ID	RTPC Name
2001	RTPCHealthRatio
2002	RTPCVelocity
2003	RTPCAngularVelocity

In the editor, we now connect and match our RTPCs with the GameDataID from earlier. This is the moment we essentially connect output and input data. All the work from above is needed so this table can be exposed to the sound designers, and they define which value should go into which RTPC. An example is shown in Table 17.3.

Finally, we need to tell our sounds to which GameData-RTPCs to subscribe. A sound may require more than a single entry. This will be pushed into the vector of GameDataIDs on the GameSound. To create the iconic LaserSword sound, it requires the values of the angular velocity. The ShieldOrb uses the health ratio of the hero to change the sound according to the heal progress and uses the velocity to drive a Doppler effect. We see these relationships in Table 17.4.

We now implement support for RTPCs for sounds. The GameSound is the object that handles the playback instance of a sound and feeds the correct GameDataValues to it. In our example, we pull this data every frame and every sound knows what GameData to ask for. In this implementation, we create a static vector for the subscriptions and populated it at startup. If the sounds in your game have changing needs during gameplay, you can consider doing this in a different way.

TABLE 17.3   Authoring of GameDataID and RTPC-ID Pairs

GameData-RTPC	GD-RTPC ID	RTPC ID	GameData ID
HealthRatio	3001	2001	1002
Velocity	3002	2002	1004
AngularVelocity	3003	2003	1001

TABLE 17.4   Authoring of GameData Subscription of Two Sounds

Sound Name	GD-RTPC ID
LaserSword	3003 (AngularVelocity)
ShieldOrb	3001 (HealthRatio)
	3002 (Velocity)

From a game engine architecture perspective, sounds can be embedded in entities, point to entities, or be their own entity type. Also, which sound middleware or sound system you use influences on which level you bind a GameEntity to a sound or a sound object. In our simple example, a GameSound simply points to a GameEntity.

```
class GameSound
{
private:
  GameEntity* m_gamEntity;
  vector<GD_RTPC> m_vecGD_RTPCs;
}
```

Just before we start the playback of a new sound, and during regular update, we run through the GameDataIDs and set the values we retrieve as RTPCs. We assume that the SetRTPC() function internally has the GameData-RTPC matching available.

```
void GameSound::Update()
{
  ApplyRTPC();
}

void GameSound::ApplyRTPC()
{
  GameDataResolver* resolver =
    m_gameEnity->GetDataResolver();
  for ( int i=0; i<m_vecGD_RTPCs.Count(); ++i )
  {
    float value = 0.0f;
    u32 GameDataID = m_vecGD_RTPCs[i].m_gameDataID;
    u32 RTPCID = m_vecGD_RTPCs[i].m_RTPCID;
    GameDataResult result =
      resolver->QueryGameData( GameDataID, value );
    if ( result != GameDataUnknown )
    {
      SetRTPC( RTPCID, value );
    }
  }
}
```

We reached an impressive milestone! Sound designers can now talk to gameplay programmers and request any new game data they need. This needs to be implemented only once, and usually takes only a few minutes. Do I capture the point? Is my shield active? Am I healing someone? Am I getting healed? Am I outdoors? The possibilities are truly endless as to what a sound designer might need. With the RTPC to `GameData` matching, they have the responsibility to define how they consume this data. Once they authored a new pair and subscribe it for a sound, the system starts publishing values into the sound system where they are needed.

17.7 GAME DATA SWITCHES

If RTPCs are not enough and your sounds can consume something like a switch, then we can easily extend this concept to allow for simple logic statements. Switches can be used for surface types, indoor/outdoor variants, or other use cases where you don't blend changes into the sound smoothly, but rather change or configure a sound discretely. Table 17.5 shows some examples of this mapping.

In your editor you can define conditions to define different scenarios. To evaluate the condition, we run through them from the top down and apply the first statement that is true. The last entry is always a condition-less statement as our default. In this example, we define switches for a "sword-hit" sound similar to the RTPC authoring. Table 17.6 shows an example for a single switch statement for a sword hit.

If we hit a friendly player, we always get a friendly version of our hit sound. If the first condition is false, we then evaluate the next. If we deal more than 100 damage, then we set the switch to be a critical hit. If this is not the case, we check if the Target has any armor and set the armor

TABLE 17.5   Authoring of Four Switches

Switch ID	Switch Name
4001	Friendly-hit
4002	Armor-hit
4003	Blood-hit
4004	Critical-hit

TABLE 17.6   Authoring of a Single Switch Statement for Sword-Hit

GameData	Condition	Switch
TargetIsFriendly	== true	4001 (Friendly-hit)
DamageDealt	> 100	4004 (Critical-hit)
TargetHasArmor	== true	4002 (Armor-hit)
None	None	4003 (Blood-hit)

switch on our sound. If all of these were false, we have an empty condition so we then set the default blood hit switch.

The code implementation is rather simple and depends heavily on how you export and author these tables. Let's say we define three conditions: EQUAL, SMALLER, and LARGER. You can extend this further to work with numerical ranges [$n..m$] or absolutes. These conditions just allow the sound designers to be able to author even more logic into their use cases, without the need to ask for a programmer. It is well worth the time it takes to program this.

Let's add switch subscriptions to the GameSound and iterate over all conditions, finding the first that is true. We set the switch and process the next switch statement.

```
class GameSound
{
private:
  [..]
  vector<GD_Switch> m_vecGD_Switches;
}

void GameSound::Update()
{
  ApplyRTPC();
  ApplySwitches();
}

void GameSound::ApplySwitches()
{
  GameDataResolver* resolver =
    m_gameEnity->GetDataResolver();
  for ( int i=0; i<m_vecGD_Switches.Count(); ++i )
  {
    for ( int j=0;
          j<m_vecGD_Switches[i].Conditions.Count();
          ++j )
    {
      float value = 0.0f;
      condition* = &m_vecGD_Switches[i].Conditions[j];
      u32 GameDataID = condition->gameDataID;
      GameDataResult result =
        resolver->QueryGameData( GameDataID, value );
```

```
    if ( result != GameDataUnknown )
    {
      bool setSwitch = false;
      switch ( condition->type )
      {
        case EQUAL:
          setSwitch = ( value == condition->value );
          break;
        case SMALLER:
          setSwitch = ( value < condition->value );
          break;
        case LARGER:
          setSwitch = ( value > condition->value );
          break;
      }

      if ( setSwitch == true )
      {
        SetSwitch( condition->switchID );
        break;
      }
    }
  }
}
}
```

17.8 GAMEDATA STATES

The overall mix of a game can change in several situations. For example, the game volume changes when you enter the game menu, or the popular shell shock effect when a grenade explodes next to the player. Situations like this can be implemented as mix states or sound moods. Some years ago, it was normal to fully implement these mechanics on the game side by interpolating DSP values across multiple busses, and blending the values additively or exclusively. Nowadays, sound systems or middleware offer states to manipulate the overall mix of a game by simply setting them.

Because of the direct resemblance of the switch implementation, I don't list an example of an authoring table with mix states, or the implementation. The main difference between switches and states is that switches are scoped toward GameSounds, whereas states are of global nature.

TABLE 17.7 Authoring of a Single State Statement

GameData	Condition	State
UIMenuActive	== true	Menu-Mix
KillCamActive	== true	KillCam-Mix
PlayerIsDead	== true	Death-Mix
TimeSincePlayerLowHealthInSec	> 3.5	Mild-LowHealth
TimeSincePlayerLowHealthInSec	>= 0.0	Intense-LowHealth

Usually, the player resolver and global resolver are used to query values, and the states are set in some global update within the sound system. We can use the same conditions we used earlier for switches for the logic to trigger mix states. Again, in our example, we evaluate from the top and apply a state as soon as the condition is true, if you define mutually exclusive mix states. If you define multiple of these condition blocks, more than one mix state can be active, if this is what you want. Table 17.7 shows an example of how easily a sound designer would be able to author all required data to create mix states for a game.

17.9 CONCLUSION

We have everything in place now to tap into any game data and control any audio behavior with it. This is extremely powerful and allows sound designers to author dynamic sounds in an easy and clear manner, while keeping the ongoing implementation cost for programmers to a minimum. It would be rather straightforward to take such a system a step further and allow asking a game entity about another game entity outside of their hierarchy. For example, we could ask a pet of any kind about properties of its owner. Or we can ask the healer for the health points of its target.

A system like this accesses a lot of random memory, and before you start implementation make sure you have a good idea about the number of GameData entries you need, how many game entities hold values, the best threading strategy, and if you prefer a push or a pull model. In a multithreaded system, you need to pay attention to how new values migrate through your memory and when they become available for a consumer. When you query for a value, it can be valuable to understand in which state the resolver is, and whether he will satisfy a query or is even able to. A push model can be simpler and might require less memory, if you can keep it under control. In a pull model you can parallelize queries more easily, if your consumers can update at the same time.

At the project I am working on, we use an enhanced system based on this basic concept for all kinds of effect beautification on the game client. My colleague Ryan Green, who implemented the underlying framework, did an impressive job supporting multiple disciplines. Sound is not the only consumer of this game data. Graphical effects, script logic, animations, the physics contact system, and the voice system all query for game data the same way and change specific behavior accordingly. My part was to develop the authoring process for our sound designers and implement the abstraction levels and feed the values into our sound system. In the long run, this freed me from the need to support the sound designers for every single request, but instead most of the time the game data is already available for them to create new and creative sounds.

I hope this chapter will help you design an appropriate and efficient system for your project, which can truly unlock the power of dynamic game data for use cases you cannot yet imagine.

Index

Page numbers with f and t refer to figures and tables, respectively.

#0002 - 010916 - C0 - 229/152/18 [20] - CB - 9781498746731